DEBATING GOVERNANCE

DEBATING GOVERNANCE

Edited by

JON PIERRE

UNIVERSITY PRESS

OXFORD

UNIVERSITY PRESS

Great Clarendon Street, Oxford OX2 6DP

Oxford University Press is a department of the University of Oxford.
It furthers the University's objective of excellence in research, scholarship,
and education by publishing worldwide in

Oxford New York

Auckland Bangkok Buenos Aires Cape Town Chennai
Dar es Salaam Delhi Hong Kong Istanbul Karachi Kolkata
Kuala Lumpur Madrid Melbourne Mexico City Mumbai Nairobi
São Paulo Shanghai Singapore Taipei Tokyo Toronto

Oxford is a registered trade mark of Oxford University Press
in the UK and in certain other countries

Published in the United States
by Oxford University Press Inc., New York

British Library Cataloguing in Publication Data

Data available

Library of Congress Cataloging in Publication Data

Debating governance: authenticity, steering, and democracy / edited by Jon Pierre.
"Grew out of a conference on the theories of governance held at the Ross Priory outside
Glasgow in October 1997"—Acknowledgments.
Includes bibliographical references and index.
1. Public administration. 2. Democracy. 3. Political planning.
4. Regionalism. I. Pierre, Jon.
JF1351.D43 2000   351—dc21   99-048959
ISBN 0-19-829772-6

3 5 7 9 10 8 6 4

Typeset by Hope Services (Abingdon) Ltd.
Printed in Great Britain
on acid-free paper by
Biddles Ltd.,
Guildford and King's Lynn

ACKNOWLEDGEMENTS

This volume grew out of a conference on theories of governance held at the Ross Priory outside Glasgow in October 1997. Stunned—and surprised—by gorgous weather and the pastoral beauty of the Priory overlooking Loch Lomond, the contributors assembled to discuss governance as an analytical framework in different subfields of political science. Andrew Gamble and Paul Hirst very generously offered to write papers commissioned after the conference. In addition to the papers included in this volume, Phillippe Schmitter gave a conceptual paper on governance, later published elsewhere, which was a valuable contribution to the discussion.

Laura Cram, Daryl Glaser, Brian Hogwood, and David Judge, colleagues at the University of Strathclyde and Grant Jordan, University of Aberdeen, kindly offered to serve as discussants. Their constructive critique has been immensely important in shaping the final version of the papers. Guy Peters and Rod Rhodes provided valuable comments on earlier drafts of the introductory chapter. Margaret Leckie kindly relieved me of the administrative hassles of the project. Dominic Byatt at Oxford University Press has been a constant source of forceful and unmitigated enthusiasm throughout the project. I am most grateful to all these people. Most of all, I appreciate Guy Peters' never-failing collegiality and support at a couple of critical junctures in the project.

The financial support from the University of Strathclyde and the Economic and Social Research Council's Local Governance research programme is most gratefully acknowledged.

The book is dedicated to my daughter Miranda for her constant reminding me about the limits of formal authority.

J.P.

Glasgow and Gothenburg,
March 1999

CONTENTS

LIST OF CONTRIBUTORS

ANDREW GAMBLE is Professor of Politics and a member of the Political Economy Research Centre, University of Sheffield. He has current research interests in the political economy of the company and comparative political economy, and his publications include *The Free Economy and the Strong State* (1994), *Britain in Decline* (1994), and *Hayek: the Iron Cage of Liberty* (1996).

PAUL HIRST is Professor of Social Theory at Birkbeck College, University of London and Academic Director of the London Consortium Graduate Programme in Humanities and Cultural Studies. His books include *Associative Democracy* (1994), *Globalisation in Question,* with Grahame Thompson (1996), and *From Statism to Pluralism* (1997).

JAN KOOIMAN is Professor Emeritus of Public Management of the Faculty of Business Administration, Erasmus University, Rotterdam (The Netherlands). Over the years, he has published on different aspects of political and administrative decision-making in The Netherlands and abroad. Recently, his interest has focused on the development of a theory of social–political governance as interaction between government and society. His major publications as editor in English include *Modern Governance* (1993), *Managing Public Organizations* (1988), and *Creative Governance* (1998).

ANTHONY PAYNE is Professor of Politics and Director of the Political Economy Research Centre at the University of Sheffield in the United Kingdom. He is also Managing Editor of the journal *New Political Economy*. He is a specialist on the international political economy of development, with particular reference to the Caribbean, and is the author of a number of books and articles in this field.

B. GUY PETERS is Maurice Falk Professor of Government at the University of Pittsburgh, Senior Fellow of the Canadian Centre for Management Development and a distinguished Professor at the University of Strathclyde. His recent publications include *Comparative Politics: Theory and Method, The New Institutionalism* (1999), and *Taking Stock: Assessing Public Sector Reforms* (co-edited with Donald J. Savoie, 1998). In 1998 he was awarded a Doctorate of Administrative Sciences, h.c., from the University of Vaasa (Finland).

JON PIERRE is Professor of Politics at the University of Gothenburg, Sweden, adjunct professor of political science at the University of Pittsburgh, USA, and visiting professor at the University of Strathclyde where he previously held a chair in politics. His publications in English include *Governance, Politics and the State*, with Guy Peters (2000); *Challenges to Local Government* (co-edited with Desmond King) (1990); and editor of *Urban and Regional Policy* (1995), and *Bureaucracy in the Modern State* (1995). He is currently co-editor (with Bert A. Rockman) of *Governance: An International Journal of Policy and Administration*.

ROD RHODES is Professor of Politics (Research) at the University of Newcastle-upon-Tyne; Director of the Economic and Social Research Council's Whitehall Research Programme; and Adjungeret Professor, Institut for Statskundskab, Københavns Universitet. He is the author or editor of many books including recently: (with P. Weller and H. Bakvis, eds.), *The Hollow Crown* (1997) and *Understanding Governance* (1997). He has also published widely in such journals as *Australian Journal of Public Administration*, *British Journal of Political Science*, *European Journal of Political Research*, *Parliamentary Affairs*, *Political Quarterly*, *Political Studies*, *Public Administration*, *Public Administration Review* and *West European Politics*. He has been editor of *Public Administration* since 1986.

JAMES N. ROSENAU is University Professor of International Affairs at The George Washington University, having previously been on the faculties of the University of Southern California, Ohio State University, and Rutgers University. A former president of the International Studies Association, his recent writings include authorship of *Along the Domestic-Foreign Frontier: Exploring Governance in a Turbulent World* (1997) and *Turbulence in World Politics: A Theory of Change and Continuity* (1990), co-authorship of *Thinking Theory Thoroughly: Coherent Approaches to an Incoherent World* (1995), and co-editorship of *Governance Without Government: Order and Change in World Politics* (1992).

ALBERTA SBRAGIA is the Director of the Center for West European Studies and the European Union Center as well as the UCIS Research Professor of Political Science at the University of Pittsburgh. She has served as the Chair of the European Community Studies Association-USA, the Program Co-chair of the 1999 American Political Science Association Convention, President of the Conference Group of Italian Politics, as well as on the executive committee of the Council of European Studies and on the German Marshall Fund of the United States Committee for European Studies. She has published in the fields of American federalism, European Union politics, and comparative environmental policy. Her most recent publications include *Debt Wish: Entrepreneurial Cities, U.S. Federalism, and Economic Development* (1996) and, as editor, *Euro-Politics: Politics and Policymaking in the 'New' European Community* (1992).

GERRY STOKER is Professor of Politics at the University of Strathclyde since 1991. He was Programme Director of the five-year ESRC Local Governance Research Programme (1992–7) and member of The Commission for Local Democracy (1993–6). In 1996 he was a founding member of the New Local Government Network and in 1997 he became a member of the Academic Advisory Group to DETR. He has held teaching posts at Leicester Polytechnic, Birmingham University and Essex University. In 1990–1 he was a Visiting Professor at Wayne State University, Detroit, USA. He currently holds the position of Visiting Professor at Greenwich, Birmingham and Warwick Universities. He is the author or editor of more than ten books. His most recent publications are *Rethinking Local Democracy* (1996, co-editor D. S. King) and *The Privatisation of Urban Services* (1997, co-editor D. Lorrain). He writes regularly for *Local Government Chronicle, Municipal Journal,* and other newspapers and magazines.

LIST OF TABLES

LIST OF FIGURES

LIST OF ABBREVIATIONS

APEC	Asia-Pacific Economic Co-operation
AEAN	Association of South East Asian Nations
CIPFA	Chartered Institute of Public Finance and Accountancy
ECJ	European Court of Justice
ESRC	Economic and Social Research Council (UK)
EU	European Union
GATT	General Agreement on Tariffs and Trade
GDP	Gross Domestic Product
IMF	International Monetary Fund
IPE	international political economy
IR	international relations
NAFTA	North American Free Trade Agreement
NHS	National Health Service
NPM	new public management
OECD	Organization for Economic Co-operation and Development
PAFTAD	Pacific Trade and Development Conferences
PBEC	Pacific Basin Economic Committee
PECC	Pacific Economic Co-operation Council
TI	Transparency International
TNC	Transnational Corporation
UN	United Nations
WTO	World Trade Organization

Introduction: Understanding Governance

JON PIERRE

Perhaps the most significant development in the advanced industrialized democracies over the past couple of decades has been the erosion of traditional bases of political power. The institutional strength of the nation state has been challenged from several different sources. The deregulation of financial markets and the subsequently increased volatility of international capital has deprived the state much of its traditional capabilities to govern the economy (Boyer and Drache, 1996; Camilleri and Falk, 1992; but see Hirst and Thompson, 1996; Weiss, 1998). Furthermore, subnational governments have become more assertive vis-à-vis the state; cities and regions—frequently propelled by ethnic and cultural identification—are positioning themselves in the international arena, seemingly bypassing state institutions and interests (Fry, 1998; Hobbs, 1994). Finally, the state's capacity to impose its will on society has become challenged by cohesive policy networks (Marsh and Rhodes, 1992; Smith, 1993).

The state has also been challenged from within, or, more correctly, its ability to address salient societal problems has been strongly questioned by the political elites in many western countries. The 1980s and 1990s saw the rapid ascendance of neo-liberal regimes in several advanced democracies, defining the state and its *modus operandi* not as the solution but rather as a chief source of several problems in society but most distinctly the poor economic performance (Savoie, 1994). For Reagan, Mrs Thatcher, Mulroney, and their ideological followers in several other countries the recipe to alleviate these problems was a firm monetaristic economic policy coupled with deregulation, privatization, drastic reductions in the civil service, the introduction of 'managerialism' in the public sector, and a profound

Guy Peters and Rod Rhodes have offered valuable critique on a previous draft of this chapter.

institutional restructuring of the state creating semi-autonomous agencies to replace governmental centers of command and control functions, i.e. the creation of a minimalist state (Hood, 1991; Peters and Savoie, 1998; Pollitt, 1990; Rhodes, 1994, 1997; Self, 1993). Thus, alongside the powerful changes in the state's external environment, the state itself has been restructuring in ways which seem to deprive it of many of its traditional sources of power, policy capacity, institutional capabilities, and legitimacy.

The outcome of all these changes has been a dramatically altered political landscape. The financial crisis of the state during the past 15–20 years has reversed the direction and objectives of the political project in many countries, from one of allocating growing public revenues towards one of imposing losses on different constituencies in society. Moreover, we have seen an ideological and cultural shift from collective solutions towards individualism and a *Zeitgeist* heralding private enterprise and 'the market' as the superior resource allocating mechanism.

These developments pose a tremendous challenge to the state's ability to maintain some degree of control over its external environment and to impose its will on society, partly because voters are becoming less willing to pay the taxes which an active state requires, and partly because the legitimacy of the state's predominant position in society is waning. What is at stake here is what new instruments and new forms of exchange between state and society can be developed to ensure political control and societal support. As the state's traditional power bases seem to be losing much of their former strength, there has been a search for alternative strategies through which the state can articulate and pursue the collective interest without necessarily relying on coercive instruments. Put slightly differently, the overarching question is what significance or meaning remains of the liberal-democratic notion of the state as the undisputed centre of political power and its self-evident monopoly of articulating and pursuing the collective interest in an era of economic globalization, a 'hollowing out of the state' (Rhodes, 1994), decreasing legitimacy for collective solutions, and a marketization of the state itself (Pierre, 1995). Is it the decline of the state we are witnessing, or is it the transformation of the state to the new types of challenges it is facing at the turn of the millennium?

This is the background against which we should assess the growing interest in governance both as an emerging political strategy for states to redefine its role in society and, subsequently, a growing interest among social scientists in the process of state restructuring and transformation in light of the external and internal changes discussed earlier. These emerging forms of governance should be seen as alternative expressions of the collective interest which do not replace but supplement the pursuit of collective interests through traditional, institutional channels. Contemporary governance also sees formal authority being supplemented by an increasing reliance on informal authority, e.g. in the shape of negotiated patterns of public–private co-ordination. The emergence of governance should therefore not, *prima facie*, be taken as proof of the decline of the state but rather of the state's ability to adapt to external changes. Indeed, as several contributors to this volume argue, governance as it emerges during the 1990s could be seen as institutional responses to rapid changes in the state's environment.

WHAT IS GOVERNANCE?

The governance literature is slightly confusing in its conceptualization of governance. Governance has a dual meaning; on the one hand it refers to the empirical manifestations of state adaptation to its external environment as it emerges in the late twentieth century. On the other hand, governance also denotes a conceptual or theoretical representation of co-ordination of social systems and, for the most part, the role of the state in that process. This latter meaning of governance, in turn, can be divided into two categories (see Chapter 3 by B. Guy Peters). In the first category—what Peters refers to as 'old governance'—questions are asked about how and with what conceivable outcomes the state 'steers' society and the economy through political brokerage and by defining goals and making priorities. The other theoretical view on governance looks more generically at the co-ordination and various forms of formal or informal types of public–private interaction, most predominantly on the role of policy networks. Thus, in the first approach, which could be labelled state-centric, the main research problem is to what extent the state has the political and institutional capacity to 'steer' and how the role of the state relates to the interests of other influential actors; in the second approach, which is more society-centred, the focus is on co-ordination and self-governance as such, manifested in different types of networks and partnerships (Rhodes, 1997). However, it should be noted that neither perspective makes any prejudgements about the locus of power.

In much of the public and political debate, governance refers to sustaining co-ordination and coherence among a wide variety of actors with different purposes and objectives such as political actors and institutions, corporate interests, civil society, and transnational organizations. What previously were indisputably roles of government are now increasingly seen as more common, generic, societal problems which can be resolved by political institutions but also by other actors. The main point here is that political institutions no longer exercise a monopoly of the orchestration of governance. In these ways, governance could be said to be shorthand for the predominant view of government in the *Zeitgeist* of the late twentieth century. Governance, in this debate, is about how to maintain the 'steering' role of political institutions despite the internal and external challenges to the state. It is also, presumably, more palatable than 'government' which has become a slightly pejorative concept.

This reorientation of the debate on the role of the state in society has been propelled by several different developments (see Pierre and Peters, 2000). For some time now government has been believed to be 'overloaded', that is, unable to resolve all the tasks and demands placed upon it by society (Birch, 1982; Crozier *et al.*, 1975; King, 1975). In the 1980s and 1990s these problems were exacerbated by another serious challenge to state authority; most advanced western democracies were hit by a severe fiscal crisis which meant that governments could not use financial incentives to ensure compliance among societal actors to the same extent as hitherto. The economic plight also forced the state to cut back, more or less extensively, on its services; something which in turn prompted a search for new strategies of public service production and delivery. Maintaining public service levels through shared responsibilities between the state and civil society became one such strategy.

An additional development which has driven the growing interest in governance has been increasing problems of co-ordination, both in government and also in order to ensure that public and private projects to some degree share the same objectives or, at the very least, do not obstruct each other. The state has played a critical role in defining regulatory frameworks for markets. In addition, governments in most western countries during the post-war period have intervened in markets in order to promote political objectives and collective interests and also to resolve market failures. While these two different roles of the state must be kept analytically separated from each other, as Andrew Gamble points out in Chapter 6, it is equally important to acknowledge the facilitating and supporting role of the state in the economy.

Yet another development which has helped increase the interest in governance is the globalization of the economy and the growing importance of transnational political institutions like the European Union (EU), World Trade Organization (WTO), Association of South East Asian Nations (ASEAN), and North American Free Trade Agreement (NAFTA). I will not review in full the now vast literature on globalization; suffice it to say that the deregulation of capital in the 1980s set in train a massive restructuring of both domestic economies and the international economic system. What seems to be the main consequence of globalization in the present context is the erosion of traditional, domestic political authority. Such authority still exists but it confronts formidable challenges; the effective limits to political control have become increasingly evident over the past decade or so. Contemporary macro-economic policy-making, to take the perhaps most obvious example, is conducted in the context of considerable uncertainty of international economic development and the possibilities of international speculation against the currency (see Hinnfors and Pierre, 1998 and the literature cited there). However, globalization causes policy makers to rethink their political strategies in a wide range of policy sectors as well, for example taxes and distributive policies.

Thus, the conventional, state-centric image of politics and the role of state in society appears to account for less and less of contemporary patterns of power and authority in an era of globalization (but see Boyer and Drache, 1996; Hirst and Thompson, 1996; Weiss, 1998). This, however, is a contested standpoint. The contributors to the present volume agree that what we are observing is less the decline of the state and more a process of state transformation. While there are differences among the chapters in the degree to which they underscore this perspective, we are still far from dismissing the state as the center of political power and authority.

Finally, governance has also gained ground as a result of the 'failure' of the state. The state-centric view on political processes has helped raise expectations on the state's capabilities beyond the state's ability to deliver. The traditional 'tax-and-spend' model of public service delivery has been questioned, in part from the vantage point of the alleged inefficiency of the public sector compared to the corporate sector.

The overarching question coming out of these developments is what new forms and shapes the pursuit of the collective interest (Peters, 1996) can and should take and to what extent we need to rethink the traditional, liberal-democratic model of the state. If the state's capacity to steer is impaired by economic globalization, what other means does the state have of imposing its will on society and the economy? If the state is no longer

able to produce extensive public services, does that mean that our image of
the state as a material provider should be reconsidered? If the state can no
longer steer, should elected officials be held accountable for societal developments beyond their control? These issues show the need for students of
governance to develop conceptual frameworks and theories which will help
structure our ways of thinking about governance and the future role of the
state in society.

These issues are at the very core of our traditional image of the liberal-
democratic state and democratic government. The pervasiveness of the
governance debate, among social scientists and practitioners alike, is proof
of the saliency of these issues and the need to rethink many of our established notions and images of the state, of the articulation and pursuit of the
collective interest, and of democratic and accountable government.

THE CHAPTERS IN THIS BOOK

The governance debate is compartmentalized, reflecting the growing specialization in political science. The development of governance as an analytical framework in different subfields of the discipline will gain from a
critical comparison of the contribution which governance theory makes in
different areas of political science. This volume brings together experts on
governance in several different subfields of political science and presents
the different strands in the governance debate to highlight both common
and divergent approaches in governance research and theory. The remainder of the book is divided into two parts. Part I highlights the emergence of
governance domestically. Part II focuses on governance in an international
context.

In Chapter 2, Paul Hirst addresses some of the key questions in the governance debate such as what new channels and processes of political control and democratic accountability the emerging forms of governance will
require. His point of departure is that the liberal-democratic image of the
state, particularly its notion of a sustained separation of state and society,
no longer captures the nature of the modern advanced democracies. The
monopoly of governance capacity which liberal-democratic theory accords
to the state is no longer a valid account. So, we must reconsider both the
role of the state in society and what other forms of governance seem to
emerge as the state's capacity to govern is undermined. Hirst outlines a

model of 'associative self-governance' in which governance can be generated among structures in civil society; that is, democratized networks. The emergence of new forms of governance forces us to rethink some of our traditional notions of democracy and the role of the state in society. It is clear that we have only taken the first few steps along this avenue of inquiry.

The role of the state in governance and contending images of that role is the leading theme in Chapter 3 by Guy Peters on 'Governance and Comparative Politics'. Peters identifies 'traditional' governance, where the main issue is the capacity of the state to steer and control, and 'new' governance, where the question is how government interacts with its external environment to form decisions which are agreeable to all parties. He then proceeds to compare 'traditional' and 'new' governance in different subfields of comparative politics. Peters argues convincingly that a state-centric approach is best suited to develop an understanding of governance in a comparative perspective. A general problem in 'new' governance is that comparison almost always has an institutional dimension but 'new' governance maintains that formal institutional structures do not account for much of what governments can do. It also seems to have little to say on government's societal role more generally.

A slightly different view on these problems is presented in Chapter 4 by Rod Rhodes on 'Governance and Public Administration'. The public service is in many ways the most intriguing arena of governance since devising new forms of public–private exchange has been a core theme of governance. For Rhodes, self-governing networks are at the heart of current governance. The chapter first elaborates on different meanings of governance and raises some interesting questions about governance: Is it new and does it matter? How does one choose between different definitions of governance? How can we explain the growth of governance? To what extent has the centre been 'hollowed out'? How does the centre manage networks? Is governance failure inevitable? In this way Rhodes pinpoints accurately the frontier of governance research, not least by drawing our attention to governance failure as a distinct possibility and also by arguing that network management is conflictual and embedded in a politically charged context.

If the public administration has been the sector of government where different models of governance has been most frequently launched, then urban politics is probably the institutional level of government where different models of governance have been both discussed and implemented. More importantly, as Gerry Stoker points out in Chapter 5, urban political theory has for a long period of time been concerned with different models of public–private exchange and co-operation to compensate for urban institutional fragmentation, for example 'urban regimes' and 'growth coalitions'. Stoker emphasizes that governance should be thought of as a process and suggests that communication, monitoring, and structural reforms are different ways of steering in the urban political context.

In Chapter 6, Andrew Gamble looks at governance in the field of political economy. Governance has been a debated concept in this research area for some time; for example, the notion of corporate (or market) self-governance and the role of the state in economic governance. On closer inspection, the state plays two separate roles in economic governance; it constitutes and defines rules and norms of the economic order and it can be an interventionist agent in the economy. Gamble outlines and compares different 'economic constitutions'; the traditional liberal economic constitution which accords the state only a minimal function, and an economic constitution in which the state is allowed to play an interventionist role in order to pursue a broader, collective interest in the economy. Understanding the role of the state in economic governance ultimately begs the questions of the extent to which the state can (that is, has the political and institutional capabilities to) govern the economy; and the nature of the state's 'embeddedness' in the economy (Evans, 1995).

Chapter 7 presents the socio-cybernetic approach to governance. Jan Kooiman's point of departure is the growing diversity, dynamics, and complexity in society and the challenges these developments pose to steering. Governance is seen as an interactive, iterative process between a wide variety of actors, none of which enjoys effective authority over the others, or over society as a whole. From here, Kooiman outlines different types of governing such as self-governance, 'co'-forms of governing as well as more traditional, hierarchical governing. This analysis is conceptually sophisticated and represents in many ways the most elaborate theoretical analysis of governing. This approach to problems of governing and governance has played a dominant role in much of the Dutch research and it is one of the leading contributions to governance research in Europe.

Complexity is also a *Leitmotif* in Chapter 8 by James Rosenau, on governance in international relations. The problem of creating and sustaining governance has been a perennial problem in international relations. Not least globalization has triggered a number of problems for democratic governance, partly because it changes the cast of actors on the international scene and partly because it has entailed an 'accountability deficit' which has yet to be resolved. Critical about state-centric models of international relations, Rosenau sees governance as a theory which has strong potential in this field of research.

In Chapter 9 on 'Globalization and Modes of Regionalist Governance', Anthony Payne looks at patterns of governance in the international political economy. Regionalist governance refers to transnational arrangements of political and economic co-ordination created to enhance the international competitiveness of the region. The analysis thus addresses both the role of the state in the global economy and governance as way of accommodating state interests in the international arena. Payne argues that 'regionalist governance' does not indicate the 'decline of the state' but rather transformations of the state to respond to changes in the international political economy.

Chapter 10, finally, focuses on the European Union and patterns of governance in that institutional milieu. Governance, including multi-level governance, as a conceptual framework has been embraced by many in the EU research field since it offers a useful conceptualization of institutional relationships which often tend to be negotiated arrangements rather than constitutionally defined relationships and where policies are implemented more on the basis of agreement and compliance than enforcement. Alberta Sbragia argues that the myriad of networks, which are a prominent feature of EU politics, enhances the governing capacity of these transnational institutions; the core institutions of the European Union remain at the centre of EU governance.

The concluding chapter seeks to bring together the main commonalities in the substantive chapters. The focus is on what the preceding analyses tell us about the role of political institutions in governance in different arenas and on different institutional levels. This chapter also identifies what appears to be some of the key research questions in future studies on governance.

REFERENCES

BIRCH, A. H. (1982), 'Overload, Ungovernability and Delegitimation: The Theories and the British Case', *British Journal of Political Science*, 14: 135–60.

BOYER, R., and DRACHE, D. (eds.) (1996), *States Against Markets: The Limits of Globalization* (London and New York: Routledge).

CAMILLERI, J. A., and FALK, J. (1992), *The End of Sovereignty* (Aldershot: Edward Elgar).

CROZIER, M., HUNTINGTON, S., and WATANUKI, J. (1975), *The Crisis of Democracy* (New York: New York University Press).

EVANS, P. (1995), *Embedded Autonomy: States and Industrial Transformation* (Princeton, NJ: Princeton University Press).

FRY, E. H. (1998), *The Expanding Role of State and Local Governments in US Foreign Policy Affairs* (New York: Council on Foreign Relations Press).

HINNFORS, J., and PIERRE, J. (1998), 'The Politics of Currency Crises in Sweden: Policy Choice in a Globalized Economy', *West European Politics*, 21: 103–19.

HIRST, P., and THOMPSON, G. (1996), *Globalization in Question* (Cambridge: Polity Press).

HOBBS, H. H. (1994), *City Hall Goes Abroad: The Foreign Policy of Local Politics* (Thousand Oaks, Calif. and London: Sage).

HOOD, C. (1991), 'A Public Management for All Seasons?', *Public Administration*, 69: 3–19.

KING, A. (1975), 'Overload: Problems of Governing in the 1970s', *Political Studies*, 23: 284–96.

MARSH, D., and RHODES, R. A. W. (eds.) (1992), *Policy Networks in British Government* (Oxford: Clarendon Press).

PETERS, B. G. (1996), *The Future of Governing: Four Emerging Models* (Lawrence, Kan.: University of Kansas Press).

—— and SAVOIE, D. J. (1998), *Taking Stock: Assessing Public Sector Reform* (Montreal: McGill/Queens University Press).

PIERRE, J. (1995), 'The Marketization of the State: Citizens, Customers and the Emergence of the Public Market', in B. G. Peters and D. J. Savoie (eds.), *Governance in a Changing Environment* (Montreal and Kingston: McGill/Queens University Press), 47–69.

—— and PETERS, B. G. (2000), *The New Governance: States, Markets, and Networks* (London: Macmillan).

POLLITT, C. (1990), *Managerialism in the Public Service* (Oxford: Basil Blackwell).

RHODES, R. A. W. (1994), 'The Hollowing out of the State', *Political Quarterly*, 65: 138–51.

—— (1997), *Understanding Governance: Policy Networks, Governance, Reflexivity and Accountability* (Buckingham: Open University Press).

SAVOIE, D. J. (1994), *Thatcher, Reagan, Mulroney: In Search of a New Bureaucracy* (Pittsburgh: University of Pittsburgh Press).

SELF, P. (1993), *Government by the Market?* (London: Macmillan).

SMITH, M. J. (1993), *Pressure, Power and Policy: State Autonomy and Policy Networks in Britain and the United States* (Pittsburgh: University of Pittsburgh Press).

WEISS, L. (1998), *The Myth of the Powerless State* (Cambridge: Cambridge University Press).

PART I

Governance, Democracy, and the State

2

Democracy and Governance

PAUL HIRST

The use of the concept 'governance' is a relatively recent fashion. It attained wide currency in the past decade and largely at the expense of the concept of government. Indeed, governance is generally perceived to be an alternative to government, to control by the state. The use of the concept is almost exclusively confined to technocratic and elite discourse. It has yet to enter the popular vocabulary of politics. In this regard the various non-governmental organization (NGO) communities that have taken up the concept must be regarded as alternative elites to the established ones. Despite its usage by bankers and economists, the concept remains relatively imprecise. It has multiple meanings and there is a good deal of ambiguity between its different usages. However, most of those meanings cluster around what might be called a 'post-political' search for effective regulation and accountability. Most of the usages of governance either signal a situation which poses a real threat to the conventional forms of democratic government or they actively propose to sidestep democracy.

The 'post-political' thrust can be found in the arguments of both conservatives and radicals. On the one hand, it is the locution of these enlightened members of the international technocracy who recognize, after a decade of economic liberalism in the 1980s, that market forces and private interests require regulation and restraint, but who are reluctant to accept a new and major extension of the powers of the state. On the other hand, governance is used by some of the alternative policy bodies in the advanced countries and by NGOs acting in the developing world, who see a new potential for organization, through 'civil society' and who have grown to distrust the state because they see it as captured by commercial interests, corrupt politicians and unaccountable bureaucracies.

This chapter will consider the different meanings of the notion of governance from the perspective of political theory. It will examine the different ways in which governance has come to be seen as an alternative to government, and also consider why these usages raise fundamental problems of democratic accountability. It will examine how the different models of governance attempt either to displace or to resolve the issue of democracy. The advantage of the classic model of government through the nation state from a democratic perspective was that it appeared to provide clear institutional channels for the participation of citizens and the representation of their interests, and also clear lines of accountability for executive action. Here it will be argued that we need to rethink the forms of democratic accountability and the roles of the state if the weakness of modern governments, alluded to in the discourses of governance, are to be overcome.

FIVE VERSIONS OF 'GOVERNANCE'

The term governance is used in five main areas. It first seems to have gained currency in the field of economic development, with the widespread advocacy by international development agencies and western governments of 'good governance' as a necessary component of effective economic modernization. The World Bank, for example, has been a leading advocate of promoting good governance, attaching various compliance conditions to its loans. Recently the Bank has also brought government back in too—advocating building state capacity in developing countries (World Bank, 1997).

Development economists came to recognize that institutions matter, that development is not just a matter of creating free markets, promoting investment, and adopting the right macro-economic policies. Dynamic economies are underpinned by appropriate laws, social institutions, and values. Good governance, therefore, means creating an effective political framework conducive to private economic action—stable regimes, the rule of law, efficient state administration adapted to the roles that governments can actually perform, and a strong civil society independent of the state. Democracy is valuable in this context if it provides legitimation for good governance. Multi-party competition and free elections are valuable in preventing cronyism and corruption, and in building public support for development strategies, but only if parties eschew extremism and play the political game by the appropriate liberal rules.

Governance is thus good provided that the state limits the scope of its action to what it has the capacity to accomplish. Essentially, it must con-

i.e all parties will be under pressure to conform to the GG agenda

centrate on policies that make markets work and that provide them with appropriate low-cost social inputs, like education and health. The scope of democratic decision is thus limited by the needs and expectations of markets. The good governance strategy is based on creating in non-western developing countries a version of the societal architecture of classical liberalism, that is, a clear separation between a limited state and a largely self-regulating civil society and market economy. The issues at stake here are not merely whether this restricts democracy to a plebiscite in favour of a certain kind of economic policy, but also, as we shall see, whether this societal architecture actually exists in the advanced western countries themselves to be copied.

The second main use of the concept of governance is in the field of international institutions and regimes. It is widely recognized that certain important problems cannot be controlled or contained by action at the level of national states alone. Examples are world environmental problems like global warming and ozone depletion, the regulation of world trade and international financial markets, and a variety of issues ranging from developing common accounting standards to checking the international drug trade. The recognition of the possibility of 'governance without government' (Rosenau and Czempiel, 1992), of international regimes (Krasner, 1983) and the growth of private governmental practices and the 'retreat of the state' (Strange, 1996) has led to extensive discussion of the role of international agencies and inter-state agreements and common commercial govermental practices (like arbitration) as methods of governance. The question is how such supra-state agencies, inter-state agreements and private governance practices at the international level are monitored and controlled by domestic publics.

In the early twentieth century international problems were frequently seen as requiring the creation of a world government. Bodies like the League of Nations would gradually become true governments, monopolizing certain functions and powers in the interests of humanity as a whole. We now, rightly, regard such ideas as impossible and naïve. A world government with claims to sovereignty would be inherently remote from domestic publics, and even more unaccountable and inefficient than existing nation states. Yet 'governance without government' poses some analagous problems. It offers the prospect of the control of vital aspects of life by specific agencies like the International Monetary Fund (IMF) or World Trade Organization (WTO), with major consequences for nationally rooted publics, and yet beyond their, or any, democratic control. The

parcellized government of international problems by a technocracy, interacting with the elites of the major wealthy states (most of whom are not
elected), seems to threaten to reduce the role of national democratic politics to that of municipal politics. Much of the critical discourse about globalization fears that world markets and transnational corporations (TNCs)
are beyond control (Martin and Schumann, 1997) and that global markets
will lead to a race to the bottom in domestic policy (Gray, 1998). In fact
global markets are far from ungovernable, and the scope of national economic and welfare policy remains considerable (Hirst and Thompson,
1996; Hirst, 1997*a*). The problem is not ungovernability *per se*, but how
world affairs are governed and how that governance is refracted in national
states.

Inevitably, governance by an international technocracy and the elites of
the G8 major economic nations is highly exclusive: it ignores many smaller
rich countries, let alone the poorer developing countries, and little attempt
is made to make international economic issues comprehensible to national
publics, or to arouse their interest in them. On the contrary, the dominant
rhetoric of globalization among politicians and technocrats has the effect
of telling citizens that they are powerless before world competitive forces,
and that they had better submit and adapt to them.

David Held (1991, 1995) has sought to highlight the consequences of the
internationalization of social and economic life for democracy. He has
pointed out that democracy is threatened with being confined to the
national level where it is no longer effective in controlling the full agenda
of issues that ought to be within the scope of democratic decision. He pro-
poses an answer in the form of a programme of policies to create a 'cosmopolitan democracy' (1995: 279–80). The problem with Held's view is
less with his objectives or even with many of his remedies; it is that we cannot make the world into the conventional democratic theory conception of
a political community. Put simply, there is no global demos and, therefore,
no real locus for popular decisions beyond or between states. Held knows
this, recognizing that the 'global order consists of multiple and overlapping
networks of power . . . different power systems which constitute the interconnections of different peoples and nations' (1995: 271). That returns
power and influence to existing institutions, and we must then face the fact
of the fundamental conflicts and differences of interest between them.

Inequalities among nations are even more extreme than those within
them. In a world in which the top fifth receive 82.7 per cent of total world
income and the bottom three-fifths just 5.6 per cent, all the world's people

are not going to be given an equal chance and an open agenda to decide what should happen (Korten, 1996). Democracy, in its most basic sense of majority decision making, requires that those who decide be sufficiently alike that they will respect the will of the majority. Global-level decisions will inevitably have a highly restricted agenda, set by what the majority of the richest nations will tolerate, and a very reduced role for the world's publics. The difficulties of global democracy should make us pause when considering the rhetoric about democracy at the national level, for that too, despite the belief that nations are relatively homogeneous political communities, is subject to similar limitations as to both agenda and participation. Democracy in practice generally amounts to much less than the claims of democratic theory. The question is whether one needs to rethink some of the assumptions of democratic theory in order to find ways to widen the scope of accountable government by consent.

The third usage of the concept of governance is that of 'corporate governance'. This is primarily an Anglo-Saxon concern, as evidenced by the Royal Society of Arts inquiry (RSA 1995) and the Cadbury Committee's report (1992). It arises from an ongoing feature of both American and British companies: highly dispersed shareholdings and an active stockmarket, on the one hand, and a permanent professional management on the other. In the UK the protection of investors' interests was based on giving shareholders voice. The 1862 Companies Act envisaged companies as republics of shareholders with directors appointed by and bound by the decisions of the investors. This is now obviously a complete fiction. Managements are largely self-appointing oligarchies rubber-stamped by proxy votes at the AGM. The real constraints managers' face are the maintenance of their company's stock market price and the fear of possible hostile bids from other companies.

'Corporate governance' is the watchword of those who wish to improve the accountability and transparency of the actions of management, but without fundamentally altering the basic structure of firms in which indifferent shareholders are the principal beneficiaries of the company, and management claims to make policy on their behalf, whilst not being subject to the constraint of active voice by investors or any other affected interest (Roe, 1994). The Anglo-Saxon doctrine is part of a political culture that has long buried the view that employees' interests should be represented at board level, even though there are strong arguments in democratic theory that favour such representation (Archer, 1995; Dahl, 1985). The dominant view is that employees should have no strong countervailing power to managers, and that organized labour inevitably becomes an obstructive interest group undermining benefits to shareholders and customers. The Anglo-Saxon view also regards other company structures, such as in Germany or Japan, in which shareholdings are more long-term and concentrated and in which banks and other partner firms hold seats on the board, as inherently inferior. They promote cosiness at best and 'crony capitalism' at worst, weakening the necessary discipline of the financial markets.

The problem with the conventional view that corporate governance can be remedied by some modest tinkering is that there is a large and growing legitimacy crisis for companies. This is signalled by the growth of stakeholding advocacy (Hutton, 1995; Kelly *et al.*, 1997), and such aspirations cannot be met by limited changes in the detail of company law. Companies exclude most major stakeholders—employees, local communities, and dependent firms—from active voice. Yet the present institutional framework is also deficient in other means for containing, controlling, or remedying the externalities created for such interests by company policy. Companies are in effect autocracies in a political climate where democracy is the primacy source of legitimacy. The argument about corporate governance as it is presently conducted has no way of either accommodating or protecting politically the interests of stakeholders, other than shareholders.

The fourth usage of the concept of governance relates to the growth of new public management strategies since the early 1980s. These raise issues of governance in respect of the two main strands of policy toward public administration and the public sector generally. The first issue arises from the privatization of publicly owned industries and public services, and the consequent need for regulating service providers to ensure service quality and compliance with contractual terms. The second results from the introduction of commercial practices and management styles within the public sector, devolving services to agencies that are self-managing within overall policy guidelines and service targets. This generates a new model of public services distinct from that of public administration under hierarchical control and directly answerable to elected officials (Rhodes, 1997: 48–60). It also involves a radically different conception of the relationship between 'customers' and service providers from the conventional view of the relationship between citizens and the welfare state (Pierre, 1995).

The fifth usage of governance relates to the new practices of co-ordinating activities through networks, partnerships, and deliberative forums that have grown up on the ruins of the more centralized and hierarchical corporatist representation of the period up to the 1970s. Such negotiated social governance is growing in salience; typically it is to be found at micro—and mezo—level in cities, regions, and industrial sectors. It embraces a diverse range of actors: labour unions, trade associations, firms, NGOs, local authority representatives, social entrepreneurs and community groups. Sabel (1995) sees this both as a new style of governance and as a source of new experiments in democratic practice. In addition, more centralized bargaining in the form of new social pacts has returned to prominence in a number of European countries (ILO, 1995; Regini, 1997; Visser and Hemerijk, 1997), most notably Finland, Ireland, Italy, and the Netherlands. This tends to be different from the corporatism of old, and indeed, in some cases, to encompass experiments in democratic involvement of the grass roots in building legitimacy for policy, as in the case of Italian pension reform (Baccaro and Locke, 1996). These developments, both central and local, should be seen as encouraging from a democratic perspective. However, their very diversity and proliferation poses problems. Many of these forms of negotiated social governance are local and evanescent, and it is often difficult to tell which of them will be short lived or enduring, good or bad. This makes social learning difficult and the generalization of effective experiences problematic (Hirst, 1997b: ch. 1). It also leads to forms of network governance that are intensely local and difficult for outsiders to penetrate, conferring exclusive benefits on existing members.

GOVERNANCE IN AN ORGANIZATIONAL SOCIETY

Together the third and fourth usages of the concept of governance, and to a lesser extent the fifth, raise a general problem of the possibility of democratic control by elected representatives and of the accountability of insiders to the wider public. We continue to persist in seeing modern advanced societies through the model architecture of a classical liberal society: a limited state controlled by representative government and bound by the rule of law, and a largely self-organizing civil society independent of the state, but protected by the state's law and administrative procedures. This model has become more salient not least in public opinion and public policy, as socialist and social democratic conceptions of the state directly controlling extensive areas of economic and social life have lost credibility. Yet one

might question how limited modern government is. First, the new public
management increases some dimensions of central control through
budgetary constraints, accounting procedures, and forms of inspection
(Jenkins, 1996). Second, few states actually spend a lower percentage of
their Gross Domestic Product (GDP) than they did in the 1960s, when the
talk was firmly of government and what it could accomplish (*The
Economist,* 1995).

The key issue is less the retreat of the state, and more one of the reality of
a state-civil society separation that is central to the classical liberal vision.
The liberal architecture looks less and less convincing as a descriptive
account of modern advanced societies. In fact it would be better to see the
state as a part of an 'organizational society', with large hierarchically controlled institutions on both sides of the public-private divide that are either
unanswerable to or only weakly accountable to citizens. The public–private
divide has ceased to be clear or salient in the way classical liberals suppose
it to be (Hirst, 1997*b*: ch. 7). Private companies often have powers that
dwarf those of many governments; they do govern substantial areas of
social life through their administrative decisions and public legal deroga-
tions, and yet they are treated for many purposes as if they were private
associations of individuals in civil society. If private governments have
always been a reality since the advent of modern large corporations, much
of the public sector is now organized on corporate lines and the corporate
bodies in question often enjoy a high degree of autonomy.

Such public simulacra of private governments are generally neither
answerable to their stakeholders nor effectively accountable to elected central and local governments. Moreover, many of the elected members of
these governments have come to think and behave like corporate managers
themselves, and to put 'efficiency' before answerability to the public. In the
maze of organizations in the UK, public, quasi-public, and private—such
as central government agencies, TECs, HATs, UDAs, regulatory quangos
like OFTEL or the ITC, NHS trusts, privatized local services, companies
performing public functions, and private companies—the citizen is often
lost as to who governs what and how, and is seldom consulted or listened
to (Weir, 1996). Most citizens are confronted by hierarchically managed
organizations that exclude them from participation, yet that claim to provide services on their behalf and often in their name. Thus the public–
private divide is criss-crossed from both directions by essentially similar
organizations, and the notion of a self-organizing civil society of freely
associating individuals is less and less meaningful. One might call it an un-

civil society composed of bureaucracies rather than democratically accountable bodies.

The principal threat to the classical liberal separation of state and civil society has been perceived to be totalitarianism: state control of the private sphere and control of the state by a single authoritarian mass party. Totalitarianism broke down the state–civil society divide from the side of the state. The threat to democracy posed by an organizational society is quite different. In breaking down the state–civil society division it does not do so in one way but in multiple and interacting ways that threaten the notion of public democratic control. This is because the effects of organizational dominance place a great deal of society beyond the reach of genuine democratic decision and they so fragment the public sphere that the possibility of a centre of control, even notionally answerable to the democratic will, is seriously diminished. The state is not so much reduced in scale and scope, nor hollowed out: rather it is fragmented and merged with non-state or non-public bodies. In a way totalitarianism was much less of a challenge to liberal democratic theory (however much of a formidable obstacle in political practice). Overthrow the ruling party, and a transition to multi-party representative government can take place. The ability to prevent the fusion of state and party by means of the ballot box is a genuine political good and should not be slighted. The problem with the organizational society is that democratic reform requires multiple foci of control and new practices of accountability, it requires proceeding to change things at different political sites and by different methods.

Organizational societies would matter less if the majority of the important organizations that made them up were subject to local democratic control, and if their internal practices were conducive to democratic manners, to promoting political activism and a culture of autonomous action on the part of their members who are the citizens of the increasingly complex and confused polity. All the evidence suggests, on the contrary, that weakly accountable hierarchical organizations do nothing of the kind: rather, they breed bureaucratic competition, conformity, and indifferentism as styles of personal response (Presthus, 1965). Thus democracy is undermined by the very organs of ordinary social life. Why would one expect a series of localized autocracies to promote a general democratic culture? Moreover, believing in the illusion that we live in a classical liberal system, with a limited government subject to democratic control and a civil society characterized by individual freedom and healthy competition, simply blots out the problem. We need to rethink the notion of democratic government to fit the reality of an organizational society. The latter poses problems through its complexity and fragmentation of authority that traditional democratic theory is completely ill equipped to respond to. The various conceptions of 'governance' thus do us a service: they point out that government in the classical liberal sense is less and less a reality, and that new methods of control and regulation are required that do not assume the state or the public sector has a monopoly of such practices. At the same time they are mainly advanced by those at or near the top of the various organizational hierarchies, members of the elite, and they generally give a low priority to the issue of devising new methods of democratic control.

GOVERNANCE AND THE NATION STATE

The growth of multiple conceptions of governance thus reflect real changes away from the central government of the nation state as the principal provider of control and regulation within the national territory. The conventional conception of democracy in modern democratic theory has relied on the notion of the 'self-governing community' (Hindess, 1991, 1997). From classical antiquity to modern representative government the state has been seen as a political community able to shape and control all its affairs by political choice. Democracy meant that that choice should ultimately be made by a majority of all adults or their representatives. As Hindess points out, this notion of the control of the political community has relied on the conflation between the formal legal right of sovereignty and the capacity of the state actually to govern certain activities. In practice both what makes up the agenda of political decision and the scope of power of state control are often not matters of community choice: many issues are imposed from without the political process and many activities cannot actually be controlled by political choice. The illusion of complete democratic control within the national territory was strengthened in the mid-twentieth century by the growth of the macro-economic management and public service functions of the central state. It seemed that the state, the government, had a monopoly of capacities of governance. It seemed as if the new welfare state could enjoy as real a governing power over society as the totalitarian state or the temporary total war state in liberal countries, and yet be subject to democratic political choice.

A mixture of the rise of economic liberalism and the rhetoric of globalization have undermined such beliefs. Indeed, together they have over-diminished our expectations as to what public power can accomplish. The myth now propagated and widely believed is that the state is less able to control affairs that in fact it is. Politicians of all political persuasions now talk to their publics as if they must bow before the inescapable logic of ungovernable global markets. They imply that the state capacities of the period of Keynesian macro-economic management, conducive to national autonomy, have been superseded in a new area of internationalization. In fact the national autonomy in economic policy enjoyed by some states after 1945 was heavily dependent on the existence of a system of international economic institutions and politics underwritten by the most powerful state, the USA. What Ruggie (1983) has called 'embedded liberalism' was not attainable at the national level alone. Domestic political choice over aspects of economic policy was thus largely an artifact of the prevailing international order. Moreover, that order also constrained the scope of domestic policy in a way that removed certain policies as options in the democratic agenda. For example, Britain was subject to a severe balance of payments constraint throughout the duration of the Bretton-Woods international monetary system. No equivalent coherent architecture of international economic governance has replaced the managed multilateralism of 1945–73. However, the world economy remains minimally governed by the joint actions of the major supra-national agencies—the World Trade Organization, the International Monetary Fund, World Bank, and Bank for International Settlements—and the major wealthy nation states of the G7 plus the impoverished Russia to make the G8. So far, such governance has curbed excessive volatility and prevented meltdown in the financial markets (Hirst and Thompson, 1996: ch. 6).

This is not to say that a substantial degree of internationalization has not taken place, nor that the powers and capacities of the nation state have remained unchanged. It is also not to say that democracy can be restored by greater reliance on the nation state as an agency of domestic governance, or that greater reliance on the existing institutions of representative government is sufficient to reinvigorate democratic accountability. The problem is that modern democratic theory has relied heavily on the notion of a single self-governing community coincident with the nation state. If this always involved elements of illusion, as Hindess has pointed out, and if it has become problematic in the era of increased internationalization, as David Held has argued, then the very multiplicity and competition of sites and agencies of governance today demonstrates that the need for rethinking is now acute. Democracy needs to be rethought on the assumption that it has no primary locus and no single demos: the nation state shares power with increasingly salient sub-national governments, with proliferating forms of network and partnership governance, with a variety of quasi public and private organizations, with NGOs, and with international agencies and other forms of supra-national governance. Modern democratic theory has worked on the assumption that state sovereignty and popular sovereignty coincide within the same political space.

Some commentators see this decline in the salience of the nation state, the proliferation of plural and often competing loci of power, and the rise of forms of private power as analogous to the Middle Ages (Cerny, 1998; Minc, 1993). The analogy is apt only insofar as states in that period had no effective monopoly of governance. But governance is an entirely different phenomenon today, power and control are changed by the modalities of what they control and are not a constant in the way the formal theory of sovereignty implies. The Middle Ages were characterized by a relatively low degree of interdependence of social, and particularly economic, activities. The social division of labour is now ever more extended, and divided yet interdependent activities require co-ordination and, therefore, governance. Governance can be generally defined as the means by which an activity or ensemble of activities is controlled or directed, such that it delivers an acceptable range of outcomes according to some established social standard (Hirst 1997*b*: 3).

If states no longer have even the appearance of monopolizing governance, it does not mean that governance can be left to happenstance. Unregulated markets cannot be the exclusive form of co-ordination of the division of labour and they certainly cannot provide the social cement that makes their own existence possible. If they could, then both government and other forms of governance could be dispensed with—we could enjoy a form of economic liberal anarchism. The *ad hoc* pluralization of political authority and of extra-political power cannot simply be accepted: governance requires a relatively settled institutional architecture if it is to be effective. Gaps in governance and lack of co-ordination between levels of governance will undermine the efficiency of the governing bodies that there are. Control and co-ordination will vanish into the gaps, as the example of offshore tax havens and parallel banking centres shows.

COMPLEX GOVERNANCE AND QUASI-POLITIES

This complexity and interdependence in modern governance poses a dual problem. How to create an at least minimally effective division of labour in governance—one that will link together a complex of very different bodies that, even in combination, cannot be considered to be a 'political community'. How to ensure at the different levels within this division of labour an effective presence of democratic voice—so that the actions of a body at one level do not systematically negate decisions at another. The combination of internationalization and an organizational society forces us to rethink democracy. I shall try to argue that this also requires us to rethink the roles of the classical liberal architecture of state and civil society and the nation state but that both are still central if supplemented by other institutions and in performing new functions.

We should not expect any one political mechanism to be effective at all scales of governance—a point effectively made by Robert Dahl (1970) against believers in participatory democracy as the primary form of governance. In that case it is necessary to extend the notion of democracy so that it is compatible with different kinds and levels of institution. A division of labour in governance implies a quasi-polity, with different kinds of decision procedure, of which the member units are political bodies or organizations with their own collective decision procedures. In effect that is what nation states have always been, formal sovereignty disguising the complex of organizations and actors within the state. But democratic theory has either seen the polity in terms of a state composed of representatives of individual electors, as in classical liberalism, or as composed of associations competing to influence a single centre of decision-making, as in classical pluralism. Quasi-polities, where the members are not individuals but political bodies, were commonplace before the rise of the modern state and its claim to a monopoly over governance in its territory.

Perhaps bodies like the Hanseatic League or the Holy Roman Empire have something to teach us. Such bodies were not inherently unviable. They declined in a process of competition with territorial sovereign states that were able more effectively to exercise governance powers (Spruyt, 1994). This is no longer the situation. Interstate military competition is no longer the dominant factor deciding the fate of political entities, and most advanced nation states have the capacity to defend their territory alone or with allies against any possible external threat. We are searching for new forms of governance above the level of the nation state that are not simply a scaling-up of the powers of nation states. We are also searching for coherence and accountability in the maze of organizations within national political systems.

National governments have performed four main roles. First, they have defined the powers and responsibilities they and other institutions and actors within their territory can legitimately posses. Sovereignty has meant since the sixteenth century the claim to the capacity to regulate lesser governmental institutions and to make state laws primary over other rules. Since the rise of liberal constitutionalism, the rule of law has been central to the definition of limited government. Government is confined in its actions to its constitutional powers and must obey its own laws. State law serves both as a guide to legitimate conduct for citizens and a source of relief from harms. Second, governments have been regulators of extra-governmental social activities and also providers of services to citizens. Thus they have been concerned with substantive policy and with affecting social states of affairs.

Third, governments have been orchestrators of social consensus, for example as the leading partners in forms of negotiated governance with major organized social interests. As we have seen, this role has been superficially identified with corporatism and seen to be obsolete in neo-liberal forms of market economy. However, the more complex and multi-centred forms of negotiated governance still require the public power as a co-ordinator and as a source of constraint to keep partners at the table when disagreements occur.

Lastly, governments have served as the means of defense of the national territory and as the exclusive representative of that territory abroad. This role was central to the state as it emerged in a system of competing states, for whom war was a normal means of intercourse. The fact that war has diminished as a threat for the advanced states in recent years, does not mean that this role no longer matters or that the state's monopoly of external representation of the territory had ceased to be important.

It by no means follows that a relative weakening of the capacities of the nation state involves all four of these roles to the same degree. Democratic theorists have tended to see the first role as essentially setting the context for the second one and the second role as the primary one. Democracy is considered to be chiefly concerned with substantive decisions, and the issue is to ensure that these are the will of the majority, either directly or through representatives. I shall claim that not only has the nation state lost some substantive governance capacities, but also that its growing rôle as a service provider, especially in the period of expansion of state activity after 1945, came to weaken and confuse its role as a source of accountability. I shall also claim that, contrary to the prevailing assumption of democratic theory, the first and third roles are central to the enhancement of democratic power within states and that the fourth role, if redefined, is capable of making the democratic nation state the main source of legitimacy and accountability for the complex quasi-polities that have grown in significance at the supra-national level.

REDEFINING DEMOCRACY

To further this argument it is important to pause and consider how we define democracy, in terms of the outcomes we expect when we consider a procedure or institution democratic. Democracy is widely recognized to be an ambiguous concept and there is no point in searching for or disputing its essential meaning. Democracy is not only a matter of majority decision, nor need it involve a single demos. In *Associative Democracy* (1994) I have used Émile Durkheim's (1957) conception of democracy as ongoing two-way communication between governors and governed to extend the meaning of this concept. Democracy in this sense is about government by information exchange and consent, where organized publics have the means to conduct a dialogue with government and thus hold it to account. Majority decisions matter but they have a subsiding part in the process of governance. Elections and referenda are relatively infrequent and only decide certain salient issues, whereas governance is a continuous process and all of its decisions cannot be subject to majority approval. The primary agents in this dialogue with the state were, for Durkheim, corporatist occupational groups, but there is no reason why it cannot be extended to a wider range of associations. In one sense this government by consent is a normal part of the current political process, but it is limited because so many of the groups entering into dialogue are exclusive and internally undemocratic.

If we return to the problem for democracy (in the senses both of majority rule and communication) posed by an organizational society, then it can be seen as having two parts. First, the prevalence of organizations that are not subject to the need to consult or even consider those whose interests are affected by their decisions. Second, a fragmented state that finds it difficult to give coherence to its actions, let alone communicate effectively with civil society. As we have seen this fragmentation is paradoxically increased by attempts to cope with governmental overload in overburdened public service states by privatizing and by creating arms' length agencies. So to the very scale and scope of public service states we can add the problem of the complexity created by trying to lessen the difficulties of control and supervision of services.

Modern institutions of representative government were mostly designed in the nineteenth century to superintend states with much more limited functions than today, and it is no wonder that they do not work well today as sources of accountability. Similarly national legal regulation continued to work tolerably well whilst it policed a relatively simple and self-governing market society. Modern representative governments are caught in the contradictory roles of being at once the provider of services and the guarantor and source of accountability for those services. Modern legislation faces an equally difficult task in attempting to protect the public against a widening range of contingencies in an increasingly complex society. Such protection is necessary because modern society is increasingly composed of undemocratic institutions that provide no other remedies to those on whom they have effects. The result is a proliferation of rules that undermine the rule of law by the very scale, complexity, and costs of the legal system itself.

DEMOCRATIZING THE ORGANIZATIONAL SOCIETY

The only way out of this is large-scale institutional reform, affecting both the state and social institutions. I advocate the adoption of the associative democratic model, which involves devolving as many of the functions of the state as possible to society (whilst retaining public funding) and democratizing as many as possible of the organizations in civil society. The aim is to restore limited government and to 'politicize' civil society, to turn its organizations from top-down bureaucracies into constitutionally ordered democratically self-governing associations.

The aim would be to try to separate service provision from supervision at all the principal levels of government within the nation state. By thus simplifying the task of representative institutions, making them primarily watchdogs, their effectiveness in ensuring that services are appropriately provided can be enhanced to a considerable degree. But how can the scope of government be limited without eliminating the services it has provided? Privatization and marketization have aimed to limit the scope of the state by reducing the services it directly provides, but in fact they have not simplified the task of governance. They have tended to make how services are delivered more complex and also created new necessities to protect the interests of service recipients by rules about service quality and by new forms of regulatory supervision.

The answer offered here is different, to devolve service provision to self-governing voluntary associations wherever possible. Members would elect to join such service providers and the associations would receive public funds proportionate to membership for providing a specific public service like education or healthcare. Members would enjoy the options of voice and exit. Associations would have to be, at a minimum, representative democracies with all members having the right to elect the governing body. Members would have an annual option to quit and join another competing voluntary service provider. The combined possibility of competitive pressure through defections and the role of activists using the option of voice, will tend to keep such voluntary bodies on their toes and there remains the possibility of government inspections or legal action. This means that such voluntary bodies could be deemed to be self-regulating, subject to rules as to minimum service quality and appropriate internal governance procedures.

Associative self-governance would establish basic democratic legitimacy for organizations, thereby reducing the need for external governance to protect those affected and reducing the need to provide formal external rules for every contingency. The existence of such self-governing associations as a model would make possible a radical administrative decentralization, removing tasks from central, local, and quango governments. Such associative self-governance would also serve as a source of pressure for democratization in the wider society, exposing the need for companies to seek equivalent legitimacy with regard to their own stakeholders. An associative reform would thus begin to restore limited government, and, therefore, the possibility of greater accountability in and through the state, and yet also extend democratic control in society. It would thus achieve the same objectives as were claimed for marketization—competition between providers and consumer choice—without making service access so dependent on the ability to pay.

The logic of such devolution to self-governing associations as a solution to problems of democracy in modern organizational societies is explained more fully in *Associative Democracy*. The point to emphasize here is that associational self-government would supplement and extend representative government, not replace it. National democracy would thus be strengthened and made viable by a democratized civil society. Government's primary tasks would thus be to raise and distribute revenue to associations and the provision of constitutional ordering and supervision to the institutions of civil society. Moreover, in its role as the orchestrator of social consensus, the state would be available to provide co-ordination between lesser authorities, associations and firms by sponsoring and overseeing forms of negotiated governance. A system that relied on self-governing associations need not be fragmented, the provision of services would create common issues and inter-associational problems that would most appropriately addressed by negotiated governance. Thus consociational institutions and practices could supplement both representative democracy at national level and assocational self-governance.

These may seem radical proposals and also an unusual form of normative advocacy tied to definite empirical propositions about the effects of institutions. However, given the scale of the problems for democratic accountability, it is difficult to see how palliative measures and more limited reforms will restore a significant level of democratic control. Conventional ideas such as further administrative decentralization, greater use of referenda, citizen's juries, and deliberative forums are all valuable but do not get to the root of the problem. Associative democracy has the virtue of confronting fragmentation directly, accepting it, democratizing the various organizations, and then seeking to reintegrate them through mechanisms of consociational governance. It also accepts the continued existence of a society of organizations, but attempts to give their members a say in them. The options of voice and exit would tend to promote democratic manners, by giving citizens opportunities for control and alternatives to conformity. As for the style of advocacy, I make no apology—analysis and normative hypotheses need to go together in any worthwhile political theorizing.

THE NATION STATE AS A LEGITIMATOR OF GOVERNANCE ROLES

A reinvigorated democratic national state, less burdened by the minutiae of governance, could better serve as the focal point in the elaborate division of labour in governance that is now inevitable. We saw that without some means of linking the different levels of governance, fundamental problems of co-ordination will occur. Elsewhere I have argued (Hirst and Thompson, 1996: ch. 8) that the democratic nation state is the best available locus for suturing together the distinct forms of sub-national, national and supra-national governance. The state is capable of doing this suturing because only it can perform three key roles simultaneously. First, in its capacity as a source of constitutional ordering and as an orchestrator of social consensus, the state is capable appropriately to distribute powers and responsibilities between itself, regional and local governments, and civil society. Second, the nation state remains the main focus of political identity for citizens and is still the main institution of democratic legitimacy that most citizens understand and are willing to accept. Effective democratic states thus can represent their populations more credibly than any other body. Third, national governments in stable democracies are thus strongly legitimate externally, their decisions and commitments are taken as reliable by other states and political entities, and thus their external commitments can provide legitimacy for supra-national majorities in quasi-polities and for inter-state agreements.

Only states have the capacity adequately to supervise international agencies or to act as the primary political agents in the forms of indirect democracy that characterize the decision procedures of quasi polities like the EU. Although NGOs are a valuable supplement to states in confronting international agencies and a valuable counterweight to states, they cannot speak authoritatively for a given territory, even if they have many members. However, for states to exercise this capacity adequately national political actors have to accept that states are no longer 'sovereign' externally, rather they are representatives of their peoples in other political bodies and forums. We need to see the supra-national not in terms of international relations but as politics, with states as members of various ongoing quasi-polities and associations of states, like the G8 or the EU. Most of these bodies and international agencies, like the WTO, enjoy the powers they do from interstate treaties and agreements. Such treaties look less and less like the grand diplomacy of the old Great Powers and more like international social contracts that establish civil orders that are almost impossible to unscramble by acts of sovereign will. The most powerful and influential states provide the resources and the legitimacy for bodies like the IMF and WTO, and, therefore, are capable of exercising some control over them. They should be seen as the 'global electors', controlling a series of quasi-polities and agencies that make up the world order. This world order is minimally governed but without a single political centre.

The expectation that national states are substantive governors within, that they can solve problems in their own territories, has focused national politics on domestic policy. Citizens have been slow to recognize how much states have become vehicles for representing the national interest in wider forums with considerable governing capacity. This neglect has been true of politicians too. However, supra-national politics is increasingly becoming the focus of national politics and not just a periodic exception. If a reorientation in this direction does take place, then states will not just be formal legitimators for supra-national bodies, but a source of active democratic input, relaying the majority domestic public view. A series of indirect democracies where the members are democratic states is the best we can hope for at the level of supra-national governance. There are severe limits to such forms of accountability at present. Inclusiveness and effect-iveness seem to be opposed virtues at the global level. Rich democratic states have legitimacy and can put real pressure on global bodies but they tend to do so exclusively for themselves. Bodies like the UN are weakly legitimate and ineffective because they combine rich and poor, democratic and undemocratic states, and hence majorities in the General Assembly have little force. The problem, therefore, is to encourage the rich and pow-erful nations to act in a less self-interested way, and to accept the need to supervise international agencies, like the IMF, on behalf of wider con-stituencies.

Obviously states are not the only sources of legitimacy, accountability and law. International law is increasingly autonomous and effective. But without a large population of states that abide by the rule of law internally, the extension of such supranational regulation would be impossible. International rules can only be received by states that are themselves law-ful, limited governments that keep their own rules. Such states are more likely to adopt the decisions of international tribunals and to keep inter-national covenants. In that sense national states remain the vital links in the chain of law making and the promotion of representative democracy and the rule of law in advanced and developing countries alike, a condition for the effectiveness of international governance through law.

The 'post-political' thrust of the concept of governance in the five meanings considered above not only evades the issue of democracy but also that of political conflict. Markets are seen as neutral institutions, with impersonal outcomes. Quasi-markets in the public arena and public agencies adopting the management forms and practices of business corporations likewise seek to replace politics with exchange and with rational goal-oriented management. Nation states have, on the contrary, existed primarily to protect against and to contain conflict. Thus by monopolizing the means of violence internally, and becoming the sole legitimate external utilizers of violence, states have sought to pacify their territories, to interact in an orderly way with other states, and to defend their territory against attack. As sources of legitimate authority, sustained by a popular vote, democratic states have provided institutionalized means to contain political conflicts, to arbitrate between conflicting interests, but also to serve as a stable medium for the pursuit of power and influence by conflicting interests. The governance discourse tends to ignore these considerable strengths of the democratic nation state and its purported monopoly of competence in determining who shall govern what and how. If the nation state is no longer a monopoly provider of government, it does not follow that issues of conflict and its containment have been displaced. The arguments advanced here for a division of labour in governance and for the democratization of organizations to legitimate them in relation to affected interests both attempt to address this deficit of attention to conflict and to 'politics' in the traditional sense in the literature on governance. Democracy matters because it provides a mechanism for consulting and respecting the interests involved in decisions, only if this is achieved to a sufficient degree can governance be sufficiently legitimate to contain conflict. Equally a division of labour in governance, necessary to ensure consistency and coordination between the different levels, must be anchored by democratically legitimate bodies that are part of that division. Democracy is central to governance and that is why the democratic nation state still has a pivotal role, albeit a different one from that envisaged in conventional democratic theory.

REFERENCES

ARCHER, R. (1995), Economic Democracy: *The Politics of Feasible Socialism* (Oxford: Oxford University Press).

BACCARO, L., and LOCKE, R. M. (1996), 'Public Sector Reform and Union Participation: The Case of Italian Pension Reforms' (paper presented to annual meeting American Political Science Association, San Francisco, 29 Aug.–1 Sept.).

CADBURY COMMITTEE (1992) 'Report of the Cadbury Committee on the Financial Aspects of Corporate Governance' (London: HMSO).

CERNY, P. (1998), 'Neo-Medievalism, Civil War and the New Security Dilemmas: Globalisation as Durable Disorder', *Civil Wars*, 1: 36–64.

DAHL, R. A. (1970), *After the Revolution* (New Haven: Yale University Press).

—— (1985), *A Preface to Economic Democracy* (Cambridge: Polity Press).

DURKHEIM, É. (1957), *Professional Ethics and Civic Morals* (London: Routlege and Kegan Paul).

The Economist (1995), 'The Myth of the Powerless State', 7 Oct.

GRAY, J. (1998), *False Dawn: The Delusions of Global Capitalism* (London: Granta).

HELD, D. (1991), 'Democracy, the nation state and the Global System', *Economy and Society*, 20: 138–72.

—— (1995), *Democracy and the Global Order: From the Modern State to Cosmopolitan Governance* (Cambridge: Policy Press).

HINDESS, B. (1991), 'Imaginary Presuppositions of Democracy', *Economy and Society*, 20: 173–95.

—— (1997), 'Democracy and Disenchantment', *Australian Journal of Political Science*, 32: 79–92.

HIRST, P. (1994), *Associative Democracy* (Cambridge: Polity Press).

—— (1997a), 'The Global Economy—myths and realities', *Foreign Affairs*, 73: 409–25.

—— (1997b), *From Statism to Pluralism* (London: UCL Press).

—— and THOMPSON, G. (1996), *Globalization in Question* (Cambridge: Polity Press).

HUTTON, W. (1995), *The State We're In* (London: Cape).

ILO (1995), 'Perspectives—Experiences of Social Pacts in Western Europe', *International Labour Review* 134: 410–17.

JENKINS, S. (1996), *Accountable to None: the Tory Nationalization of Britain* (London: Penguin).

KELLY, G., KELLY, D., and GAMBLE, A. (eds.) (1997), *Stakeholder Capitalism* (Basingstoke: Macmillan).

KORTEN, D. C. (1996), *When Corporations Rule the World* (London: Earthscan).

KRASNER, S. D. (ed.) (1983), *International Regimes* (Ithaca, NY: Cornell University Press).

MARTIN, H-P., and SCHUMANN, H. (1997), *The Global Trap* (London: Zed Books).

MINC, A. (1993), *Le Nouveau Moyen Age* (Paris: Gallimard).

PIERRE, J. (1995), 'The Marketisation of the State: Citizens, Consumers and the Emergence of the Public Market', in B. G. Peters and D. J. Savoie (eds.), *Governance in a Changing Environment* (Montreal and Kingston: McGill-Queens University Press), 47–69.

PRESTHUS, R. (1965), *The Organizational Society* (New York: Vintage).

REGINI, M. (1997), 'Still Engaging in Corporatism? Recent Italian Experience in Comparative Perspective', *European Journal of Industrial Relations*, 3: 259–78.

RHODES, R. A. W. (1997), *Understanding Governance: Policy Networks, Governance, Flexibility and Accountability* (Buckingham, UK: Open University Press).

ROE, MARK J. (1994), *Strong Managers Weak Owners: The Political Roots of American Corporate Finance* (Princeton, NJ: Princeton University Press).

ROSENAU, J., and CZEMPIEL, E-O. (eds.) (1992), *Governance without Government* (Cambridge University Press).

ROYAL SOCIETY OF ARTS INQUIRY (1995), *Towards Tomorrow's Company* (London: RSA).

RUGGIE, J. G. (1983), 'International Regimes, Transactions and Change: Embedded Liberalism in the Postwar Economic Order', in S. D. Krasner (ed.), *International Regimes* (Ithaca, NY: Cornell University Press), 195–231.

SABEL, C. (1995), 'Bootstrapping Reform: Rebuilding Firms, the Welfare State and Unions', *Politics and Society*, 23: 5–48.

SPRUYT, H. (1994), *The Sovereign State and its Competitors* (Princeton: Princeton University Press).

STRANGE, S. (1996), *The Retreat of the State* (Cambridge: Cambridge University Press).

VISSER, J., and HEMERIJCK, A. (1997), *'A Dutch Miracle': Job Growth, Welfare Reform and Corporatism in the Netherlands* (Amsterdam: Amsterdam University Press).

WEIR, S. (1996), 'From Strong Government and Quasi Government to Strong Democracy', in P. Hirst and S. Khilnani (eds.), *Reinventing Democracy* (Oxford: Blackwell/The Politcal Quarterly).

WORLD BANK (1997), *World Development Report—The State in a Changing World* (Oxford: Oxford University Press).

3

Governance and Comparative Politics

B. GUY PETERS

The question we are faced with here is how can a governance perspective inform and improve the study of comparative politics? What do we gain by using governance to frame a discussion of differences among nation states as opposed to using the variety of other theoretical and analytical perspectives that have been advocated (Dogan and Pelassy, 1990)? At one level the governance approach forces the scholar of comparative politics to examine what governments do, and how they perform their functions; in that way it is similar to adopting a policy perspective in the field (Heidenheimer, Heclo and Adams, 1990). Are certain types of political systems apparently better at steering and control than are others? If so, why does that appear to be the case?

The answer to this question about the utility of the governance perspective depends in part, however, upon which of several extant approaches to governance is adopted. If the more traditional 'steering' conception of governance is adopted (Rose, 1978; see also Bovens, 1990) then the question becomes one of the capacity of the center of government to exert control over the rest of government, and over the economy and society. If the 'modern governance' or 'new governance' perspective is adopted (Kooiman, 1993; Rhodes, 1997) then the question becomes one of how that centre of government interacts with society to reach mutually acceptable decisions, or whether society actually does more self-steering rather than depend upon guidance from government, especially central government.[1] This leads on to an associated question of whether steering decisions made by government can be implemented once they have been made.

---

[1] Sub-national government appears to be in a somewhat ambiguous position here. It is governmental certainly, but also tends to stand at odds to the central government.

Both of these approaches raise valid and important questions about governance, but they are substantially different questions. The two versions of governance also imply very different approaches to comparative politics, but when phrased in comparative terms the issues are not as incompatible as they may appear initially. Both approaches make the functionalist assumption that society must be governed and then proceed to ask what the source of that governance will be. The functionalist question begins with very broad assertions about whether state or society is dominant, and then the comparison can become more fine-tuned to assess relative contributions of different political structures to governance.

What neither approach does very well is to address issues of mass politics and the inputs into the political process through familiar mechanisms such as voting and public opinion (Dalton, 1996). In this way adopting a governance perspective may be a healthy antidote to the large volume of literature on mass politics in political science. This literature has been little concerned with what governments actually do, and has tended to assume a correspondence between the 'inputs' made into the system and the outputs. While there are already sufficient reasons to doubt such a close correspondence (Rose, 1974; Castles and Wildenmann, 1986), the governance perspective places the question of performance at the centre of the debate.

These disjunctures also raise questions about the connections between governance approaches and democratic theory, and the now burgeoning literature on democratization in transitional societies (O'Donnell, Schmitter and Whitehead, 1986). The interest in governance to some extent resurrects the discussion in some of the earlier modernization and development literature concerning the crucial linkage between legitimacy and effectiveness (Lipset, 1959) in creating viable political systems. That is, how do governments govern if they are not legitimate? But is being effective in governance not the best way of building lasting legitimacy?

It also is interesting that at the same time that the academic literature is raising numerous analytic questions about governance, the more practical concerns of governments themselves are with 'performance' and 'quality' and similar questions of effectiveness, rather than with the procedures that have tended to dominate much of the public administration literature. Any number of governments have initiated programmes to enhance the performance of their own organizations and their personnel, and are searching for effective ways of measuring and fostering performance within the public sector. It appears that both the academic and the practical world are attempting to determine ways of understanding better how government

actually works, with at least one of the two attempting to utilize that knowledge to make government work better.

I will be making the argument that governance offers an important and
interesting avenue for reframing the study of comparative politics and government. This reframing appears analogous to the way in which the implementation literature refocused the literature in public administration
(Pressman and Wildavsky, 1974; Barrett and Fudge, 1980) The public
administration literature was useful and important before the concept of
implementation was introduced into it, but became more analytically useful thereafter.[2] The reason is simply that implementation provided a more
or less objective standard against which to compare the outcomes of the
process; did the law or programme go into effect as intended? If it did not
(as is usually the case), then why not? These questions moved the discussion of public administration beyond description of processes and structures to ask more interesting questions about the way in which the public
sector actually functions.

A governance approach does much the same for comparative politics
and government, and indeed would for the study of politics in any one
country. If we assume (almost always rightly) that governments or other
political actors are attempting to make something happen through the
political process, then we can ask what happened along the way to cause it
to fail, or why it succeeded in part and failed in part, or indeed ask why it
was successful (see LeGrand, 1991). Adopting the governance approach
simply provides some standard against which to examine behaviour in the
public sector, and analyse what has happened. The same type of analysis
may be undertaken from other perspectives, e.g. from an institutionalist
view (Weaver and Rockman, 1993), but thinking about governance and
governing makes the question of what has happened to policy ideas and
proposals all the more evident.

What makes the use of the governance approach particularly useful for
comparative politics is that there is some variance on the independent variables. This is true whether we adopt an 'old governance' or a 'new governance' perspective. If we look at governance questions within a single
political system, or even within a single class of political systems then any
answer to the basic question of what happens to attempts to 'steer' may be
incomplete or just incorrect. The same attributes that appear associated
with failure in one setting may appear to be associated with success in

---

[2] For the purposes of this paper some of the comparative studies of implementation
become particularly important. See Grindle (1980).

another. If that is indeed the case then clearly there are other factors at work that need to be explored. We assume, for example, that 'divided government' is a major reason for failure in presidentialist regimes (Pierce, 1991; but see Mayhew, 1991), but the same divisions may be manifested, albeit in different ways, in coalition governments in parliamentary systems. Thus, although we will be looking primarily at what governance tells us about comparative government, the reverse question can also be asked: what does comparative government tell us about governance theory?

GOVERNANCE AND COMPARISON

Although we will be arguing largely on its behalf, the governance approach as a means of conceptualizing and interpreting comparative politics is not without its problems. These problems need not be fatal, but they do prevent any simple and unthinking adoption of the approach within this subdiscipline. If nothing else, any use of the concept requires the researcher to be very explicit about what he or she intends to do when 'governance' is invoked, and to elaborate what the theoretical implications of the choices are.

Clarity and Travelling

The most basic problem with 'governance' has already been alluded to; the term is used in two almost inherently contradictory ways, and therefore there is a real possibility of misunderstanding. But the conceptual problems do not end there. One of the two basic conceptualizations of governance itself appears to have two versions, and the empirical and normative elements of those two sub-species are not always distinguished, so that a scholar may readily blend the observable with the assumptive worlds if he or she is not wary.

We can begin to look at these conceptual problems by starting with the somewhat simpler idea of 'old governance'. Following from the above discussion, there are both normative and empirical elements in this approach. The empirical element is contained largely in determining if (again much like in implementation studies), a government is capable of governing. Like all good empirical questions this one is open to investigation and should display a good deal of variance on the dependent variable. Some such as

Sweden are expected to show up as effective while others like the United States may be more suspect.

The normative element of old governance is implicit, and somewhat more subtle. It appears first that there is the simple argument that an effective government is a good thing—a view to which people living in societies without one would probably subscribe. There is also the implication that the state is necessary to guide the public toward some attainment of the 'public interest'. In this view the public interest is much more than just a simple aggregation of their individual interests, or the triumph of the strongest socio-economic elements in society. The (again largely implicit) assumption is that society can not reach that higher order good on their own, but instead requires the imposition of the authority of the state.

There is some empirical and analytic evidence to back the implicit normative claims of old governance scholars that society is incapable of going beyond self-interested policy outcomes, and hence requires governance. The most famous is perhaps the Avrow problem in welfare economics, arguing that under realistic assumptions about preferences and voting systems there is no way of reaching desirable outcomes without the imposition of the solution (Avrow, 1957). The argument of the 'tragedy of the commons', and related problems of controlling common property resources, are another way of understanding the need for some institutional mechanisms for imposing solutions (Ostrom, 1990; Peters, 1999). The basic argument is, therefore, that the state and old governance are required to produce better outcomes from social and political activity than would otherwise be possible.

When we move to consider 'new governance' the conceptual problems do not become a great deal easier. We should first distinguish here between the negative and the positive versions of the 'new governance' that appear to exist within the literature. These two versions of new governance exist side by side, and at times a single analyst may move back and forth between the two versions almost without thinking. The two versions of new governance do seem, however, to have rather different implications for the comparative analysis of politics. The negative version of new governance stresses the capacity of social forces to resist the regulations and impositions of the state, while the positive version extols the virtues of governance systems that operate through those same instrumentalities.

If we begin with the negative conception of 'new governance' then we see there are an additional two elements within it. Both normative and empirical elements are involved, and closely intertwined, in the arguments supporting the negative version of new governance. The normative element is that somehow citizens know better what they want and need than does the state, and therefore are entirely justified in finding way to avoid those incursions of authority and bureaucracy into their lives. The argument sounds somewhat like that of the 'philosophical radicals' in France who argued that the principal duty of the citizen was to resist the power of the state (Alain, 1951); this was more than empirical *incivisme*, it was also a philosophical position. More recently, the communitarian literature (Etzioni, 1997; Tam, 1998) and the deliberative democracy literature (Bohman, 1996) embrace some of the same claims about the capacity of people and communities to identify their own needs and to govern themselves more autonomously.

Empirically, the argument of the negative 'new governance' advocates is that groups, and even individuals, in society do have the capacity to resist government's interventions. Governments do have legitimate authority on their side, but the public is seen as sufficiently clever and resourceful to escape any regulations that they do not like. We can see this in the capacity of industries to avoid regulation, or in the capacity of ordinary citizens to evade taxation (Peters, 1991), or perhaps in the capacity of subnational governments to undermine the intentions of grant programmes from the central government. At the same time that groups in society are portrayed as rather clever, governments tend to become stereotyped as clumsy and bureaucratic.

The positive version of the new governance is that there are resources in society that are sufficiently powerful to shape policy, at both the input and the output stages. Networks, communities, and other aggregations of interest organizations that surround policy areas are assumed to be in positions to either shape policy as they see fit, or to assist government in putting policies into effect. In this view the strength, and even dominance, of society becomes an asset for governance, at least within the individual policy domain. That is, in this view it appears that there would be little overall coordination of policy (see Peters, 1998), but within each policy area—each 'silo' or 'iron triangle' there would be effective governance. In fact, within each domain there is likely to be extremely effective governance, with most of the actors involved agreeing on the nature of the problem as well as the solutions.

Again, one can identify both normative and empirical elements within the more positive conception of 'new governance'. The normative element is that society should be capable of managing many of its own affairs without the need for intervention from the state. Further, social capital is argued to be necessary for good (especially democratic) governance (Putnam *et al.*, 1993). Strong social groups create that social capital and can function as the training ground for political participation, especially in socio-economic settings in which effective governance might be expected to be difficult (Gyimah-Boadi, 1996).

These various versions of governance also appear to present something of a travelling problem, one of the major pitfalls in comparative theory building. This hazard appears primarily as we think about the 'new governance' approach as it functions in different societies. On the one hand in those societies in which civil society has not been seen to be sufficiently developed to sustain effective governance, the question appears to be how to build a strong society and to do so for reasons of building the capacity of government to govern. On the other hand, in more developed societies, the existence of a strong civil society appears to become a barrier to effective governance. It may be that the relationship between society and governance may be curvilinear (see below) but if so that relationship needs to be explored within that context.

Governance and Comparison

Now, one of the reasons for doing comparative research is that there is variance by country, or by whatever geographical unit of analysis is being used for the research. One problem with some components of the 'new governance' literature is that it virtually defines away some of the more interesting parts of the available variance. By appearing to argue that the state, or the centre of government, is largely incapable of ruling, it appears to refuse to consider that indeed there are cases in which the centre may be effective. That variance may be by country, with the state in some countries (Singapore, Iraq, but also the United Kingdom) having a great deal of capacity to achieve compliance from society. The variance may also be by policy area (see Freeman, 1985) with governments generally being better placed to achieve compliance in areas such as defence and immigration than in policy areas with stronger domestic interest organizations.

The use of the network concept to identify the mechanism through which 'governance without government' can be achieved also appears to define away a good deal of interesting variance in the area of governance. Societal forces may be structured in a number of different ways, and their interactions with the state also differ (see below). For example, some scholars of Austrian politics argue that corporatism remains in place, or has even been strengthened, despite its alleged demise in other settings (see Schmitter, 1989). The network concept may be sufficiently general to subsume corporatism, pluralism, and a host of other ways of conceptualizing the state–society interface, but that appears to defeat the purpose of comparison. To paraphrase Wildavsky, if networks are everything, then maybe they are nothing.

The purpose for comparative analysis appears, therefore, to investigate the capacity of the centre to govern, rather than to define it away. The comparative exercise could begin with either the 'old' or 'new' perspectives on governance. From one the assumption is that the centre should be able to govern, while from the other the assumption would be that it should not necessarily. From either view, however, the question of matching stated goals with outcomes can be asked, and factors facilitating or hindering the achivement of those goals can be identified. The use of comparison provides for such an assessment while single country or single policy area studies would not.

Governance and Mid-Range Theory

From a more analytic perspective the governance model tends to push comparative research back in the direction of whole-system comparison. Following the pleas by LaPalombara (1968) and others (see Peters, 1998) for mid-range theory and attention to components of the political system, a good deal of development in comparative analysis has been directed at theories that address either a single institution or a particular group of countries (Heisler, 1974; Berg-Schlosser, 1984). The argument was that any theory that attempted to cover all aspects of politics in all places might be so general as to be useless for analytic purposes.

If we are to think about governance as the carrying through of policy intentions, then we are almost required to engage in the analysis of an entire system and its internal interconnections. Although more focused, governance then becomes a model of analysis not dissimilar to systems theory, in that there is input, processing, and output that is assessed. There is also more than a whiff of a teleological, goal-seeking component to the approach. Whereas systems theory was conceptualized as seeking equilibrium, governance is seen to seek control of society (and perhaps social equilibrium rather than equilibrium within the system itself).

In many ways governance theory could be conceived as reviving structural-functional approaches to politics, long thought to be moribund (but see Lane, 1994). Structural functionalism assumed that politics happened in any setting, but did not argue for the importance of any particular locus or process for politics. The importance of structural functionalism for comparison was that this approach forced scholars to think about the alternative sources of governing. Governance theory does much the same thing; it assumes that governance will occur, and therefore the comparative question becomes one of how, and through what institutional mechanisms, it occurs in particular settings.

A good deal of progress in comparative politics has been made by creating building blocks defined by institutions, processes, and geography. The question is whether the subdiscipline is now ready to move ahead to create more comprehensive theories based on governance. This movement need not be imperialistic, with governance being the only option for building a more comprehensive approach. The question is whether we have a sufficient stock of analytic tools and empirical findings to create more sweeping approaches to comparison.

Institutionalism versus Deinstitutionalization

Another important point for comparison is the way formal institutions, constitutions, and similar structural elements fit into the study of comparative politics. For a good portion of the post-war period in comparative analysis there was a movement away from formalism and constitutionalism, and advocacy for examining the behavioural aspects of politics—what actually happened and what the individual level attributes were that produced the decisions in the public sector.

More recently comparative analysis has returned to some of its roots and is looking more carefully at institutions, and the role that formal structures (including constitutions) play in governing. This has not excluded the questions of individual level variance, but it has forced the behavioural brethren to think about the structures within which individuals do their behaving. The new institutionalism has become a significant focus of comparison, as well as other aspects of political science.[3]

The choice of either old governance or new governance appears to imply a push toward one element of this (perhaps false) dichotomy or the other. If the old governance approach is selected there appears to be some push towards greater formalism and perhaps constitutionalism. The state is

---

[3] Like governance 'institutionalism' may mean many different things to different people, so some care must be taken when discussing this term (see Peters, 1999).

returned to the stage as the central actor and is often defined in a rather for-malistic manner. There is the danger of reifying government, and of assum-ing that there is a 'central mind of government' (Dror, 1994) that establishes policy priorities and whose aspirations serve as the standard for governing. As has been noted any number of times in critiques of the 'State' literature, government is rarely a unitary actor, and rarely has a single coherent and integrated set of preferences for policy. The governance per-spective may implicitly advise governments that they should create such a coherent approach to governing (see Peters, 1997), but in the real world that happens infrequently. Thus, saying that one is adopting a governance perspective begs a number of questions about which of a number of alter-native policy priorities is being privileged in the analysis.

On the other hand, if new governance is selected then the state is almost certainly banished again, but we may lack any real dramatis personae to motivate the action. That is, if the old governance approach creates a straw person of the unitary state as motivator of the action, the decentralized, fragmented approach of new governance appears to have little to force the action. Something may emerge from the rather unguided interactions within all the networks, but it is not clear how that will happen, and there is perhaps too much faith in the self-organizing and self-coordinating capacities of people. In some ways, the negative conception of new govern-ance may be better off here, given that it is seen largely as a means of sub-verting the intentions of the state, rather than as the source of autonomous action.

There may be yet other ways in which the perspectives of old and new governance come into conflict. I would argue that 'old' governance implies attempts (although certainly not always successes) at creating greater coherence among policies and across policy domains. Part of the demand for the commodity called governance is that the various sectors of govern-ment do not function well together, and appear to produce conflicts and incoherence in policy. That incoherence, in turn, creates disaffection with government and excessive expenditures. The new governance approach, on the other hand, might institutionalize and legitimate the conflicts among policy domains, and reinforce those natural divisions.

There are, of course, ways around these coherence problems. Those would include the creation of overlapping networks and the use of devices such as corporate pluralism. Those strategies, however, appear to imply the authoritative intervention of state actors, something that might be written out of the script by new governance advocates. Indeed, it appears to be in the political interest of networks within each policy sector to maintain their own local equilibrium, and to pursue some global optimum only where forced to by external (e.g. state) actors.

Summary

In short, governance may have the capacity to reinvigorate some aspects of comparative politics. It addresses a question that all polities must face, and raises fundamental questions about the roles of state and society in achieving social control. It seems to be meaningful and applicable in all manner of political systems, and is sufficiently robust to range across the world. These strengths may, however, also be part of its weaknesses. Is governance so general a term as to be meaningless? Has the concept so many meanings that we might be better starting anew and specifying more precisely what we mean and have a single denotative meaning for the term? In Sartori's (1970) phrasing of these issues, have we achieved so much by extension that we have lost all intension?

GOVERNANCE AND THEMES IN COMPARATIVE POLITICS

The remainder of this chapter will discuss various themes in comparative politics through the lens of governance. In the space available this can hardly be a comprehensive essay, but it should point to the possible utility, and possible pitfalls, of using governance as an organizing concept in the comparative study of political systems. In conducting this *tour de horizon* I will also attempt to distinguish between the differential impacts of 'old' and 'new' conceptions of governance. These two views on governance will provide rather different lenses through which to view comparative politics. Indeed, we could almost think of the two as providing their own version of the triangulation that may be necessary for building better theory in comparative politics (Webb *et al.*, 1967; Peters, 1998).

Democratization

One concern currently motivating a good deal of comparative analysis is the question of democratization. As a number of countries in East and

Central Europe, Latin America and increasingly Africa undergo a transition to some form of democratic government, we should consider the implications of those transformations for our understanding of governance (Stepan and Skach, 1993). Likewise, we should also ponder the implications of governance approaches for the study of democracy and the process of building democratic institutions. Although the democratization literature focuses on the input side of government, it must also be concerned with the capacity of government to govern effectively.

At first glance, it does not appear that governance theories are especially apt vehicles for understanding democracy and democratization. First, by concentrating attention on the central mind of government, 'old governance' might be perceived as undermining the need to consider democratization and the importance of inputs from the mass public into the political process. If taken to the extreme, it could even be argued that from the 'old governance' perspective carrying out the intentions of the centre of government should be considered more important than the manner in which that centre was selected, or how it arrived at its policy intentions. It is not at all difficult to build democratic requirements into the old governance model; all that would be required is some stipulation about the source of the governing elite and requirements for accountability. The model *per se*, however, does not have those democratic values as part of its central assumptions.

The 'new governance' model, despite its assumptions about the capabilities of the society to overcome a central government bent on steering, is not necessarily more compatible with most notions of political democracy. If we assume that the center is selected in some more or less democratic manner, then the capacity of groups to counteract and subvert its intentions may actually be anti-democratic. This sense of being anti-democratic might be especially apparent in cases in which a popularly elected government is thwarted by traditional elites, or by other entrenched socio-economic interests. Thus, the 'new governance' approach appears to work well as a way of thinking about the functioning of established democratic systems that have more or less equal opportunities for group mobilization.[4] It appears much more questionable in societies where the societal powers are themselves anti-democratic or at least question the efficacy of a democratic and activist government.

---

[4] The real range of applicability may be even narrower, i.e. countries in northern Europe such as the Netherlands and Scandinavia that have dense networks of interest groups and a history of working toward consensus (or at least accommodation).

State and Society

One of the classic questions in comparative politics is how state and society interact in the process of governing. In some ways this issue is a natural place to introduce the governance perspective into comparative analysis, given that it has been asking some of the same questions since at least the time of Aristotle. At issue here is how state and society interact, and to some extent which player is dominant in the political process. The traditional institutionalist position would have been that the state was the source of governance, and that its essential task was to govern and to provide order to society. In some versions of state theory, state and society were seen as virtually an organic whole, with the state however being the legitimating entity for action (see Dyson, 1980). In yet other approaches the real legitimacy for political action comes from society and from citizens, and hence we should focus attention on society-dominant, polyarchic systems.

The above discussion points to the normative elements of comparative political analysis, but the empirical elements also have this tension between state and society. Just as one of the two versions of governance emphasizes the role of the state and the other stresses the role of society, so too there are state-centric and society centric forms of explanation in comparative politics. Much of the 'new institutionalism', for example, tends to emphasize the role of formal institutional structures in the state as the best way of understanding differences among policy outcomes and political success. On the other hand the large body of literature on interest intermediation, as well as that on mass politics, tends to assume that social forces are dominant.

Clearly then an 'old governance' perspective is consistent with state-centric models of explanation. Take for example, the new institutionalist literature mentioned above. Does it matter if a country selects a presidentialist or a parliamentary form of government? The old governance approach would certainly believe that it does, and would have a range of arguments (empirical and normative) to back up that belief (Weaver and Rockman, 1993; Sartori, 1997; Stepan and Skach, 1993). That literature could easily go on to point to the subtle differences existing among types of presidentialism (Duverger, 1988; Noniaisenen, 1993) and different types of parliamentary government (Lijphart, 1984; Strom, 1990). In short, in this version of governance the structure of the state is what matters for explaining different levels of performance.

Similarly, the 'new governance' literature is consistent with the society-centric models of explanation. For the new governance literature the principal question appears to be how the social forces are structured so as to both channel the inputs of society into government, and to assist (or not) in implementation. As noted, depending upon which subset of the new governance literature is being discussed, society becomes either a major contributor or a major hindrance to providing direction and to implementing policies. In either case an understanding of governance begins with society and not with government itself.

Strong States and Weak States

Another of the classic questions in comparative government is that of the strength of the state. Even if states are the dominant actors in the policy process they may not be 'strong' in the sense of being able to overcome opposition. The interesting question is whether the governance perspective, and especially the 'new governance' approach, permits some reconceptualization of this question. If what really matters is that there is some direction provided, then the locus of that guidance may not be particularly important.

Migdal, working primarily in the context of developing societies, uses a simple typology to discuss the relationship between the relative strength of states and societies (see Migdal, 1988: fig. 1). Migdal argues that all four of the cells in this matrix should have some empirical referent, although he presents on cases of strong societies and strong states existing together. He

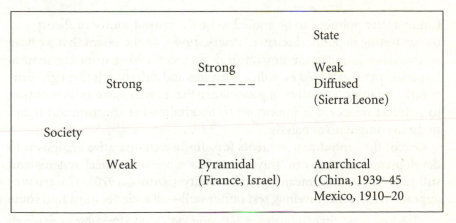

Fig. 3.1. **Social Control of States and Societies**

also implies, but does not develop (at least within the present framework) the notion that there are implications for governance in these differences.

Migdal appears to argue implicitly that state and society are playing a zero-sum game, there being no real cases in the 'strong/strong' cell in his typology. This assumption appears compatible with the 'old governance' view, and to some extent with the negative conception of 'new governance', but not with the positive conception of new governance. The latter approach appears to argue that a strong society would make strong governance by the state *more* possible. Governance is assumed to function better if there is more social capital in the society, rather than less (Putnam *et al.*, 1993).

In thinking about the relationships between state and society it appears to avoid the simple zero-sum conceptualization. Several of the more important conceptualizations of state–society interactions, e.g. the corporatist model and the corporate pluralist model, implied that the capacity of the state to govern was actually enhanced by the involvement of interests in the processes of formulation and implementation. By involving the groups in the policy process governments were able to co-opt them into the decisions and hence prevent subsequent opposition. The short-term decision-making costs appeared to be more than outweighed by the long-term gains in compliance.[5]

CONCLUSION

Comparative politics can be argued to be the central source of theory and theory testing in political science (Peters, 1998). To the extent that we have a laboratory to judge the impact of differences arising from the natural 'experiments' conducted by political leaders and citizens it is through comparative analysis. Therefore, if governance theory is to make a contribution to political science it is important to ascertain what contribution it can make to comparative analysis.

One of the central requirements for effective comparative analysis is to develop concepts that can 'travel' across a range of political systems and still have substantial meaning and validity (Sartori, 1970). Governance appears to meet the travelling test rather well—all societies must find some

[5] This logic is not dissimilar to that of Buchanan and Tullock (1965) discussing constitutions.

way of providing direction. Governance also appears capable of differentiating among different political systems, with some apparently more successful in governing than are others.

That capacity to differentiate appears substantially greater for the 'old governance' approach than for 'new governance'. If nothing else the existence of a clear (or at last clearer) set of goals from government makes assessment of success and failure more feasible. Further, there are marked normative implications in both versions of governance theory that must be considered when using this body of theory for comparative purposes. The summary assessment must be that governance holds a great deal of promise for comparative analysis, but that the potential is as yet largely unfulfilled.

REFERENCES

ALAIN (1951), *Politique* (Paris: Presses universitaires de France).

ARROW, K. (1957), *Social Choice and Individual Values* (Cambridge, Mass.: Harvard University Press).

BERG-SCHLOSSER, D. (1984), 'African Political Systems: Typology and Performance', *Comparative Political Studies*, 17: 121–51.

BOHMAN, J. (1996), *Public Deliberation: Pluralism, Complexity and Democracy* (Cambridge, Mass.: MIT Press).

BOVENS, M. A. P. (1990), 'The Social Steering of Complex Organizations', *British Journal of Political Science*, 20: 91–118.

BUCHANAN, J. M., and TULLOCK, G. (1965), *The Calculus of Consent* (Ann Arbor: University of Michigan Press).

CASTLES, F. G., and WILDENMANN, R. (eds.) (1986), *Visions and Realities of Party Government* (Berlin: De Gruyter).

DALTON, R. J. (1996), *Citizen Politics in Western Democracies: Public Opinion and Political Parties in the United States, Great Britain, West Germany and France* (2nd edn.) (Chatham, NJ: Chatham House).

DOGAN, M., and PELASSY, D. (1990), *How to Compare Nations: Strategies in Comparative Politics* (2nd edn.) (Chatham, NJ: Chatham House).

DROR, Y. (1994), *The Capacity to Govern* (Rome: Club of Rome).

DUVERGER, M. (1988), *Les Régimes semi-presidentiels* (Paris: Presses Universitaires de France).

DYSON, K. H. F. (1980), *State Traditions in Western Europe* (Oxford: Martin Robertson).

ETZIONI, A. (1997), *The New Golden Rule: Community and Morality in a Democratic Society* (New York: Profile Books).

FREEMAN, G. (1985), 'National Styles and Policy Sectors: Explaining Structured Variation', *Journal of Public Policy*, 5: 467–96.

GRINDLE, M. S. (1980), *Politics and Policy Implementation in the Third World* (Princeton: Princeton University Press).

GYIMAH-BOADI, E. (1996), 'Civil Society in Africa', *Journal of Democracy*, 7: 118–32.

HEIDENHEIMER, A. J., HECLO, H., and ADAMS, C. T. (1990), *Comparative Public Policy* (3rd edn.) (New York: St Martin's Press)

HEISLER, M. O. (1974), 'The European Polity Model', in M. O. Heisler (ed.), *Politics in Western Europe* (New York: David McKay).

KOOIMAN, J. (ed.) (1993), *Modern Governance* (London: Sage).

LANE, R. (1994), 'Structural-Functionalism Reconsidered: A Proposed Research Model', *Comparative Politics*, 26: 461–77.

LAPALOMBARA, J. (1968), 'Macro-theories and Micro-applications: A Widening Chasm', *Comparative Politics*, 1: 52–78.

LEGRAND, J. (1991), 'The Theory of Government Failure', *British Journal of Political Science*, 21: 423–42.

LIJPHART, A. (1984), *Democracies: Patterns of Majoritarian and Consensus Government in Twenty-one Countries* (New Haven, Conn.: Yale University Press).

LIPSET, S. M. (1959), 'Some Social Requisites of Democracy: Economic Development and Political Legitimacy', *American Political Science Review*, 53: 69–105.

MAYHEW, D. (1991), *Divided We Govern* (New Haven, Conn.: Yale University Press).

MIGDAL, J. S. (1988), *Strong Societies and Weak States: State Society Relations and State Capabilities in the Third World* (Princeton: Princeton University Press).

NONSIAINEN, J. (1993), 'Bureaucratic Tradition, Semi-Presidential Rule and Parliamentary Government: The Case of Finland', *European Journal of Political Research*, 16: 221–49.

O'DONNELL, G., SCHMITTER, P. C., and WHITEHEAD, L. (1986), *Transitions from Authoritarian Role: Southern Europe* (Baltimore: Johns Hopkins University Press).

OSTROM, E. (1990), *Governing the Commons: The Evolution of Institutions of Collective Action* (Cambridge: Cambridge University Press).

PETERS, B. G. (1991), *The Politics of Taxation* (Oxford: Blackwells).

—— (1997), *Managing Horizontal Government* (Ottawa: Canadian Centre for Management Development).

—— (1998), *Comparative Politics: Theory and Methods* (Basingstoke: Macmillan).

—— (1999), *Institutional Theory in Political Science: The New Institutionalism* (London: Cassells).

PIERCE, R. C. (1991), 'The Executive Divided against Itself: Cohabitation in France 1986–1988', *Governance*, 4: 270–94.

PRESSMAN, J. L., and WILDAVSKY, A. (1974), *Implementation* (Berkeley: University of California Press).

PUTNAM, R. D., with R. LEONARDI and R. V. NANETTI (1993), *Making Democracy Work* (Princeton: Princeton University Press).

ROSE, R. (1974), *The Problem of Party Government* (London: Macmillan).

—— (1978), *What is Governing?* (Englewood Cliffs, NJ: Prentice-Hall).

RHODES, R. A. W. (1997), *Understanding Governance: Policy Networks, Governance, Reflexivity and Accountability* (Buckingham: Open University Press).

SARTORI, G. (1970), 'Concept Misformation and Comparative Politics', *American Political Science Review*, 64: 1033–41.

—— (1997), *Comparative Constitutional Engineering: An Inquiry into Structures, Incentives and Outcomes* (Washington Square, NY: New York University Press).

SCHMITTER, P. C. (1989), 'Corporatism is Dead, Long Live Corporatism', *Government and Opposition*, 24: 54–73.

STEPAN, A., and SKACH, C. (1993), 'Constitutional Frameworks and Democratic Consolidation: Parliamentarianism and Presidentialism', *World Politics*, 46 1–22.

STROM, K. (1990), *Minority Government and Majority Rule* (Cambridge: Cambridge University Press).

TAM, H. (1998), *Communitarianism: A New Agenda for Politics and Citizenship* (London: Macmillan).

WEAVER, R. K. and ROCKMAN, B. A. (eds.) (1993), *Do Institutions Matter?* (Washington, DC: The Brookings Institution).

WEBB, E. J., CAMPBELL, D. T., SCHWARTZ, R. D., and SECHREST, L. (1966), *Unobtrusive Measures: Nonreactive Research in the Social Sciences* (Chicago: Rand-McNally).

4

Governance and Public Administration

R. A. W. RHODES

INTRODUCTION

Over the years, the study of Public Administration has seen many fashions
come and go, often fun, sometimes instructive, rarely long-lived; this chapter focuses on the currently fashionable notion of 'governance'. It is widely
used, supplanting the commonplace 'government', but does it have a distinct meaning? What does it tell us about the challenges facing the study
and practice of Public Administration?

The coming of the New Right with its love of markets heralded lean
times for Public Administration. Long concerned with the design of public institutions, especially with creating efficient and democratically controlled bureaucracies, it found its prescriptions roundly rejected for private
sector management skills and marketization. Bureaucrats were self-serving
producers who sought to maximize the agency budget. The public interest
was a myth. Students of Public Administration were sidelined, reduced to
commenting on changes pioneered by others. Governance is part of the
fight back. It is a description of the unintended consequences of corporate
management and marketization. It is a response, therefore, to the perceived
weaknesses of marketization. Also, marketization fragmented service
delivery systems by drawing in actors and organizations from the public,
private, and voluntary sectors. The networks so central to the analysis of
governance are a response to this pluralization of policy making. Finally,

I would like to thank Mark Bevir, Andrew Dunsire, Lotte Jensen, Torben Beck Jørgensen,
Janice McMillan, Patrick Le Galès; Cynthia Rhodes, and Gerry Stoker for help and com-
ments. The second section is both an abbreviated and updated version of Rhodes 1996. I use
Public Administration (upper case) to refer to the academic subject and its study.

the governance literature grapples with the changing role of the state after the varied public sector reforms of the 1980s and 1990s. In the UK context, where there is no state tradition comparable to the Continental tradition of *rechtsstaat*, governance explores how the informal authority of networks supplements and supplants the formal authority of government. The governance literature explores the limits to the state and seeks to develop a more diverse view of state authority and its exercise.

For such a bold project, as even the most cursory inspection reveals, the term 'governance' has an unfortunately large number of meanings. It can refer refer to a *new* process of governing; or a *changed* condition of ordered rule; or the *new* method by which society is governed (cf. Finer, 1970: 3–4). So far, so simple; but the problems of definition become chronic when specifying this new process, condition, or method. There are at least seven separate uses of governance relevant to the study of Public Administration: corporate governance; the new public management; 'good governance'; international interdependence; socio-cybernetic systems; the new political economy; and networks.

This chapter has two aims: to review the literature on governance relevant to the study of Public Administration; and to provide a critical interpretation of the social science view of governance. So, I review the seven definitions, focusing on governance as networks. I then pose seven questions about the usefulness of the notion, contrasting social science with an anti-foundational approach (Bevir, 1999). Finally, I assess its potential and limits.

SEVEN DEFINITIONS OF GOVERNANCE

The word can be used as a blanket term to signify a change in the meaning of government (Jørgensen, 1993; March and Olsen, 1989) often focusing on the extent and form of public intervention and the use of markets and quasi-markets to deliver 'public' services. To employ Stoker's (1998*a*: 18) apt phrase, governance is 'the acceptable face of spending cuts'. Governance as the minimal state encapsulates the preference for less government, but says little else being an example of political rhetoric. I concentrate on more substantial definitions.

Governance as Corporate Governance

This use refers to the way in which business corporations are directed and controlled (see e.g. Cadbury Report 1992: 15) but it has been 'translated' for the public sector by the Chartered Institute of Public Finance and Accountancy (CIPFA, 1994: 6) which wants to see more efficient governance in the public sector. Their report argues for 'a more commercial style of management' to bring about 'a different culture and climate'. This 'departure from the traditional public service "ethos"' means the public service must exercise 'extra vigilance and care to ensure that sound systems of corporate governance are both set in place and work in practice'. Its report applies three principles to public organizations. They recommend openness or the disclosure of information; integrity or straightforward dealing and completeness; and accountability or holding individuals responsible for their actions by a clear allocation of responsibilities and clearly defined roles.

Governance as the New Public Management

Initially the 'new public management' (NPM) had two meanings: corporate management and marketization. Corporate management refers to introducing private sector management methods to the public sector through performance measures, managing by results, value for money, and closeness to the customer. Marketization refers to introducing incentive structures into public service provision through contracting-out, quasi-markets, and consumer choice.

NPM is relevant to this discussion of governance because steering is central to the analysis of public management and steering is a synonym for governance. For example, Osborne and Gaebler (1992: 20) distinguish between 'policy decisions (steering) and service delivery (rowing)', arguing bureaucracy is a bankrupt tool for rowing. In its place they propose entrepreneurial government which will stress competition, markets, customers, and measuring outcomes. This transformation of the public sector involves 'less government' (or less rowing) but 'more governance' (or more steering) (Osborne and Gaebler, 1992: 34). Similarly, although Peters (1996: 1) defines governance as 'institutions designed to exercise collective control and influence'—a definition so broad it covers all forms of government—he also uses steering as a synonym for governance (Peters, 1995: 3). In effect, like Osborne and Gaebler, Peters (1996) uses governance to describe recent public sector reforms but, in sharp contrast to Osborne and Gaebler, he does not argue for any one reform. He identifies the several variants—the market, participatory, temporary, and regulatory states—and discusses their effects. Governance signals both the importance of these changes and their concern with the new public management (see also OECD, 1995).

Governance as 'Good Governance'

Government reform is a worldwide trend and 'good governance' is the latest flavour of the month for international agencies such as the World Bank (1992), shaping its lending policy towards third world countries (see also OECD, 1996). Leftwich (1993) identifies three strands to good governance: systemic, political, and administrative. The systemic use of governance is broader than government covering the 'distribution of both internal and external political and economic power'. The political use of governance refers to 'a state enjoying both legitimacy and authority, derived from a democratic mandate'. The administrative use refers to 'an efficient, open accountable and audited public service' (p. 611). And to achieve efficiency in the public services, the World Bank seeks to: encourage competition and markets; privatize public enterprise; reform the civil service by reducing over-staffing; introduce budgetary discipline; decentralize administration; and make greater use of non-governmental organizations (Williams and Young, 1994: 87). In short, 'good governance' marries the new public management to the advocacy of liberal democracy.

Governance as International Interdependence

There is a growing literature on governance in the fields of international relations and international political economy (see Chapters 8–10). But two strands of this literature are directly relevant to the study of Public Administration: hollowing-out; and multilevel governance.

The hollowing-out thesis argues that international interdependencies erode the authority of the state. Thus, Held (1991: 151–7) suggests that four processes are limiting the autonomy of nation states: the internationalization of production and financial transactions; international organizations; international law; and hegemonic powers and power blocs. As a result, the nation state's capacities for governance have weakened but 'it remains a pivotal institution' (Hirst and Thompson, 1995: 409). It is essential to 'suturing' power upwards to the international level and downwards

to sub-national agencies (p. 423). They envisage the state as a 'source of
constitutional ordering', providing minimum standards in a world of inter-
locking networks of public powers (p. 435).

The European Union illustrates how transnational policy networks
emerge when, for example, there is a high dependence in the policy sector;
policy making is depoliticized and routinized; supra-national agencies are
dependent on other agencies to deliver a service; and there is a need to
aggregate interests. In the EU, multilevel governance posits links between
the Commission, national ministries and local and regional authorities. It
is a specific example of the impact of international interdependencies on
the state (see: Hooghe, 1996).

Governance as a Socio-Cybernetic System

The socio-cybernetic approach highlights the limits to governing by a central actor, claiming there is no longer a single sovereign authority. In its
place there is a great variety of actors specific to each policy area; interdependence among these social–political–administrative actors; shared
goals; blurred boundaries between public, private and voluntary sectors;
and multiplying and new forms of action, intervention, and control.
Governance is the result of interactive social–political forms of governing.
Thus, Kooiman (1993*b*: 258) distinguishes between governing (or goal-
directed interventions) and governance which is the result (or the total
effects) of social–political–administrative interventions and interactions.
In contrast to the state or the market 'socio-political governance is directed
at the creation of patterns of interaction in which political and traditional
hierarchical governing and social self-organization are complementary, in
which responsibility and accountability for interventions is spread over
public and private actors' (Kooiman, 1993*b*: 252). So, government is no
longer supreme. The political system is increasingly differentiated. We live
in 'the centreless society' (Luhmann, 1982: xv) in the polycentric state
characterized by multiple centres. The task of government is to enable
socio-political interactions; to encourage many and varied arrangements
for coping with problems and to distribute services among the several
actors. Such new patterns of interaction abound: for example, self- and co-
regulation, public–private partnerships, co-operative management, and
joint entrepreneurial ventures.

Governance as the New Political Economy

The new political economy approach to governance re-examines the government of the economy and the interrelationships between civil society, state, and the market economy as these boundaries become blurred. To illustrate the variety of approaches under this broad label, I contrast a social science and a Marxist influenced approach.

For Lindberg and others (1991: 3) governance refers to 'the political and economic processes that coordinate activity among economic actors'. They explore the 'transformation of the institutions that govern economic activity' by focusing on the 'emergence and rearrangement' of several institutional forms of governance. They identify six ideal type mechanisms of governance: markets, obligational networks, hierarchy, monitoring, promotional networks, and associations (p. 29). Their discussion of these mechanisms does not focus only on which promotes economic efficiency under what conditions but also on social control; that is on governance as 'struggles over strategic control and power within economic exchange' (p. 5). The state is not simply another governance mechanism because it acts as a gatekeeper to sectoral governance, and can facilitate or inhibit production and exchange. This approach is relevant to Public Administration because it explores the ways in which the state (understood as actor and as structure) constitutes the economy and influences the selection of governance regimes (Lindberg and Campbell, 1991).

For Jessop (1995, 1997) governance is 'the complex art of steering multiple agencies, institutions and systems which are both operationally autonomous from one another and structurally coupled through various forms of reciprocal interdependence'. There has been a 'dramatic intensification of societal complexity' stemming from 'growing functional differentiation of institutional orders within an increasingly global society' which 'undermine the basis of hierarchical, top-down co-ordination' (Jessop, 1997: 95; and 1995: 317, 324; see also Le Galès, 1998: 495). The distinctive features of his approach is his concern to locate 'governance' in a systematic, broader theoretical framework. Jessop (1995: 323) recognizes the differences between governance and regulation, contrasting for example 'the distinctively Marxist genealogy of the regulation approach' and its well-defined economic problematic and concern to explain the stability of capitalism with the pre-theoretical stage of governance theory and its substantive concern with inter-organizational co-ordination. However, Jessop's analysis of governance draws on his strategic–relational approach with its focus on the complex dialectical interrelationships between structure, agency and strategy. I have no space to explain his analysis in detail (see Jessop, 1990). The simple point is that the explanatory heart of this approach to governance lies in theories of political economy such as regulation theory (see Le Galès, 1998; Stoker, 1998b for variations on this theme). It is relevant to the study of Public Administration because it brings a critical eye to bear on the instrumental concern of governance with solving co-ordination problems, arguing that governance is not necessarily more efficient than markets and identifying several strategic dilemmas that make governance prone to fail (Jessop, 1997: 118–22).

Governance as Networks

Networks are the analytical heart of the notion of governance in the study of Public Administration. There is a massive literature on them but I focus only on those studies explicitly concerned with governance (for broader reviews see: Börzel 1998; Dowding 1995; and Rhodes 1990 and 1997a: chapters 1 and 2). This literature falls into two broad schools depending on how they seek to explain network behaviour: power-dependency or rational choice. I illustrate the two approaches with the work of the British 'Local Governance' and 'Whitehall' research programmes; the Erasmus University, Rotterdam 'governance club'; and the work originating at the *Max-Planck-Institut für Gesellschaftsforschung*.

Power-Dependence. The UK Economic and Social Research Council (ESRC) Research Programmes on 'Local Governance', and 'Whitehall' fuelled research in Britain. At the start of the 'Local Governance' Programme, Rhodes (1992: 2) argued the system of government beyond Westminster and Whitehall changed 'from a system of local govern*ment* into a system of local govern*ance* involving complex sets of organizations drawn from the public and private sectors'. This use sees governance as a broader term than government with services provided by any permutation of government and the private and voluntary sectors. Complexity arising out of the functional differentiation of the state makes interorganizational linkages a defining characteristic of service delivery. The several agencies must exchange resources if they are to deliver services effectively. All organizations are dependent on other organizations for resources to achieve their goals and have to exchange them, employing strategies within known rules of the game (Rhodes, 1999: ch. 5: Stoker, 1998a: 22). These themes remained prominent throughout the Programme. Thus, Stoker (1998*a*: 18) describes governance as a set of institutions and actors drawn from but also beyond government, where boundaries and responsibilities for tackling social and economic issues are blurred, the several institutions are power-dependent, and the resulting networks are autonomous and self-governing. So, the government cannot command; it must use new tools and techniques to steer and to guide (see Stoker, 1999*b* for examples).

The ESRC Whitehall Programme generalized the governance argument from local government to British government as a whole, challenging the conventional wisdom of the Westminster model (Rhodes, 1997*a*: ch. 1). Networks are a common form of social co-ordination, and managing interorganizational links is just as important for private sector management as for public sector. They are a mechanism for co-ordinating and allocating resources—a governing structure—in the same way as markets or bureaucracies. So, networks are an alternative to, not a hybrid of, markets and hierarchies:

If it is price competition that is the central co-ordinating mechanism of the market and administrative orders that of hierarchy, then it is trust and co-operation that centrally articulates networks. (Frances *et al.*, 1991: 15; see also Powell, 1991)

Other key characteristics include diplomacy, reciprocity and interdependence (Rhodes, 1997*b*). More important, this use of governance also suggests that networks are *self-organizing*. At its simplest, self-organizing means a network is autonomous and self-governing. Networks resist government steering, develop their own policies and mould their environments. So, Rhodes (1996: 660) defines *governance as self-organizing, interorganizational networks*. These networks are characterized, first, by interdependence between organizations. Governance is broader than government, covering non-state actors. Changing the boundaries of the state meant that the boundaries between public, private, and voluntary sectors became shifting and opaque. Second, there are continuing interactions between network members, caused by the need to exchange resources and negotiate shared purposes. Third, these interactions are game-like, rooted in trust and regulated by rules of the game negotiated and agreed by network participants. Finally, the networks have a significant degree of autonomy from the state. Networks are not accountable to the state; they are self-organizing. Although the state does not occupy a privileged, sovereign position, it can indirectly and imperfectly steer networks.

The key problem confronting British central government is, therefore, its reduced capacity to steer. The story of British government as a unitary state with a strong executive is replaced by the story of the hollowing-out of the British state by international interdependencies and multiplying internal networks. There is now a differentiated polity with a hollow crown.

This focus on the constraints on central capacity is also a feature of the work by Walter Kickert, Jan Kooiman, and their colleagues at the Erasmus University, Rotterdam. The 'governance club' research programme began in 1990 and on focuses on policy making and governance in and of networks (see: Kickert, 1993; Kickert, 1997a and 1997b; Klijn et al., 1995; Kooiman, 1993a). Their basic argument is that the lack of legitimacy, complexity of policy processes, and the multitude institutions concerned reduce Government to only one of many actors. Other institutions are, to a great extent, autonomous; they are self-governing. Government steers at a distance (Kickert, 1993: 275). Governance refers to 'the directed influence of social processes' and covers 'all kinds of guidance mechanisms connected with public policy processes' (Kickert and Koppenjan, 1997: 2). Policy networks make public policy. They are '(more or less) stable patterns of social relations between interdependent actors, which take shape around policy problems and/or policy programmes' (p. 6). The core of these interorganizational links is power dependence (Klijn, 1997: 21). However, the main concern of the Erasmus Rotterdam 'governance club' is managing networks (see below pp. 72–6).

The Max-Planck-Institut and actor-centred institutionalism.[1] For Renate Mayntz, Fritz Scharpf, and their colleagues at the *Max-Planck-Institut*, policy networks represent a significant change in the structure of government. They are specific 'structural arrangement' which deals typically with 'policy problems'. They are a 'relatively stable set of mainly public and private corporate actors'. The linkages act as 'communication channels and for the exchange of information, expertise, trust and other policy resources'. They

---

[1] Most of the work from the Max-Planck-Institut is not available in English, so I must acknowledge the invaluable help provided by Tanja Börzel (European University Institute, Florence) who first pointed out to this literature to me. Her article (Börzel, 1998) was my main source, supplemented by Marin and Mayntz, 1991; and, at the last minute, Scharpf, 1997. Of course I am familiar with Scharpf's earlier work on *politikverflechtung* (see e.g. Hanf and Scharpf, 1978) but the work on governance and actor-centred institutionalism was not published until the 1990s. There is a bibliography of German publications in Börzel, 1998.

have their own 'integrative logic' and the dominant decision rules stress bargaining and sounding-out. So, as with the power-dependence approach, the Max Planck school stress functional differentiation, the linkages between organizations, and dependence on resources (Kenis and Schneider, 1991: 41–3).

They also stress the advantages of networks over markets and hierarchies. Thus, networks can avoid not only the negative externalities of markets but also the 'losers'—that is, those who bear the costs of political decisions—produced by hierarchies because:

in an increasingly complex and dynamic environment, where hierarchical co-ordination is rendered difficult if not impossible and the potential for deregulation is limited because the problems of market failure, governance becomes only feasible within policy networks, providing a framework for the efficient horizontal co-ordination of the interests and actions of public and private corporate actors, mutually dependent on their resources.   (Börzel, 1998: 262–3)

To explain how policy networks work, Scharpf (1997: chs. 2 and 3) combines rational choice and the new institutionalism to produce actor-centred institutionalism. The basic argument is that institutions are systems of rules that structure the opportunities for actors (individual and corporate) to realize their preferences. So, 'policy is the outcome of the interactions of resourceful and boundedly rational actors whose capabilities, preferences, and perceptions are largely, but not completely, shaped by the institutionalized norms within which they interact' (Scharpf 1997: 195).

Networks are one institutional setting in which public and private actors interact. They are informal institutions; that is, informally organized, permanent, rule-governed relationships. The agreed rules build trust, communication, reduce uncertainty and are the basis of non-hierarchic co-ordination. Scharpf uses game theory to analyse and explain these rule-governed interactions.

There is much agreement, therefore, that governance as networks is a ubiquitous and important form of governing structure in advanced industrial societies, but there are competing explanations about how networks affect government and its policies.

SEVEN QUESTIONS ABOUT GOVERNANCE

The human sciences offer only provisional knowledge and governance, like any other approach, is no exception. To explore these limits, I pose seven questions.[2] Is governance new and does it matter? How do you choose between the definitions and their associated approaches? How do we explain the growth of governance? Has the centre been hollowed out? How does the centre manage networks? What are the implications of governance for representative democracy? Is governance failure inevitable? I provide an answer to each of these questions by summarizing the social science literature. This section has three other ambitions. First, to identify the limits to the social science story about governance. Second, running through the discussion of each question, I develop a critical, anti-foundational account of governance as an alternative to the social science interpretation. Third, I ground the argument by using boxed examples of how individual actors responded to the difficulties of governance.

IS GOVERNANCE NEW AND DOES IT MATTER?

A sceptic would point out that networks are not new. The major difference is that social scientists now talk about them endlessly. Both points are correct, and misleading. The governance approach does not claim networks are new, only that they have multiplied. Precise figures are not available, but the fragmentation of public services through the increasing use of special-purpose bodies and contracted-out services is obvious and widespread. Thus, the care package for Mrs T. (see Box 1) involves eleven agencies as well as family and a friend. So, it does not matter if networks are new or that social scientists go on about them. All that matters is that there are networks and government works with and through them.

The dominant narrative of the 1980s and 1990s told the story of how corporate management and marketization triumphed over bureaucracy. It is a story which ignores the need for negotiation in and between networks. Whether there is more fragmentation is less important than the search for

---

[2] On the questions see also: Ferlie and Pettigrew, 1996; Kickert *et al.*, 1997*b*; Klijn *et al.*, 1995; Painter *et al.*, 1997; Perri 6, 1997; Reid, 1998; Rhodes, 1997*a* and *b*; and Stoker, 1998*a* and Stoker, 1999*b*.

Box 1. The case of Mrs T.

A local GP refers one of his patients asking for Home Help. Mrs T. is 80 years old, and arthritic. She lives on her own in a bungalow. She uses a walking frame. She can no longer manage pans and cooking for herself. She coped well until she fell fracturing her wrist. She visited casualty for treatment. The hospital sent her home after treatment. A friend has been helping but she is elderly and finds the constant care that Mrs T. needs too much of a struggle.

The Home Care Manager visits and assesses Mrs T. She is slow and finds holding the frame difficult because of the arthritis in her hands and fractured wrist. She has difficulty with washing, dressing, toilet, bathing, preparing food, cooking, and shopping. The friend who calls in cooks and shops and helps with personal care. She would still like to visit her friend twice a week and will do small amounts of shopping and get her pension when she gets her own. Mrs T's three children all live away from their home town, have families of their own and work. The eldest will retire next year. The family have arranged to take it in turns to visit on Sundays, keep the house and garden tidy and in good repair.

The Home Care Manager asks for an urgent visit from the Occupational Therapy Services to assess Mrs T. for equipment for daily living. While waiting for this assessment a home carer will call at meal-times and help with dressing in the morning. The friend will call about 7.00 p.m. to help her undress.

Two days later an Occupational Therapy Assistant (OTA) calls to assess Mrs T's equipment needs for daily living. Mrs T. can eat with special cutlery and a plate guard. She can manage a cup of tea with a kettle tipper if laid out for her. She can manage toast or cereal for breakfast if laid out before. Tea is manageable with bread, butter, cheese or cold meats. Mrs T. can manage her gas cooker with the help of replacement dials. The kitchen is well-organized. With a perching stool she can sit at the work surface next to the cooker to eat her meals. She can wash and dress herself with equipment but needs help with doing up buttons, laces and zips and putting on stockings. With carefully selected clothing from her wardrobe Mrs T. will need minimum help to dress and undress. She needs a raised toilet seat and frame in the bathroom and a bath board on the bath with a grab rail on the wall. All the equipment except the grab rail arrived later that day. An emergency warden call system will be installed by the end of the week by the council's housing services. The Gas Board will call within 48 hours to replace the dials on the cooker.

The Home Care Manager rearranges the home carer. She provides a morning call from her own services Monday to Friday and arranges for a private agency on Saturday. The home carer will help with buttons and will collect shopping and pension and do some basic cleaning. They will do the laundry and ironing. The home carer helps Mrs T. to use her bath board to have a bath one morning a week. She lays out breakfast and tea and fills the kettle for the day. A twilight service (provided by the Community Health Trust) will call any time between 7.00–9.00 p.m., Monday to Saturday to help with undressing. The Home Care Manager arranges and buys these services.

The WRVS delivers Meals on Wheels Mondays and Fridays. Frozen meals are cooked at a local primary school and delivered by the home carer. On Saturdays Mrs T. will treat herself to a meal cooked and delivered by a local hotel.

Mrs T. does not get out to at all and with increasing disability does not feel that she can consider going out. She is isolated. Various local centres have activities for the elderly either run by the council or voluntary agency such as Age Concern. Age Concern runs a post-hospital discharge support service. Having become used to her own company, Mrs T. is nervous about mixing with others. She is grateful for all the help she gets and does not want to be a nuisance. She does not like to ask for information and more help. She is also hard-up, getting only her pension. The Home Care Manager is busy and now all the arrangements are in place will only make a quick visit to check six-monthly.

a new story (and associated language) about government which confronts its perceived weaknesses and the market alternative. Governance as networks provides a different story and language to marketization and therefore underpins the attempt to develop alternative steering strategies (see below pp. 72–6).

How do You Choose between Definitions?

Governance as self-organizing interorganizational networks is a stipulative definition and Rhodes (1996) claims the key test is the contribution it makes to understanding change in British government in the 1990s. In effect, I treat networks as given facts, use an ideal type, and compare change in British government to it knowing that no policy network and its service delivery system is likely to conform exactly to the ideal type (see Rhodes, 1997*a*). It is a common social science research strategy. There is an alternative approach.

The human sciences offer us narratives about the past, present, and possible futures; stories that relate beliefs, actions, and institutions to one another by bringing the appropriate conditional and volitional connections to our attention. The human sciences do not offer us causal explanations that evoke physically necessary relationships between phenomena; prediction is mainly an aspiration and probably an impossibility. I evoke narratives to make the point that understanding and explanation in the human sciences always take the form of a story. Narrative structures relate people and events to one another understandably over time, but these relations are not necessary ones (see Bevir, 1999; Bevir and Rhodes, 1998).

An awareness of our limits does not make the human sciences useless. We can define and redefine problems in novel ways. We can tell the policy makers and administrators distinctive stories about their world and how it is governed. For example, the corporate management rhetoric told a story of economy, efficiency, and effectiveness which contrasted sharply with the story of the local government officer as professional with clients and the permanent secretary as policy adviser and fire-fighter for the minister. As Stoker (1999a) argues corporate management and marketization had *beneficial* unintended consequences because it challenged existing ways and set in train a discourse and pressures for change which led not to efficient responsive services but to the broader notion of local governance. The language of governance tells a distinctive story of fragmentation, networks, and dependence which contrasts sharply with the language of corporate management and markets. In short, therefore, governance provides a language for redescribing the world and challenges the dominant narrative of the 1980s. In its story, networks rival markets and bureaucracy as a suitable means for delivering services and its language describes a complex world in all its complexity; advocating no simple solution whether based on markets or hierarchies or networks.

An anti-foundational story of governing structures—of markets, hierarchies, and networks—must not hypostatize them; that is, represent them as a concrete reality. They are frequently described as ideal types. Such constructs are ahistorical. They are static, fixed categories, into which we force beliefs, cases, and texts. Instances cannot be constructed by comparison with the features of an ideal-typical governing structure. The choice of definition is not, therefore, a matter of evidence but a function of the story; of the questions to be asked and the plot to be unfolded. So, governance is constructed by the questions asked. But we also have to know who is asking the question. The view of the minister will differ from that of the manager from that of the service recipient. Thus, in the case of Mrs T. there are clear differences of interpretation as fragmentation meets turf protection to the disadvantage of the user. The Home Care Manager has one view about improving the quality of Mrs T.'s life. A social worker will have other resources at her fingertips and will have another view. For example, she could be taken to the local centres run by either the council or the voluntary sector. She may like playing bingo, or whist. What about a stay in a residential home or a holiday with her friend perhaps? Is Mrs T. entitled to more money? What about Income Support, Attendance Allowance, and Council Tax Benefit? Would Mrs T. have more choice about the services she would like if she had more income? Would she have to pay more for some of the services? The user has no idea of what is available. The street-level bureaucrat does not have access to a full range of services, but wants to keep control. There is no one person able to co-ordinate a care package, and yet the social worker was never consulted. At the root of these issues lies fragmented service delivery but that fragmentation can only be understood through the eyes of the several participants; a 'thick description' is essential (Geertz, 1973: ch. 1).

How Do We Explain the Growth of Governance?

One popular social science explanation for the growth of governance posits that advanced industrial societies grow by a process of functional and institutional specialisation and the fragmentation of policies and politics (Rhodes, 1988: 371–87). For some authors, differentiation is part of a larger context. For example, regulation theory sees it as a result of the shift from Fordism to post-Fordism (see also Jessop, 1997: 308–15; Stoker, 1998b: 126–7 and Chapter 5 below). However, an anti-foundational approach stresses how the different British governmental traditions understand and respond to governance.

It is rapidly becoming a commonplace that even simple objects are not given to us in pure perceptions but are constructed in part by the theories we hold true of the world. When we turn our attention to complex political objects, the notion that they are given to us as brute facts verges on absurd. There is a sense, therefore, in which there is no 'governance' because all complex political objects are constructed in part by our prior theories of the world and the traditions of which they are part. How we understand 'governance' depends, therefore, on the theories within which we do so.

A tradition is a set of shared theories that people inherit and that form the background against which they construct the world about them. Traditions are contingent, constantly evolving, necessarily in a historical context, and consist of theories and narratives with associated practices. Narratives are the form theories take in the human sciences; narratives are to the human sciences what theories are to the natural sciences. Governance is a narrative interpreted through traditions (Bevir, 1999). In the UK, it is possible to identify several traditions; for example, Tory, Liberal, Whig, and Socialist. Each tradition will interpret governance differently. As illustrations only, I outline briefly the interpretations of governance as networks by the liberal and socialist traditions.

Henney (1984: 380–1), writing in the liberal tradition, interprets networks as examples of the corporate state; 'the institutionalised exercise of political and economic power' by the various types of local authority, government, the unions, and to a lesser extent business. They 'undertake deals when it suits them; blame each other when it suits them; and cover up for each other when it suits them'. These interactions are conducted 'behind closed doors' and each sector has a 'cultural cocoon' rationalizing their interests with the public interest. The vested interests 'institutionalise irresponsibility'. Producers interests rule OK, only for Henney it isn't, and he wants to cut local government down to a manageable size by removing some functions and transferring others to the social market. But the problem of networks as producer capture is not easily resolved. Marketization is the alleged solution but it fragments service delivery structures, creates the motive for actors (individuals and organizations) to co-operate and, therefore, multiplies the networks Henney's reforms seek to break up. Beliefs in the virtues of markets have to confront the obvious defects of quasi-markets.

The socialist tradition in the guise of New Labour sees networks as a problem of integration. For Perri 6 (1997) government confronts 'wicked problems' which do not fit in with functional government based on central departments and their associated policy networks. Such functional government is costly, centralised, short term, focuses on cure not prevention, lacks co-ordination, measures the wrong things and is accountable to the wrong people (Perri 6, 1997: 26). The solution is holistic government which will span departmental cages (for the specific reforms see below p. 73). This report from a New Labour 'think-tank' epitomizes the long-standing Fabian tradition in the Labour Party which sees salvation in administrative engineering. The problem of integration is not easily

resolved. Perri 6's reforms have a centralizing thrust. They seek to co-ordinate the departmental cages, a centralizing measure, and to impose a new
style of management on other agencies, a central command operating
code. But network structures are characterized by a decentralized, diplo-
matic, negotiating, style. Beliefs in leaders know best confront the belief
that decentralized structures need indirect or hands-off management.

This focus on Anglo-Saxon pluralist traditions is too narrow.
Governance has important implications for other state traditions.
Loughlin and Peters (1997: 46) distinguish between the Anglo-Saxon (no
state) tradition; the Germanic (organicist) tradition; the French
(Napoleonic or Jacobin) tradition; and the Scandinavian tradition which
mixes the Anglo-Saxon and Germanic. Thus, in the Germanic tradition
state and civil society are part of one organic whole; the state is a transcend-
ent entity. Its defining characteristic is that it is a *Rechtsstaat*; that is a legal
state vested with exceptional authority but constrained by its own laws.
Civil servants are not just public employees, but personifications of state
authority. The Anglo-Saxon pluralist tradition draws a clearer boundary
between state and civil society; there is no legal basis to the state; and civil
servants have no constitutional position. The Jacobin tradition sees the
French state as the one and indivisible republic, exercising strong central
authority to contain the antagonistic relations between state and civil society. The Scandinavian tradition is also 'organicist', characterized by
Rechtsstaat, but differs from the Germanic tradition in being a decentralized unitary state with a strong participation ethic. (In this paragraph I
paraphrase Loughlin and Peters, 1997: 46–55; see also Dyson, 1980.)

These traditions interpret governance differently. For example, local networks with high participation are common in Denmark. Governance poses
the issue of how to keep the multiplying networks under democratic control but decentralized networks are already a feature of the tradition.
Similarly, in the Germanic tradition, the legal framework sets the boundaries to, and guides, official action. The direct imposition of control is
unnecessary. There is a high degree of tolerance for the multilevel networks
(*Politikverflechtung*) so common in, for example, federal systems such as
Germany. On the other hand, the Jacobin tradition with its assumption of
conflict between state and civil society sees networks as a potential threat
to state authority unless subject to state control, for example through
strong mayoral leadership. In other words, in seeking to interpret and
understand governance, we have to ask whose interpretation in which tradition. Moreover, I have illustrated an argument. As Loughlin and Peters

(1997: 60) are the first to admit, this account of state traditions is broad brush and does not do justice to their variety and nuances.

Has the Centre been Hollowed Out?

Governance is the product of the hollowing-out of the state from above (for example, by international interdependencies), from below (for example, by special-purpose bodies), and sideways (for example, by agencies). As a result there has been a decline in central capacity. Thus, Peters (1996: 117) concludes:

Many of the reforms already implemented have helped to create a greater need for coordinative structures and action while at the same time reducing to some extent the capacity of governments to coordinate effectively. In an increasingly complex and interdependent world, government appears to be squandering its capacity to present an integrated and coherent set of policies at the time that capacity is most needed.

Rhodes (1997*c*: 211–12) in a review of trends in five parliamentary democracies argues there are six countervailing trends which may result in a hollow crown:

Fragmentation vs. control. There is a conflict between institutional fragmentation and core executive steering which is captured by the phrase that core executives have 'more control over less'; that is, they have reduced the scope of their interventions but have greater control over what remains.

Internal independence vs. external dependence. Core executives respond to the constraints of international interdependence by asserting their independence from domestic pressures. Global pressures produce distinctive national responses.

Centralisation vs. autonomy. The search for internal independence saw both a centralisation of power on the core executive as it sought to assert its control over priorities and greater autonomy for other state actors in managing and implementing policy.

Intended vs. unintended consequences. Assertive leadership produced unintended consequences which became ever more visible as institutional differentiation and pluralisation, coupled with indirect or 'hands-off' management, multiplied the disparities between policy aims and implementation.

Symbols vs. substance. Confounded by the sour laws of unintended consequences, core executives balance policy effectiveness against electoral survival by playing symbolic politics which value the appearance of coherence as much, if not more than, the substance. Media pressures fuel the desire to appear coherent, cohesive and effective.

Constraints vs. opportunities. The constraints on core executives are also opportunities to reassert control; for example, international agreements can provide the rationale for renewed efforts at internal control.

The hollowing-out thesis addresses the proposition that institutional differentiation and pluralization is common, creating multiple challenges to the capacity of core executives to steer. It identifies important trends, focusing attention on the unintended consequences (beneficial as well as damaging) of these processes. However, the thesis and its associated trends are a social science analysis of government. So, the changes in government and the list of trends treat networks as given facts and do not tell the story from the standpoint of the several actors. Are central elites aware of their alleged loss of capacity? If they have 'more control over less', they could argue they chose both to increase control and to withdraw from certain policy areas. Such choices are not evidence of incapacity. An anti-foundational account would want to know whose story of government structures understood within which tradition was being examined. Hollowing-out is the story of an outsider looking in, although arguably it could be an elite or top-down view of the problems facing government and the need to resolve them by reducing the scope of government action. The same issue of 'whose story within which tradition' arises in the discussion of network management and network failure (see below pp. 72–6 and 80–3). I note the issue at the relevant point and discuss it more fully in the 'Conclusions' when I discuss a research agenda for governance.

How does the Centre Manage Networks?

I discuss the social science analysis of network management using Table 4.1 which identifies three approaches. I illustrate the approaches from the UK literature on networks. As Kickert (1997: 46) points out, we seek to manage the *structure* of network relations, the *process* of consensus building and the *outcome* of joint problem solving. I recognize networking strategies will vary with what is being managed but I do not explore these differences here.

The instrumental approach is a top-down approach to network steering. Although there are limits on the centre's ability to steer, it still attempts to do so. This approach accepts that government occupies a special position and will seek to exercise its legitimate authority but it also recognises the constraints imposed by networks. So government departments are the focal organization, developing strategies which unilaterally alter the structure of incentives to alter dependency relationships to get effective problem

TABLE 4.1. *Approaches to Network Management*

	Instrumental Approach	Interactive Approach	Institutional Approach
Focus	Improving steering conditions	Co-operation	Network arrangements and their impacts
Level of analysis	Focal organization and its set	Interactions of actors (individual and organizations)	Network structure
View of policy networks	Closed and multi-form object of steering	Horizontal interaction	Product and context of interaction and governance
Characteristics of network management	Strategic steering	Game playing to develop co-operation and prevent blockages	Diplomacy and incremental adaptation of incentive structures, rules and culture of networks
Criteria of evaluation	Effective problem solving	Satisficing policy, consensus	Institutionalised key interests and relationships

Source: Modified from Kickert, Klijn, and Koppenjan 1997*a*: 186.

solving. Perri 6 (1997) provides specific examples of this approach in action. He argues functional government has failed. In its place he wants, to use his watchwords, holistic, preventive, culture-changing, and out-come-oriented government (p. 10). The key to real progress is integrating budgets and information. The twelve recommendations include: holistic budgets designed around outcomes, not functions; cross-functional out-come measures; integrated information systems (for example, one-stop shops); and culture, value for money and preventive audits (pp. 10–12 and chs. 4–7). A specific example of this approach in practice is the policy initiative on Health Action Zones (NHS Executive EL (97)65, 30 October 1997) which exhorts agencies from the public, private, and voluntary sectors to work together to bring better health care to the poor. The instrumental approach assumes the centre can devise and impose tools which will foster integration in and between policy networks to attain central objectives.

The key problem is the costs of steering. A central command operating code, no matter how well disguised, runs the ever-present risk of recalcitrance from key actors and a loss of flexibility in dealing with localized problems. Control deficits are an ever-present unintended consequence of the top-down imposition of objectives.

The interaction approach focuses on the dependence of network actors, developing goals and strategies by mutual learning; collective action depends on co-operation. Rhodes (1997b) argues for management by negotiation, or diplomacy, stressing how important it is to sit where the other person is sitting to understand their objectives and to build and keep trust between actors. Stoker's (Ch. 5) review of techniques for steering urban governance includes indirect management through cultural persuasion, communication, and monitoring as well as direct management through financial subsidies and structural reform. Klijn et al. (1995: 442) distinguish between game management and network structuring. Indirect management through game management includes selectively favouring some actors in the network, mobilizing supporters and their resources, greater expertise in the rules of the game, and managing perceptions to simplify compromise. Ferlie and Pettigrew (1996: 88–9) found that the National Health Service was embedded in a web of interagency alliances which changed the style of NHS management. For example, there was a shift to matrix management styles with chief executive officers increasingly concerned to build and maintain links and institutionalize strategic alliances. Respondents identified the following key networking skills:

strong interpersonal, communication and listening skills; an ability to persuade; a readiness to trade and to engage in reciprocal rather than manipulative behaviour; an ability to construct long-term relationships. (p. 96)

Painter et al. (1997: 238) provide specific advice on game management. They conclude local authorities should: conduct an audit of other relevant agencies; draw a strategic map of key relationships; identify which of their resources will help them to influence these other agencies; and identify the constraints on that influence.

The key problem of the interactive approach is the costs of co-operation. The obvious version of this argument is the more actors in a network, the longer it takes to agree and such delays are costly. Network management is time consuming, objectives can be blurred, and outcomes can be indeterminate (Ferlie and Pettigrew, 1996: 95–6). Decision making is satisficing, not maximizing. Also, the interaction approach ignores the context of network relations; for example, the way in which political control can change the perceptions and strategies of local authorities in their dealings with other local agencies.

The institutional approach focuses on the institutional backcloth, the rules and structures, against which the interactions take place. Thus, Klijn *et al.* (1995: 442) suggest that networking strategies involve changing relationships between actors, the distribution of resources, the rules of the game, and values and perceptions. Similarly, Stoker (Ch. 5) itemizes new funding arrangements and creating new agencies as two key ways of altering the structure of network relations. For example, for urban governance alone, he lists urban development corporations, housing action trusts, the Housing Corporation and housing associates, English Partnerships, Training and Enterprise Councils, Local Enterprise companies, the Government Offices for the Regions and the proposed Regional Development Agencies as tools for giving specific issues a higher profile and for involving a wider range of actors. This approach aims for incremental changes in incentives, rules and culture to promote joint problem solving.

This approach has three key problems. First, incentives, rules, and culture are notoriously resistant to change. Second, networks are closed. They are rooted in the interests of a few, privileged actors who equate their sectional interest with the public interest. Third, appointments to the special-purpose agencies are patronage appointments and these bodies are rarely accountable to elected assemblies. As with the instrumental and the interaction approaches, the institutional approach to network management encounters important problems. None is a panacea for central steering in the differentiated polity.

This discussion of network management may seem lengthy but it reflects the preoccupations of students of Public Administration. This literature is mainstream social science research. Its rapid growth shows how the study of governance focuses on practical, technical, even narrow issues. An antifoundational account of network management raises broader but none the less practical issues.

First, the above discussion of network management focuses on the problems confronted by managers, rather than users or politicians (see Kickert et al., 1997*b*; and O'Toole, 1997 where even the research agenda is focused on management issues). The literature seeks to tell managers how to do their job more effectively. But there are several participants in managing networks; politicians, employees, users. Each may tell different stories about network management and its difficulties. Again, therefore, we need thick descriptions which will recognize there are several actors interpreting networks through various traditions. Simply contrast general injunctions about changing the rules of the game with the difficulties of the Home Care Manager putting together a package for Mrs T. Contracting-out may seem a straightforward change in the rules of service delivery but it had many implications for both street-level manager and user.

Second, although an anti-foundational approach enjoins understanding governance from the standpoint of all participants, it still holds lessons for managers. If the governance story can be interpreted through several traditions, if networks are differentially and continuously constructed, there can be no one tool kit for managing them. There is no essentialist account of networks so managing networks is about understanding the traditions and their interpretations. The social science model of networks treats them as given facts; as if they are cars and the researcher is the car mechanic who finds the right tool to effect repairs. An anti-foundational approach avows that practitioners learn by telling, listening to, and comparing stories; policy advice becomes the telling of relevant stories (Rein, 1976: 266–7).

WHAT ARE THE IMPLICATIONS OF GOVERNANCE FOR REPRESENTATIVE DEMOCRACY?

It is a commonplace observation in the social sciences that there is a democratic deficit in the multi-form maze of the new governance. Hirst (1990: 2) comments that representative democracy delivers 'low levels of governmental accountability and public influence on decision making'. He notes that 'big government is now so big' that it defeats effective co-ordination by the centre and grows 'undirected' and by 'accretion' (pp. 31–2). Recent changes in British government have led to a chorus of complaint about the loss of democratic accountability whether through the emasculation of local authorities, the erosion of ministerial accountability by agencies, or the growth of non-elected, special-purpose bodies and patronage appointments. Rhodes (1988: 402–6) notes that the networks of sub-national actors were subject to 'otiose and ineffective mechanisms of accountability' and concludes that accountability can no longer be specific to an organization but must fit the policy and its network. But networks are an example of private government. All governments confront a vast array of interests. Aggregation of those interests is a fact of everyday life. Policy networks focus on the oligopoly of the political market-place: that is, on how they limit participation in the policy process; define the roles of actors; decide which issues will be included and excluded from the policy agenda through the rules of the game; shape the behaviour of actors; privilege certain interests not only by according them access but also by favouring their preferred policy outcomes; and substitute private government for public accountability. So, accountability disappears in the interstices of the webs of institutions

Box 2. Eating out with Yorkshire Regional Health Authority

It is best to begin at the beginning and with a culinary story that is with the hors d'oeuvres. Based on a sample of hotels and restaurants for 1992/93 and 1993/94, the Committee of Public Accounts (1997) reports that Yorkshire Regional Health Authority paid invoices totalling £694,909. To give the full 'flavour', the Devonshire Arms is one of the better hotels in the Yorkshire region and each event cost between £4,000 and £6,000. The invoices for the Old Swan Hotel included 'Super Sleuth' events at £10,000 each.

The Committee of Public Accounts (1997) expressed 'concern' about a further eight instances of 'unacceptable' behaviour which they noted 'with surprise' and 'serious concern', including on one occasion, an 'appalled'. They also consider the remedial action 'deeply unsatisfactory'. What further transgressions moved the Committee to use such uncharacteristically strong language? I provide several examples from the report.

Relocation and Severance Payments
The Authority made 'irregular payments' of relocation expenses totalling £447,847 to senior managers and medical consultants. In two cases severance payments were made without the necessary approval.

Scotton Banks land disposal
The sale and development of the Scotton Banks hospital site in 1989 was mishandled, raising an estimated £4 million of which only £1.5 million had been received (September 1994) when it should have raised some £7.6 million.

Agreement with Yorkshire Water for clinical waste incineration
The Authority let a contract, worth £7.2 million of capital and £2 million a year in revenue, without competition. It was for *fifteen* years. The Authority did not get NHS Executive approval.

Potential conflicts of interest
The Personnel Director awarded contracts to the value of £43,000 to a company owned by her husband without declaring her interest. She would fulfil one of these contracts after her retirement from the Authority. She negotiated a new contract for herself three days before the demise of the Authority. The Committee concluded 'her actions seemed to have been intended to maximise her own reward'.

Adequacy of remedial action
One manager was given a 'severe reprimand'. Because the Authority no longer existed, the NHS Executive concluded that neither it nor the current employing Authority could take legal or disciplinary actions against any of the individuals involved. The Committee thought it 'deeply unsatisfactory that so little of the money improperly paid . . . had been recovered'.

which make up governance, as the behaviour of Yorkshire Regional Health Authority makes clear (see Box 2).

The usual analysis of policy networks sees institutions exercising a major influence on individual actions. It treats functional domains and policy networks as objective social facts from which we can read-off the ideas and actions of individuals. An anti-foundational account of networks makes no such assumptions. It would focus on the social construction of policy networks through the capacity of individuals to create meaning.

Bang and Sørensen's (1998) story of the 'Everyday Maker' provides an instructive example of an anti-foundational account of governance as networks focused on the beliefs and actions of individuals. They interviewed twenty-five active citizens in the Nørrebro district of Copenhagen to see how they engaged with government. They argue there is a long tradition of networking in Denmark. They argue Denmark has recently experienced the conflicting trends of political decentralization through governmental fragmentation which has further blurred the boundaries between public, private and voluntary sectors; and political internationalization which has moved decision-making to the EU (p. 11). They described this shift from

Government to 'governance networks' as ideal typical and suggest the governance of Denmark is a paradoxical mixture of Government (hierarchy) and governance (networks).

In this context, the 'Everyday Maker' focuses on immediate and concrete policy problems at the lowest possible level and civic engagement is about:

balancing relations of autonomy and dependence between elites and lay-actors in recursive, institutional networks of governance within or without the state or civil society. (p. 3)

The 'Everyday Maker' has:

a strong self-relying and capable individuality; a perception of politics as the concrete and direct handling of differences, diversity and dispute in everyday life; a notion of commonality as relating to solving common concerns; an acceptance of certain democratic values and procedures in handling not only of high but also of low politics'. (p. 3)

Thus, Grethe (a grassroots activist) reflects that she has acquired the competence to act out various roles: contractor, board member, leader. There has been an 'explosion' of 'issue networks, policy communities, ad hoc policy projects, and user boards, including actors from "within", "without", "above", and "below" government'. So the task of the 'Everyday Maker' is 'to enter in and do work at one point of entry or another' (p. 15). Political activity has shifted from 'formal organizing to more informal networking' (p. 20). And amidst these networks 'You do in fact miss local government—a visible local government. They become visible at once when there are hullabaloos . . . in ordinary everyday life, they are conspicuous by their absence' (p. 21). Politics is no longer about left and right but engaging in what is going on in institutions (p. 23).

Bang and Sørensen (1998: 24–6) then describe the ideal typical forms of civic engagement. The Everyday maker espouses the following political maxims:

- Do it yourself.
- Do it where you are.
- Do it for fun but also because you find it necessary.
- Do it ad hoc or part time.
- Think concretely rather than ideologically.
- Show responsibility for and trust in yourself.
- Show responsibility for and trust in others.
- Look at expertise as an other rather than as an enemy.

There are some instructive contrasts between Band and Sørensen and an anti-foundational approach. First, they employ an ideal–typical research method, specifying not only the characteristics of the 'Everyday Maker' but also the maxims which guide their political behaviour. Specific instances are then compared to these ideal-typical formulations. An anti-foundational account would not assume the 'Everyday Maker' had these characteristics.

Second, the 'Everyday Maker' is a normative ideal. Her behaviour epitomizes civic engagement in Denmark. A note of caution is in order. The 'Everyday Maker' may be an endangered species. Jensen (1998) shows how the democratic experiment in Danish social housing is confounded by the fatalism of tenants and the lack of suitable democratic skills. Normative ideals could lead the researcher to ignore the fatalist for whom networks will have a different meaning.

Third, Bang and Sørensen's account of networks focuses on the beliefs and actions of only one group of actors and does not provide a 'thick description' (Geertz, 1973: ch. 1). An anti-foundational account implies a micro-analysis but does not imply necessarily a bottom-up approach. The analysis is not restricted to any one category of actor. So, to the 'Everyday Maker', we need to add: the street-level bureaucrats, who can make and remake policy; services users, whose experiences can differ markedly from the expectations of the service provider; and the beliefs and actions of the political and managerial elite who seek to steer other actors in the network.

Finally, there are significant constraints on access to and communication in networks. If you increase the number of participants, you lose advantages of closure; of simplifying the interests that must be aggregated and accommodated. Elite actors may be reluctant to forgo the privileges and advantages of closure. There are important limits to the new role of citizen as user: for example governments still restrict access to information and there are clear limits to the knowledge of citizens.

However, Bang and Sørensen provide a concrete illustration, with excellent quotes from their interviewees, of how citizens can engage with policy networks and change them from closed to open government.

Is the Failure of Governance Inevitable?

It is a long-standing theme of the social science literature that markets and hierarchies have their limits. Networks are seen as the solution to such problems. There is a growing recognition that they too have marked problems. So, no governing structure works for all services in all conditions. The issue, therefore, is not the superiority of markets and hierarchy over networks but managing networks in the conditions under which they work best. Networks work where the following factors combine:[3]

- Actors need reliable, 'thicker' information.
- Quality cannot be specified or is difficult to define and measure.
- Commodities are difficult to price.
- Professional discretion and expertise are core values.
- Flexibility to meet localised, varied service demands is needed.
- Cross-sector, multi-agency co-operation and production is required.
- Such co-operation confronts disparate organizational cultures.
- Actors perceive the value of co-operative strategies.
- Long-term relationships are needed to reduce uncertainty.
- Monitoring and evaluation incur high political and administrative costs.
- Implementation involves haggling.

Equally networks, like all other resource allocation mechanisms, are not cost free. They are:

- closed to outsiders and unrepresentative;
- unaccountable for their actions;
- serve private interests, not the public interest (at both local and national levels of government);
- difficult to steer;
- inefficient because co-operation causes delay;
- immobilized by conflicts of interest;
- difficult to combine with other governing structures.

Also, network negotiation and co-ordination can be confounded by the political context in which they are embedded. Rapid rates of change, endemic social conflicts and short-term political, especially party political, interests can all undermine negotiations and the search for an agreed course of action.

One clear effect of marketization is that it undermines the effectiveness of the networks it spreads. The government promoted competition and

---

[3] On the conditions under which networks thrive, see: Ferlie and Pettigrew 1996: 96–7; Flynn *et al.*, 1996: 139–41; Kramer and Tyler, 1996: chs. 4 and 16; Larson, 1992: 98; Lowndes and Skelcher, 1998; Powell, 1991: 268–74; Rhodes, 1997*a*: ch. 3; Thompson *et al.*, 1991: Introd. and chs. 21–3; Thompson, 1993: 54–60; and Wistow *et al.*, 1994.

contracting-out. The result was to 'corrode . . . common values and commitments' and 'to create an atmosphere of mistrust' (Flynn *et al.*, 1996:
115). Market relations had 'corrosive effects' on 'professional networks
which depend on co-operation reciprocity and interdependence' (pp.
136–7; see also Lowndes and Skelcher 1998: 24). In short, contracts undermine trust, reciprocity, informality and co-operation (see Box 3).
Competition and co-operation mix like oil and water! It is the mix of governing structures that matters. Governments confront not only a choice of
strategies for managing networks but also a choice between governing
structures. As Lowndes and Skelcher (1998: 24) argue this choice can vary
during the life cycle of a policy programme; competition and co-operation
co-exist. Similarly, Flynn *et al.* (1996) show that community health services

Box 3. The ethics of competition

The Yorkshire Regional Health Authority General Manager defended his
actions claiming he brought a more commercial attitude and a willingness to embrace risk to health services management. He embraced 'the
rhetoric of the day (in summary the ministerial encouragement to break
away from the bureaucratic stranglehold).' The point is of sufficient
importance to warrant a lengthy quote from the former chief executive
of Yorkshire RHA, Keith McLean.

*The culture of the day in the NHS should be recognised as a real factor. In
the 1988–93 period, senior managers were encouraged from the highest
levels to focus on the achievement of nationally desired results. The service
was in the throes of radical structural change with the introduction of a market approach and . . . it felt to me and perhaps others that the regulatory
framework of the pre-reform era was relaxed to give local managers the
space to achieve change quickly through the exercise of managerial discretion. The advent of the Chief Executive . . . was a signal of the changing culture. Several of the regulations which are said to have been transgressed in
Yorkshire have since been modified in the direction of greater flexibility . . .
and the coming changes were, inevitably, 'in the air' before they actually
came about. (Committee of Public Accounts 1997: 40 [emphasis added])*

Mr McLean accepted that he embraced 'the culture of the day too
enthusiastically and uncritically in pursuit of successful outcomes' but
insisted that his decisions must be placed in the broader context. They
should, and that context is the erosion of public service ethics by corporate management and marketization.

involve hierarchy (instructions from the government), markets (contracting), and networks (GP fundholders and primary health care).

Finally, this catalogue of qualifications and defects does not lead to the conclusion that networks are an unworkable alternative. It is important to remember the underlying theme of the social science literature is that *all* governing structures fail. It also identifies the advantages of networks. First, markets and hierarchies also fail. Networks work in conditions where other governing structures do not. The list of conditions above are conditions under which markets fail; for example, where it is difficult to specify the price of a good or service! Second, networks bring together policy makers and the implementing agencies, and by so doing increase the available expertise and information. Third, networks bring together many actors to negotiate about a policy, increasing the acceptability of that policy and improving the likelihood of compliance. Fourth, networks increase the resources available for policy making by drawing together the public, private and voluntary sectors. Finally, Dunsire (1993: 26) points out that 'Government could never govern if the people—in their organizations, their families, their groupings of all kinds—were not self-governing'. Networks are a point of convergence for exercising that self-governing ability.

And this last point reintroduces the anti-foundational theme running through the questions; namely, whose story of network failure within which tradition are we seeking to understand? There are three assumptions running through the above discussion. The first assumption is that the researcher's task is to identify the unintended consequences of government action. Thus, the list of conditions answers the researcher's question of when networks fail. The second assumption is that governance failure takes government intentions as its measuring rod. The aim is to improve the chances of success of government policy. Street-level bureaucrats and citizens can undermine policies with which they disagree. From their standpoint, policy failure is a success! There is no one, given yardstick for measuring the success or failure of a policy. The third assumption is that the three governing structures are ideal types. An anti-foundational perspective seeks to avoid hypostatizing social structures and to ground them in the beliefs and actions of individuals. Just as a network is socially constructed and enacted by its members, so are markets and hierarchies. Governance failure is itself a constructed category.

CONCLUSIONS

As I discussed my seven questions about governance, I contrasted the social science and anti-foundational approaches. This conclusion summarizes the advantages of focusing on governance and the outstanding issues from the social science perspective. It then outlines what an anti-foundational approach can add to our understanding.

As a narrative of British government, governance has two advantages. First, it identifies and focuses on key changes in government; for example, the failures of marketization and the unintended consequences of differentiation. Second, it poses distinctive, new questions about government; for example, about reshaping the state and the pluralization of policy making. It is a necessary corrective, therefore, to traditional narratives; an exercise in 'edification'—a way of finding 'new, better, more interesting, more fruitful ways of speaking' about British government (Rorty, 1980: 360).

The governance approach tells a distinctive story, but it also leaves some important issues unresolved. Although it argues there has been a loss of central capability, there are countervailing trends to the hollow crown, captured by the phrase 'more control over less'. Although there are equivalent trends in other advanced industrial democracies, we know little or nothing about how national governmental traditions shape responses to these trends. We can identify the different approaches to network management but all these tools of central steering encounter problems. Although there is a large democratic deficit in governance, we know little about the prospects for democratizing functional domains. We know that network governance fails, but not how to compensate for such failures. Marketization undermines trust, co-operation and reciprocity in networks. Organizational complexity obscures accountability. The search for co-operation impedes efficient service delivery. As Stoker (Ch. 5) notes, all we can tell the practitioner is to 'keep on "muddling through" . . . in an appropriately thoughtful and reflexive manner'. Perri 6 (1997: 70) accuses this analysis of fatalism:

the best that can be hoped for is a constant and shifting process of negotiations, bargaining games and mutual adjustment across networks of organizations without overarching objectives.

He is insufficiently cautious about the provisional nature of knowledge in the social sciences and his optimism for the latest managerial fashion is almost certainly misplaced. But his 'tool' view of governance, with its stress as choosing between and managing resource allocation structures, is widespread. Its prominence is clear from the large and growing literature on how to manage networks. The research frontier for the study of governance cannot be drawn so tightly. In no way do I wish to suggest that learning how to steer networks is unimportant. But it is not the only or even the most important question. The technical or administrative engineering orientation of Public Administration has always been strong. Governance is not just about corporate management and marketization but also the changing nature of government and how to understand such changes. The anti-foundational approach suggests several ways of broadening the research agenda to encompass these topics.

The key question posed by an anti-foundational approach is 'whose story within which tradition'. Its distinctive approach is to answer this question by constructing narratives. It is an exercise in the political ethnography of networks which: studies individual behaviour in everyday contexts; gathers data from many sources; adopts an 'unstructured' approach (that is, 'data is collected in a raw form' not to a preconceived plan); focuses on one group or locale; and, in analysing the data, stresses the 'interpretation of the meanings and functions of human action' (paraphrased from Hammersley, 1991: 1–2; see also Geertz, 1973: 20–1). The reference to 'everyday contexts' implies micro-analysis but not a bottom-up approach. Thus, following Bulpitt (1983) we can explore the operational code, or rules of statecraft, of central political elites. The key aims of statecraft are to achieve governing competence and to preserve the centre's autonomy in 'High Politics' (for example, foreign, defence, and trade policy, although increasingly the term also covers macro-economic policy). The approach invites the historical analysis of the beliefs and actions of elite actors. Equally, the example of the 'Everyday Maker' shows the importance of a 'bottom-up' approach. We know street-level bureaucrats can make and remake policy. We know users' experience of services can differ markedly from the expectations of the service provider. And yet, after over a decade of public sector reforms, there is no study of the beliefs and actions of employees (or even middle level managers) in response to these (allegedly) dramatic changes. The political ethnography of networks invites us to build a multifaceted picture of how the several actors understood the changes labelled here 'governance'.

There is no expectation there will be the one 'true' account. Rather, there will be conflicting but overlapping stories built out of the several organizational, network, and political traditions actors have learnt and constructed. Individuals as bearers of traditions enact and remake structures in their everyday lives. So, governing structures can only be understood through the beliefs and actions of individuals. Traditions are passed on from person to person. They are learnt. Much will be taken for granted as common sense. Some will be challenged; for example, when beliefs collide and have to be changed or reconciled. The several traditions will produce different stories which we will compare. We may prefer one story to another because it is more accurate and open. But that story will still be provisional.

So, when the analysis of governance is allied to a anti-foundational epistemology, it challenges conventional ways of explaining networks. A political ethnography of networks will focus on the question of 'whose interpretation of governance in which tradition'. If the social science approach identifies important changes and raises new questions, the anti-foundational approach provides distinctive answers by using narratives and focusing on individual beliefs and actions.

REFERENCES

BANG, H. P., and SØRENSEN, E. (1998), 'The Everyday Maker: a New Challenge to Democratic Governance', paper to the ECPR Workshops, 26th Joint Sessions, University of Warwick, 23–8 March.

BEVIR, M. (1999), *The Logic of the History of Ideas* (Cambridge, Cambridge University Press).

——, and RHODES, R. A. W. (1998), 'Narratives of "Thatcherism"', *West European Politics*, 21: 97–119.

BÖRZEL, T. J. (1998), 'Organising Babylon: on the different conceptions of policy networks', *Public Administration* 76: 253–73.

BULPITT, J. G. (1983), *Territory and Power in the United Kingdom* (Manchester: Manchester University Press).

CIPFA (Chartered Institute of Public Finance and Accountancy) (1994), *Corporate Governance in the Public Services* (London: CIPFA).

CADBURY REPORT (1992), *The Report of the Committee on the Financial Aspects of Corporate Governance* (London: Gee & Co).

COMMITTEE OF PUBLIC ACCOUNTS (1994), *The Proper Conduct of Public Business* (London: HMSO).

—— (1997), *The Former Yorkshire Regional Health Authority. The Inquiry Commissioned by the NHS Chief Executive* (London: HMSO).

DOWDING, K. (1995), 'Model or Metaphor? A Critical Review of the Policy Network Approach', *Political Studies*, 43: 136–58.

DUNSIRE, A. (1993), 'Modes of Governance', in J. Kooiman (ed,), *Modern Governance* (London: Sage).

DYSON, K. H. F. (1980), *The State Tradition in Western Europe* (Oxford: Martin Robertson).

FERLIE, E., and PETTIGREW, A. (1996), 'Managing through Networks: Some Issues and Implications for the NHS', *British Journal of Management*, 7: 581–99.

FINER, S. E. (1970), *Comparative Government* (London: Allen Lane, The Penguin Press).

FLYNN, R., WILLIAMS, G., and PICKARD, S. (1996), *Markets and Networks: Contracting in Community Health Services* (Buckingham: Open University Press).

FRANCES, J., *et al.* (1991), 'Introduction', in G. Thompson *et al.*, *Markets Hierarchies and Networks: The Co-ordination of Social Life* (London: Sage) pp.1–19.

GEERTZ, C. (1973), *The Interpretation of Cultures* (New York: Basic Books).

HAMMERSLEY, M. (1991), *Reading Ethnographic Research: A Critical Guide* (Harlow, Essex: Longman).

HANF, K, and SCHARPF, F. W. (eds.) (1978), *Interorganizational Policy Making* (London: Sage).

HELD, D. (1991), 'Democracy, the Nation State and the Global System', *Economy and Society*, 20: 138–72.

HENNEY, A. (1984), *Inside Local Government. The Case for Radical Reform* (London: Sinclair Browne).

HIRST, P. (1990), *Representative Democracy and its Limits* (Cambridge: Polity Press).

——, and THOMPSON, G. (1995), 'Globalisation and the Future of the Nation State', *Economy and Society*, 24: 408–42.

HOOGHE E. (ed.) (1996), *Cohesion and European Integration: Building Multi-Level Governance* (Oxford: Clarendon Press).

JENSEN, L. (1998), 'Cultural Theory and Democratizing Functional Domains: the case of Danish Housing', *Public Administration*, 76: 117–39.

JESSOP, B. (1990), 'Regulation Theories in Retrospect and Prospect', *Economy and Society*, 19: 153–216.

—— (1995), 'The Regulation Approach, Governance and Post-Fordism: An Alternative Perspective on Economic and Political Change?', *Economy and Society*, 24: 307–33.

—— (1997), 'The Governance of Complexity and the Complexity of Governance: Preliminary Remarks on Some Problems and Limits of Economic Guidance', in A. Amin and J. Hausner (eds.), *Beyond Market and Hierarchy: Interactive Governance and Social Complexity* (Cheltenham: Edward Elgar).

JØRGENSEN, TORBEN BECK (1993), 'Modes of Governance and Administrative Change', in J. Kooiman (ed.), *Modern Governance* (London: Sage) pp. 219–32.

KAVANAGH, D. (1990), *Thatcherism and British Politics: the end of consensus?* 2nd edn. (Oxford: Oxford University Press).

KENIS, P., and SCHNEIDER, V. (1991), 'Policy Networks and Policy Analysis: Scrutinizing a New Analytical Toolbox', in B. Marin and R. Mayntz (eds.) (1991), *Policy Networks: Empirical Evidence and Theoretical Considerations* (Frankfurt am Main: Campus Verlag) pp. 25–59.

KICKERT, W. (1993), 'Autopoiesis and the Science of (Public) Administration: Essence, Sense and Nonsense', *Organization Studies,* 14: 261–78.

—— (1997*a*), 'Public Governance in the Netherlands: an alternative to Anglo-American "managerialism" ', *Public Administration,* 75: 731–52.

—— and KOPPENJAN, J. F. M. (1997*b*), 'Public Management and Network Management: An Overview', in Kickert *et al.* (1997*b*) pp. 1–13.

—— KLIJN, E-H., and KOPPENJAN, J. F. M. (1997*a*), 'Managing Networks in the Public Sector: Findings and Reflections', in Kickert, Klijn, and Koppenjan (1997*b*) pp. 166–91.

—— —— and —— (eds.) (1997*b*), *Managing Complex Networks: Strategies for the Public Sector* (London: Sage).

KLIJN, E.-H. (1997), 'Policy Networks: An Overview', in Kickert, Klijn, and Koppenjan (1997*b*) pp. 14–34.

—— KOOPENJAN, J., and TERMEER, K. (1995), 'Managing Networks in the Public Sector: A Theoretical Study of Management Strategies in Policy Networks', *Public Administration,* 73: 437–54.

KOOIMAN J. (1993*a*), 'Social-Political Governance: Introduction', in Kooiman (1993*c*) pp. 1–8.

—— (1993*b*), 'Findings, Speculations and Recommendations', in Kooiman (1993*c*) pp. 249–62.

—— (ed.) (1993*c*), *Modern Governance* (London: Sage).

KRAMER, R. M., and TYLER, T. (eds.) (1996), *Trust in Organizations: Frontiers of Theory and Research* (London: Sage).

LARSON, A. (1992), 'Network Dyads in Entrepreneurial Settings: A study of governance exchange relationships', *Administrative Science Quarterly,* 37: 76–104.

LEFTWICH, A. (1993), 'Governance, Democracy and Development in the Third World', *Third World Quarterly,* 14: 605–24.

LE GALÈS, P. (1998), 'Regulations and Governance in European Cities', *International Journal of Urban and Regional Research,* 22: 482–506.

LINDBERG, L. N. and CAMPBELL, J. L. (1991), 'The State and the Organization of Economic Actitvity', in J. L. Campbell, R. Hollingsworth, and L. Lindberg (eds.), *Governance of the American Economy* (Cambridge: Cambridge University Press) pp. 356–95.

—— —— and HOLLINGSWORTH, J. R. (1991), 'Economic Governance and the Analysis of Structural Change in the American Economy', in J. L. Campbell, J.

R. Hollingsworth, and L. Lindberg (eds.), *Governance of the American Economy* (Cambridge: Cambridge University Press) pp. 3–34.

LOUGHLIN, J., and PETERS, B. G. (1997), 'State Traditions, Administrative Reform and Regionalization', in M. Keating and J. Loughlin (eds.), *The Political Economy of Regionalism* (London: Frank Cass) pp. 41–62.

LOWNDES, V. and SKELCHER, C. (1998), 'The Dynamics of Multi-organizational Partnerships: An Analysis of Changing Modes of Governance', *Public Administration*, 76: 313–33.

LUHMANN, N. (1982), *The Differentiation of Society* (New York: Columbia University Press).

MARCH, J. G., and OLSEN, J. P. (1989), *Rediscovering Institutions: The Organizational Basis of Politics* (New York: The Free Press).

MARIN, B., and MAYNTZ, R. (eds.) (1991), *Policy Networks: Empirical Evidence and Theoretical Considerations* (Frankfurt am Main: Campus Verlag).

OECD (1995), *Governance in Transition: Public Management Reform in OECD Countries* (Paris: OECD/PUMA).

—— (1996), *Ministerial Symposium on the Future of the Public Services* (Paris: OECD).

OSBORNE, D., and GAEBLER, T. (1992), *Reinventing Government* (Reading, Mass.: Addison-Wesley).

O'TOOLE, L. (1997), 'Treating Networks Seriously: Practical and Research Based Agendas in Public Administration', *Public Administration Review*, 57: 45–52.

PAINTER, C., ISAAC-HENRY, K., and ROUSE, J. (1997), 'Local Authorities and Non-elected Agencies: Strategic Responses and Organizational Networks', *Public Administration*, 75: 225–45.

PERRI 6 (1997), *Holistic Government* (London: Demos).

PETERS, B. G. (1995), 'Introducing the Topic', in B. G. Peters and D. J. Savoie (eds.), *Governance in a Changing Environment* (Montreal and Kingston: Canadian Centre for Management Development and McGill-Queen's University Press) pp. 3–19.

—— (1996), *The Future of Governing: Four Emerging Models* (Lawrence, Kan.: University of Kansas Press).

POWELL, W. (1991), 'Neither Market Nor Hierarchy: Network Forms of Organization', in G. Thomson *et al.*, *Markets, Hierarchies, and Networks: The Co-ordination of Social Life* (London: Sage) pp. 265–76.

REID, B. (1998), 'Reframing the Delivery of Local Housing Services: Networks and the New Competition', in G. Stoker (ed.), *The New Management of British Local Governance:* (London: Macmillan) pp. 128–44.

REIN, M. (1976), *Social Science and Public Policy* (Harmondsworth: Penguin).

RHODES, R. A. W. (1999) [1981], *Control and Power in Central–Local Relations* (Aldershot: Ashgate, 2nd edition).

—— (1988), *Beyond Westminster and Whitehall* (London: Unwin Hyman).

RHODES, R. A. W. (1990), 'Policy Networks: A British Perspective', *Journal of Theoretical Politics*, 2: 293–317.

—— (1992), 'Beyond Whitehall: Researching Local Governance; *Social Sciences*, No. 13 November: 2.

—— (1994*a*), 'The Hollowing-Out of the State', *Political Quarterly*, 65: 138–51.

—— (1996), 'The New Governance: Governing without Government', *Political Studies*, 44: 652–67.

—— (1997*a*), *Understanding Governance* (Buckingham: Open University Press).

—— (1997*b*), 'It's the Mix that Matters: From Marketisation to Diplomacy', *Australian Journal of Public Administration*, 56: 40–53.

—— (1997*c*), 'Shackling the Leader? Coherence, Capacity and the Hollow Crown', in P. Weller, H. Bakvis, and R. A. W. Rhodes (eds.), *The Hollow Crown: Countervailing Trends in Core Executives* (London: Macmillan) pp. 198–223.

RORTY, R. (1980), *Philosophy and the Mirror of Nature* (Oxford: Blackwell).

ROSENAU, J. N. (1992), 'Governance, Order and Change in World Politics', in J. N. Rosenau and E.-O. Czempiel (eds.), *Governance without Government: Order and Change in World Politics* (Cambridge: Cambridge University Press) pp. 1–29.

SCHARPF, F. W. (1997), *Games Real Actors Play. Actor Centred Institutionalism in Policy Research* (Boulder, Colo.: Westview Press).

STOKER, G. (1998*a*), 'Governance as Theory: Five Propositions', *International Social Science Journal* No. 155: 17–28.

—— (1998*b*), 'Theory and Urban Politics', *International Political Science Review* 19: 119–29.

—— (1999*a*), 'Introduction: The Unintended Costs and Benefits of New Management Reform for British Local Government', in Stoker (1999*b*) pp. 1–21.

—— (ed.) (1999*b*), *The New Management of British Local Governance* (London: Macmillan).

THOMPSON, G. (1993), 'Network co-ordination', in R. Maidment and G. Thompson (eds.), *Managing the United Kingdom* (London: Sage) pp. 55–74.

—— FRANCES, J., LEVACIC, R., and MITCHELL, J. (eds.) (1991), *Markets Hierarchies and Networks: The Co-ordination of Social Life* (London: Sage).

TRICKER, R. I. (1984), *International Corporate Governance* (Englewood Cliffs, NJ: Prentice Hall).

WILLIAMS, D., and YOUNG, T. (1994), 'Governance, the World Bank and Liberal Theory', *Political Studies*m, 42: 84–100.

WISTOW, G., KNAPP, M,., HARDY, B., and ALLEN C. (1994), *Social Care in a Mixed Economy* (Buckingham: Open University Press).

WORLD BANK (1992), *Governance and Development* (Washington, DC: World Bank).

5

Urban Political Science and the Challenge of Urban Governance

GERRY STOKER

The study of urban politics has been prone to some of the same cycles and trends as the wider field of political science (Stoker, 1998*a*). Fifty years ago—as in political science in general—the focus was on institutions. Urban politics was the study of city government: its legal competences and structure and its core actors—mayors, councillors, bureaucrats. The literature was often descriptive and generally concerned with examining semi-constitutional questions and administrative doctrines about the appropriateness of local autonomy or how best politicians could hold bureaucrats to account without undermining the distinctive contribution of each. This relatively quiet backwater was given a radical shake-up by the arrival of behavioural political science with its focus on 'how things are rather than how they should be' and its new commitment to empirical analysis. The most prominent expression of the revolution was the emergence of a community power debate and associated competing elitist and pluralist interpretations. These studies and more broadly the behavioural style of analysis became the cutting-edge of the sub-discipline of urban politics in the 1960s.

In the 1970s, however, something happened to urban political science that set it on a rather different path to much of mainstream political science. It got Marxism or rather Marxism got it. The crucial impact of Marxism is that it orientated urban political science away from institutional analysis and steered it towards a concern with external social and economic influences and the distributional impact of policy (Pickvance, 1995). The study of urban politics became situated in the context of capital accumulation and the social conflicts endemic to market societies. This shift in focus in many respects 'made sense' in the light of the considerable observable social conflicts in cities and the substantial processes of dislocation and change associated with the late urbanisation of some capitalist economies and the processes of deindustrialisation in others (Brindley *et al.*, 1996).

The study of urban politics may have left behind some of the specific Marxist-inspired studies but the broader political economy perspective associated with these studies has helped to frame key research and theoretical themes in the 1980s and 1990s. City politics is seen as shaped by two fundamental and connected external factors. The first can be termed the 'market' effect. Land-use, employment, leisure and welfare in urban areas are profoundly shaped by the forces of the private market. Urban politics is the study of how the state at various levels meets the challenge posed by key decision making capacity and resources being held in private hands (Lindblom, 1977). The second external factor is captured by the phrase 'globalization'. The politics of cities it is argued is subject to a wide range of pressures for homogenization as a result of technological, political, and economic developments that are global in scope (Leo, 1997). The information revolution, the processes of global economic competition and increasing tendency for political systems to look beyond their boundaries for lessons and ideas from elsewhere all contribute to a homogenising stimulus. At the same time much urban governance is seen as about asserting particularity—about identifying a niche for a particular locality.

Beyond these broad forces city politics are shaped by the attempt to grapple with some intractable and difficult policy issues (Stoker and Young, 1993). The list for many city governments would include: economic development and property development, finance (balancing spending with revenues), training and employment, crime prevention and public safety, transport congestion, and pollution and environmental problems.

The challenge posed by each policy issue is considerable but made still more problematical by features integral to these core and critical policy arenas. The first is a high degree of institutional fragmentation. The core actors associated with each policy issue are spread not only among a wide variety of institutions but also across public, private and voluntary sectors. Second, each policy arena is one of high-bounded rationality. It is difficult to know what to do and gaining understanding is time-consuming and demanding. Defining the problem let alone designing appropriate solutions is a difficult and daunting task. Third, each of the core policy issues relies on action in situations characterized by power dependence. Power to impose solutions is limited and the crucial challenge is to create a power to act. In a complex, fragmented urban world the paradigmatic form of power is that which enables certain interests to blend their capacities to achieve common purposes (Stone, 1993). Governing becomes an inter-active process because no single actor has the knowledge and resource capacity to tackle problems unilaterally (Kooiman, this volume).

As the research agenda has unfolded the study of urban politics has returned to a reformulated concern with institutions but this time framed within the wider context of what has been termed the 'new institutional-ism' (Lowndes, 1996). Reflecting a wider trend in political science institu-tions are back in fashion in urban politics.

The new institutionalism harks back to the early concern with institu-tions but attempts to move beyond its descriptive style and its focus on constitutional and administrative doctrines. It recognizes the value of the behavioural revolution in its commitment to empirical research and its concern with actual practice. What it challenged is the 'under-socialized' character of behaviourism:

The behavioralist focus usefully serves to fix attention upon agency, upon individ-uals and groupings of individuals whose behavior it is observing. But those indi-viduals are shaped by, and in their collective enterprises act through, structures and organizations and institutions. What people want to do, and what they can do, depends importantly upon what organizational technology is available or can be made readily available to them for giving effect to their individual and collective volitions. (Goodin, 1996:13)

New institutionalism argues for the importance of institutionalized social conventions to explain human action and inaction. Intellectual currents and developments in the world of urban politics have combined to encour-age a focus on how individuals act collectively and the institutional structure—both informal and formal—that shapes collective action. Approaches to the study of the new institutionalism range from the histor-ical to rational choice. There is, however, a shared concern with the fram-ing of collective action (Stone, 1993; Dowding *et al.*, 1998).

To put the issue another way, a key concern in the study of urban politics has become governance which can be broadly defined as a concern with governing, achieving collective action in the realm of public affairs, in con-ditions where it is not possible to rest on recourse to the authority of the state (see Stoker, 1998*b*). Governance involves working across boundaries within the public sector or between the public sector and private or volun-tary sectors. It focuses attention on a set of actors that are drawn from but also beyond the formal institutions of government. A key concern is processes of networking and partnership. Governance recognizes the capacity to get things done which does not rest on the power of government to comment or use its authority.

To make the argument somewhat less abstract and to provide a framework for the remainder of this chapter it is argued that the governance debate in the urban field amounts to a concern with the strategies of co-ordination available to urban actors in the context of a globalized, market economy. The debate has been made concrete by the concern with the range of interactable cross-cutting policy issues identified earlier. How can cities balance their books, create jobs, deal with crime and overcome problems of traffic congestion and environmental pollution? The initial governance focus was on coalition formulation as *the* mechanism for achieving co-ordination. Yet this chapter argues that this narrow focus needs to be expanded to consider wider co-ordination mechanisms both in recognition of what is happening in city politics and in order to gain a wider understanding that might in turn aid policy-makers, practitioners, and urban citizens.

The first section of the chapter reviews the literature on coalition-building which is largely a US-based force. The literature offers a number of powerful insights but has the characteristic US feature of not taking the role of the state seriously enough. To complement it and gain a wider understanding of urban governance it is necessary to consider how far and in what ways the state can steer the processes of governance, a characteristic European concern. The second section of the chapter examines various co-ordination strategies available to the state. However both coalition-building and state steering emerge as prone to only short-term success and a cycle of failure. The final section of the chapter discusses the inevitability of governance failure. Given the complexity of what is being attempted in governance the only option open is to mix and match strategies in a never-ending attempt to provide the capacity to act.

GOVERNANCE: GROWTH COALITIONS AND URBAN REGIMES

A key way for urban actors to tackle the challenge of governance and create the conditions for collective action is to form a coalition. The bringing together of a coalition of public and private partners to tackle economic and land-use development is characteristic of urban politics, at least as seen from a US perspective. The 'growth coalition' thesis (Logan and Molotch, 1987) in essence argues that in most cities the rentiers alongside allies among developers, utility companies, the media, and politicians, who all benefit from growth, form a coalition which drives development policy. The 'rentiers' lie at the heart of the process and constantly push to enhance the value of their land and property holdings in cities by arguing for more intensive or up-market development.

Logan and Molotch (1987) suggest that growth coalitions dominate US city politics. Outside the US growth coalitions have been identified by researchers but they are seen as weaker and less well developed (Harding, 1995). Moreover they are often constructed in different ways to US-coalitions reflecting different governmental traditions, patterns of land-ownership and structures in the development industry.

Even within the US a strong stream of writing has emphasised that 'growth coalitions' are only one form of coalition to be observed in cities (Stone, 1997; Pierre, 1999). Other coalitions are formed to preserve the status quo or promote environmental protection and control growth. Indeed the possibility of coalitions seeking to promote opportunities for deprived groups is an area of interest. Embryonic or short-lived versions of such regimes can be found, it is argued, even in the US.

The broader stream of writing which looks beyond growth coalitions has proved a powerful and influential tool within urban political science. It goes under the title of urban regime theory. It is worth exploring some of its major propositions which have helped to illuminate the working of urban governance and won supporters and interest in the academic community both inside and beyond the US. Regime analysis has developed largely through case studies of particular coalitions in the institutional and historical setting of individual cities. Yet its core propositions can be gathered together and are briefly reviewed below (Stoker, 1995).

Governance is a problematic activity from the perspective of regime theory. Social complexity, the low coherence of political society and the fundamental division of resources between public and private actors makes the capacity to act difficult to achieve in urban settings. The formation of governing coalitions helps to resolve the problem of governance, according to regime theory.

Regimes are informal yet relatively stable coalitions 'with access to institutional resources that have a sustained role in making governing decisions' (Stone, 1989: 4). Regimes are likely to draw on actors from both public and non-public sectors. Crucially a regime 'is not simply a matter of aggregating resources, but it includes the *blending* of capacities around potentially shared purposes of various sectors of the community' (Stone, 1997: 6). The coalitions that interest regime theory go beyond the common political coalition formed to achieve a majority of votes in an assembly. Indeed such a political coalition is seen as inadequate to the task of governing:

In order to achieve anything beyond straightforward statutory tasks, elected leaders need the support of other powerful interests, especially within the business community. Governing coalitions regularise those relations of mutual support. (Harding, 1998)

The crucial role of governing coalitions or regimes is to blend capacities between governmental and non-governmental actors in order to achieve a governing task.

The blending of capacities is a complex challenge and is fraught with difficulties but it is what gives the regime its power. Regimes are given their character by who is included or excluded but two other factors are crucial: how co-operation is achieved and the ability to assemble resources sufficient to the task of governance. The most common form of achieving civic co-operation is mutual self-interest. Selective incentives create the conditions for collective action. Yet regimes might be held together in other ways by, for example, a deeply held commitment to a shared social purpose (Stoker and Mossberger, 1994). The provision of selective incentives is easier to bring into operation, however, particularly in the context of US cities.

Once co-operation has begun the regime itself becomes a resource. A new phase of bargaining is more easily developed between partners with past 'successful' bargaining experience who have a reservoir of trust on which to build. The reputation of partners for making and sticking to deals enables a regime to build on its past successes. It also makes it more daunting for challengers to attempt to break up and replace the regime. Regimes in a full-blown form have a pre-emptive power, they can dictate and direct policy in their chosen arena.

Assembling and blending resources sufficient to achieve an effective regime is a daunting task. Even if a form of co-operation is developed a governing coalition to be viable in the long term 'must be able to mobilise resources commensurate with its main policy agenda' (Stone, 1993: 21). The availability of relevant selective incentives and the presence of potential partners with substantial institutional resources makes economic and property development a particularly propitious arena for regime-building in the urban field. Hence the prominence of the growth coalition form, argue regime theorists.

All regimes are subject to change and potential decay. Governing coalitions or regimes that can dominate a city or even one policy area within a city will not automatically be found. It is not necessarily the case that a long-standing coalition will be in operation (Orr and Stoker, 1994). Indeed it may be that tight-knit regimes are no more common than more loosely assembled coalitions (Stone, 1997).

A model of regime transition would recognize how both external and internal factors might undermine a regime. A period of externally driven policy change may undermine the chosen site of governance for a regime. For example, if growth coalitions lose a favourable grant or financing framework from higher levels of government they can begin to struggle. Equally if partners lose their resources—their role in the market or their electoral support—then the regime can be threatened from within. It may be possible to rebuild the regime and regime partners have certain advantages in this respect but it remains the case that if external pressure or internal problems are severe enough the regime will fold and shorter-term coalitions—perhaps competing for regime status—may fill the vacuum.

The idea of city governance being about the formation of coalitions is a 'natural' one in the US context. Earlier elitist and pluralist interpretations, after all, were arguing about whether ruling coalitions were singular and near permanent or multiple and subject to frequent change. Growth coalition studies and regime analysis have continued the US tradition of community power studies. What makes them different is the nature of coalitions and coalition-building that they focus on. Regime analysis in particular shifts attention away from the classic question of 'who gets what?' which dominated the earlier community power debate to a question that is more in tune with the challenge of governance as understood in this paper: how in conditions of great complexity and uncertainty do actors blend their resources together to achieve shared purposes?

The European and more particularly the UK interest in regimes in the academic world and partnerships in the practitioner world reflects a growing awareness of the limits to direct action by the state and the need for it to bring together forces in the public and private sectors and civil society in order to achieve key policy goals (Harding, 1998). The US literature stresses the lack of a strong government tradition, the weakness of political (especially party) organization and the tendency for policy programmes to be framed through indirect mechanisms. The process of governing in these circumstances tends towards coalition-building. In the European case the possibility of government steering of urban governance is perceived to be available.

GOVERNANCE AND STEERING: THE MAKING AND GUIDING OF URBAN PARTNERSHIPS

Coalitions that are a 'natural' part of the landscape of US city politics have in many European countries been subject to a process of more deliberate creation. More generally European governments have attempted to actively steer processes of co-ordination and collective action across public, private, and voluntary boundaries using a wide range of tools. The UK government has been increasingly strongly committed to this style of working, although not without certain contradictions and uncertainties. The election of a Labour Government has further legitimized the search for a 'modernized' form of government. Other European countries—for example France— have shown a greater uncertainty about partnership but have nevertheless developed their own initiatives and approaches (Le Galés and Loncle, 1996). In Spain governance is the characteristic mode of operation for political leadership in the larger cities.

What is meant by 'steering'? It is not government setting out policy and letting others do the implementation as suggested by Osborne and Gaebler (1991) in their well-known advice to governments to steer and not to row. Steering in the context of governance recognizes that government cannot impose its policy but must rather negotiate both policy and implementation with partners in public, private, and voluntary sectors.

Steering involves government learning a different 'operating code' which rests less on its authority to make decisions and instead builds on its capacity to create the conditions for positive—sum partnerships and setting or changing the rules of the game to encourage what are perceived as beneficial outcomes. Governments, the advocates of steering suggest, can establish a framework for effective collective action and seek to guide that action towards 'desirable' goals and away from 'undesirable' goals. In the field of urban politics in the UK a debate about enabling local government and community governance, launched in the late 1980s, has tried to capture this vision of a 'light-touch' government (Stewart and Stoker, 1988; King and Stoker, 1996).

Drawing on a range of typologies it is possible to review a number of the tools used by governments in urban settings in order to stimulate partnerships and effective collective action (see Rhodes, 1997; Jessop, 1998). Table 1 presents a list of five 'tools' used in UK urban politics since the late 1980s and at the same time identifies how each is associated with certain tensions and contradictions.

TABLE 5.1. *Steering Urban Governance*

Technique	Example (s)	Tension (s)
Cultural Persuasion: promoting partnership	Joint vision and and strategic planning. Use of media to promote partnership	Lack of legitimacy Clash with established 'norms' of public conduct.
Communication: facilitating learning and encouraging access	City Pride Initiative, City Challenge, etc	Limits to openness. Fragility of trust.
Finance: subsidising partnership	City Challenge, Single Regeneration Budget	Competitive bidding undermines co-operation
Monitoring: checking partnership performance	Performance review, best practice promotion, threat of intervention	Introduction of rigidities that undermine governance
Structural reform: establishing new agencies	Establishing quangos, Government Offices for regions, Regional Development Agencies.	Problems of accountability. Intensifying fragmentation.

Culture-Persuasive Techniques

The first and most obvious way in which a government can steer is by using its 'moral' authority to promote, persuade, and exhort others to work together to solve problems and take action. Paradoxically in the UK context this technique was taken up by so-called 'New Left' local authorities in the early 1980s—most famously the GLC—and then picked up by the Conservatives, especially under the second tenure of Heseltine at the

Department of the Environment, in the 1990s. The post-1997 Labour Government developed a commitment to partnership in opposition and that commitment has remained central to its rhetoric and actions.

The strength of the rhetoric of partnership and the bi-partisan support it enjoys masks, however, a number of tensions and difficulties. The new order of partnership is in part undermined by processes of 'cultural lag' which give prominence to previous operating codes, such as central government control or in local settings the primary of elect representatives in making decisions. Politicians and officials at both national and local/regional levels appear to find it all too easy to slip back into an operating code in which they impose solutions and direct approaches (Rhodes, this volume). Lowndes and Skelcher (1997: 16) comment:

Different representatives within a partnership draw their legitimacy from different sources—from election, appointment, common experience, professional expertise, leadership skills—but these various mandates are not mutually recognized and there is a lack of clarity about their relative value.

An 'iron-law' in partnerships involving local elected representatives appears to an unavailing tendency for them to question the legitimacy and representativeness of all other partners. In turn all other partners have a strong tendency to question the legitimacy of people who 'do politics'.

Even if the argument for partnership has been won to a degree among elites—that is in general terms they sign up to the agenda—there is evidence to suggest that the public are not entirely sold on the idea (Miller and Dickson, 1998). The public—and to an extent the popular media—continue to cling to a model of power in which control rests in the hands of elected officials that can be blamed when things go wrong. Some suspect that all the talk of partnerships and complex governance challenges is an excuse for not doing anything. If a 'success' is achieved then an opportunity is merely provided for self-congratulation among partners about their leadership skills (Peters, 1997). Partnership may appear to sound like 'motherhood' and 'apple-pie' but its legitimacy remains uncertain notwithstanding extensive promotion and extolling of its virtues by government. A cultural-persuasive technique takes time to win over opponents and indeed may never reach all or get below the skin of others.

Communication

Another mechanism for bringing partners together is to provide fora in which communication can occur thereby reducing 'noise' and facilitating

mutual learning. There are numerous examples of both nationally promoted or locally initiated examples of such fora in the urban field. One
project officer described the role of reducing misunderstandings and facilitating relationships in the following terms:

We acted like a kind of dating agency—bringing people together. We helped form
partnerships that wouldn't necessarily have come together unless someone pushed
them together. We took the bottle to the party! (quoted in Lowndes and
Skelcher, 1997: 18)

The establishment of fora for communication can also provide an opportunity for ensuring access for the relatively powerless or those less able to
express their voice in the normal processes of politics.

The 'magic' of such arrangements from the viewpoint of governance is
that it enables people to put themselves in the position of others and
encourages all to publicly justify their action or inaction. The seeds for new
thinking and a new consensus can be sown in such fora.

There are tensions and difficulties associated with communication. One
key dilemma is how open or closed the fora should be. As Jessop (1998)
comments such arrangements 'face problems in remaining open to the
environment at the same time as securing the closure needed for effective
co-ordination among a limited number of partners'. To move from a 'talk-
ing-shop' to action may require some closure and this in turn may facilitate
partners in making longer-term commitments central to governance.
Lowndes and Skelcher (1997: 18) found in their study of urban partnerships:

While pre-partnership collaborations were characterised by relatively fluid memberships and indistinct boundaries, partnership creating involved negotiation and
contest over 'who's in and who's out'. This was sometimes focused on a particular
issue like the allocation of seats to a board or management committee, sometimes
it was played out in terms of debates about leadership, remit and priorities.

Given that governance requires a move from talking to action a key
dilemma is the robustness of communicative fora during this process and
whether the openness and wider access is lost in the move from talking
principles to talking practice.

Finance

There can be little doubt that providing grants and subsidies enables government to steer governance in the urban setting. The US literature, as

noted earlier, recognized the importance of selective incentives is encouraging coalition formation. By offering to provide finance governments create a pool of resources from which they can provide selective incentives to partners to get together, agree a project and see it through to implementation.

Allocation of funds involves a process of rationing. Rationing could be operated (and was to an extent in past urban policy in the UK) on the basis of 'centrally' prescribed definitions of need. During the late 1980s and early 1990s, however, there was a tendency to move to competitive bidding in schemes such as City Challenge and Single Regeneration Budget (see Mossberger and Stoker, 1997). The aim of such competition is to encourage innovation and value for money in bids, drawing on local knowledge and interests to ensure maximum programme effectiveness.

The dilemma is that competitive processes can stimulate short-term, self-interested behaviour among partnerships which in turn threatens to destroy the basis for continuing partnership (Jessop, 1998). Lowndes and Skelcher (1997: 18) comment in the case of urban partnerships:

Trust between agencies often reached an all-time low in the bidding process as potential providers refused to co-operate with each other and those involved in allocating contracts became increasingly suspicious of potential providers' claims. Many interviewees pointed to the fact that different agencies were 'all after the same money' and 'at each other's throats' as a result. Agencies were seen as jostling to 'take credit' for past achievements and assert 'ownership' of joint projects.

The same authors note that competition brings in its wake a wider range of difficulties. First, there is the sheer duplication of effort involved in wide scale competitive bidding. Second, there is the disabling impact on losers which may make it more difficult for them to regain a sense of commitment to partnership and joint-working. Third, in order to make judgements about allocating funds, quantifiable measures tend to be favoured over more vague qualitative measures but this in turn can distort the purposes and values of partnership. Even winners may find themselves not getting the 'value-added' they have wanted or identified through their partnerships but instead dancing to the tune of externally imposed quantitative measures.

Monitoring

Governments can steer governance by setting up procedures for monitoring. This activity can take a variety of forms (Taylor, 1997). One option is systematic review. Once bodies are sponsored they can be required to produce a corporate and business plan supplemented by a financial agreement and an annual review of performance. In short there are ways of guiding individual organizations or partnerships and these are widely practised in the urban field. More generally government may take on the role of organizing cross-institutional learning by identifying and promoting best practice. A third form of monitoring means holding in reserve the power to directly intervene. Partners know what the government wants and the possibility of it 'taking over' again encourages the policy direction favoured by government.

Again each of these monitoring activities have their limits. An over-emphasis on plans and performance review can encourage excessive rigidities or game-playing (Rhodes, 1997). The identification of best practice is fraught with difficulties and may over-promote methods that, at most, were appropriate in one setting but may be inappropriate in others (Overman and Boyd, 1994). As Jessop notes in the case of local partnerships there is a tension between 'exploiting past organisational and inter-organisational learning to standardise around best practice and maintaining adaptability in the face of a turbulent environment by avoiding 'lock-in' to outmoded routines' (Jessop, 1998). Finally the threat of active intervention is a limited use tool, if the threat has to be mobilized regularly it has lost its value. Moreover there is a danger that a reserve power may be exploited to promote the career of a politician—making initiatives almost for their own sake in order to gain political credit with the media, public or fellow politicians. If activism gives way to hyperactivism then the basis of governance relationships based on steering can be undermined (Dunleavy, 1995).

Structural Reform

One way in which governance can be steered is through the launch of new agencies. Single purpose bodies can give the governance mix a new flavour (Stoker, 1998c). The world of UK urban governance is heavily populated by such agencies including urban development corporations, housing action trusts, the Housing Corporation and housing associations, English Partnerships, Training and Enterprise Councils and Local Enterprise companies. The steering potential of such agencies is considerable. They provide:

• a mechanism for giving a greater profile to an area of activity;
• a tool for involving non-partisans in decision-making on the basis of

their expertise or their involvement in relevant private or voluntary sector activity.

The Conservatives made heavy use of such agencies. In launching Regional Development Agencies in England it would appear that Labour has a similar interest in the value of such agencies.

The tensions involved in using such agencies revolve around a number of issues. First, there are questions about who is appointed to them and the power of patronage. Second, there are difficulties about how these agencies are held to account. Finally, there is the issue that the existence of a diverse and complex range of such agencies exacerbates the problem of community governance—the bringing of the parts together.

One response to the last problem is to propose a further structural reform: the creation of an over-arching body charged with bringing the parts together. The launch of Government Offices for the Regions in the earlier 1990s and indeed Labour's newly proposed Regional Development Agencies reflect the influence of such thinking. The dilemma for such agencies is how to lead without undermining the purpose of governance which is the bringing together of various actors to achieve shared purposes. Setting up an overarching agency reframes the governance question but does not resolve it.

ACCEPTING GOVERNANCE FAILURE: IT'S THE MIX THAT MATTERS

Given the difficulties in establishing long-term coalitions and the limits to the various techniques for government steering it is clearly possible for governance to fail. As Jessop depressingly reminds us 'markets, states and governance all fail. This is not surprising. For failure is a central feature of all social relations' (Jessop, 1998). But what counts as failure in governance? There are at least two possibilities.

The first expression of failure may be the absence of a process of engagement and re-engagement among partners. To put it the other way around when asked for their criteria of success partners often cite the number of meetings held and the continuing existence of a process of dialogue and negotiation as a positive measure. So a lower tier of governance failure would be the breakdown of ongoing reflection and negotiation among partners.

However it appears slightly bizarre to leave the issue there. The reflection and negotiation must ultimately be about achieving some social purpose. The higher tier of governance failure must be based on an assessment of its capacity to produce more effective long-term outcomes than could have been produced using markets or imperative co-ordination by the state. It is necessary to consider not only the doing of governance—either by coalition-building or by government steering and pulling policy levers—it is also necessary to consider the impact of governance.

There are grounds to suspect governance failure at both lower and higher tiers. In modern market democracies there are many factors which make failure likely especially in urban settings.

First, as noted earlier cities are subject to strong and complex pressures as a result of economic market processes which can only be partially 'tamed'. The pace of change confronted by cities is staggering.

Second, city politics is a fulcrum for the social conflicts endemic to market societies. Conflicts should not automatically be seen as undermining governance (Hirschman, 1995). On the contrary they can provide the energy and drive for governance. A never-ending series of conflicts is characteristic of market societies and these conflicts can be managed as long as they are divisible, that is conflicts over getting more or less. Such conflicts lend themselves to compromise and the art of bargaining. Yet they are never resolved 'once and for all' and so the scene is always set for the next round of negotiation. The cumulative experience of muddling through numerous such conflicts is at the heart of an effective governance system.

What can be disabling to governance is conflict which is not divisible. Conflicts which are driven by matters of religion, race, language, or ideology, which have an 'either-or' character, present considerable difficulties to governance. They are not inherently irresolvable but in so far as they figure strongly they are likely to make the compromise and messiness central to governance appear inadequate.

A third reason to expect governance failure, again, harks back to the fundamental context of city politics identified at the beginning of the chapter (Jessop, 1998). Urban politics operates in an increasingly globalized world and in the context of a complex architecture of government. This environment requires governance to make links between different spatial scales. The perception of appropriate time-scales may also vary between these levels. Effective action at the local level may depend on decisions taken at a higher level. Some actors may enter the governance relationship with a very localist perspective, for others the boundary is regional, for still others it may be international. Reconciling these different spatial perspectives is complicated. In the same way with respect to time-scales what is short-term to some will appear like an eternity to others. Governance arrangements are in general about encouraging a longer-term time horizon but the perception of 'long-term' for a community group, politician, or multi-national company is likely to vary to such a degree that governance failure may result.

A fourth reason for governance failure at the urban level is the tension between two conceptions of 'good' government. One, the 'overhead' conception of democracy, relies on a range of new management techniques to enable elected representatives to understand public wishes and oversee government and in turn be held to account by the public. Another, which might be called the stakeholder model, argues that effective governance requires the direct involvement of various interests both in the making and implementing of policy. The latter model downplays the role of the formal electoral processes and the representatives it produces. The tension between these models and their competing claims for legitimacy can be a source of governance failure.

Finally, a general source of governance failure can be associated with the contingencies of politics. Electoral considerations may encourage politicians to break apart complex governance arrangements for short-term advantage. The trust on which governance arrangements often rely may prove too weak to carry the burden placed on it. Governance fails because the dialogue, bargaining, consensus-seeking, and other-regarding perspectives it may demand cannot always be established and made effective.

Emphasizing the 'improbability of success' (Jessop, 1998) for governance should not be read as leading to the conclusion that it is necessary to look elsewhere for the salvation of our cities or that everything is hopeless. The simplistic certainties of some versions of the new management are not an option. Nor does the dream of some communitarians for a new healing community spirit appear viable.

On the contrary by recognizing the incompleteness of governance the aim is to encourage continued experimentation and learning. Jessop (1998) argues that those concerned with urban governance should deliberately cultivate a 'flexible repertoire' of responses. This in turn involves a commitment to review and reassessment, to check that mechanisms are achieving desired outcomes and a 'self-reflective irony' in which participants 'recognise the likelihood of failure but proceed as if success were possible'. Rhodes (1997) comes to similar conclusions in his analysis of governance and argues that government needs to keep on picking up the skills of indirect management and learning how to manage the mix.

To be told to keep on 'muddling through' with governance in an appropriately thoughtful and reflexive manner is, I am sure, sound advice to policy-makers and practitioners. There are perhaps two further contributions that the academic community might make to this process. In different ways both are about improving the infrastructure of governance. First, there is a considerable challenge—practical and intellectual—around the issue of how to identify and effectively communicate best practice (Bardach, 1987). How can a more viable learning environment be created? The second challenge is that of institutional design. Is it possible to imagine institutional, and perhaps more broadly constitutional reforms, that would deliver a better infrastructure for governance? Bob Goodin (1996) has suggested some design principles which would appear particularly well suited to governance. Institutions should be revisable, robust, sensitive to motivational complexity, publicly defendable, and varied in order to encourage experimentation and learning. A key challenge is to assess existing institutions against these principles and consider whether other models or options may have more to offer.

The ultimate irony is that the challenge of urban governance has brought back into focus issues of institutional design that were a concern of students of urban politics fifty years ago. In Britain, for example, the focus of this debate is about the need for a renewed civic leadership and arguments about the case for executive mayors (Hodge *et al.*, 1997). The challenge in these debates is to get beyond doctrines and proverbs that characterized much of the understanding of traditional public administration (Hood and Jackman, 1991).

REFERENCES

BARDACH, E. (1987), 'From Practitioner Wisdom to Scholarly Knowledge and Back Again', *Journal of Policy Analysis and Management*, 7: 188–99.

BRINDLEY, T. RYDIN, Y., and STOKER, G. (1996), *Remaking Planning. The Politics of Urban Change* (2nd edn.; London: Routledge).

DOWDING, K., DUNLEAVY, P., MARGETTS, H., and RYDIN, Y. (1998), 'Urban Politics and Rational Choice: Lesson from London', in G. Stoker (ed.), *The New Politics of British Local Governance* (London: Macmillan).

DUNLEAVY, P. (1995), 'Policy Disasters: Explaining the UK's Record', *Public Policy and Administration*, 10: 52–71.

GOODIN, R. (1996), 'Institutions and their Design', in R. Goodin (ed.), *The Theory of Institutional Design* (Cambridge: Cambridge University Press).

HARDING, A. (1995), 'Elite Theory and Growth Machines', in D. Judge, G. Stoker, and H. Wolman (eds.), *Theories of Urban Politics* (London: Sage).

—— (1998), 'Regime Formation in Manchester and Edinburgh', in G. Stoker (ed.), *The New Politics of British Local Governance* (London: Macmillan).

HIRSCHMAN, A. (1995), 'Social Conflicts as Pillars of Democratic Market Societies', in *A Propensity to Self-Subversion* (Cambridge, Mass.: Harvard University Press).

HOOD, C., and JACKMAN, M. (1991), *Administrative Argument* (Aldershot: Dartmouth).

HODGE, M., LEACH, S., and STOKER, G. (1997), 'More than the Flower Show: Elected Mayors and Democracy', Fabian Society Discussion Paper 32 (London: Fabian Society).

JESSOP, B. (1998), 'Governance Failure', in G. Stoker (ed.), *The New Politics of British Local Governance* (London: Macmillan).

KING, D., and STOKER, G. (1996) (ed.), *Rethinking Local Democracy* (London: Macmillan).

KOOIMAN, J. (1999), 'Societal Governance: Levels, Modes and Orders of Social-Political Interaction' (this volume).

LE GALÉS, P., and LONCLE , P. (1996), 'The Role of Partnership in Combating Social Exclusion: Final Report' (mimeo).

LEO, C. (1997), 'City Politics in an Era of Globalization', in M. Lauria (ed.), *Reconstructing Urban Regime Theory* (Thousand Oaks, Calif.: Sage).

LINDBLOM, C. (1977), *Politics and Markets* (New York: Basic Books).

LOGAN, J., and MOLOTCH H. (1987), *Urban Fortunes: The Political Economy of Place* (Berkeley: University of California Press).

LOWNDES, V. (1996), 'Varieties of the New Institutionalism', *Public Administration* 74: 181–97.

—— and SKELCHER, C. (1997), 'Modes of governance and multi-organisational partnerships: reflections from the British Urban Regeneration Experience' (paper to the Fourth International Conference on Multi-Organisation Partnerships and Co-operative Strategy, Balliol College, Oxford, 8–10 July).

MILLER, W., and DICKSON, M. (1998), 'The Democratic Principle of Local Governance', in G. Stoker (ed.), *The New Politics of Local Governance* (London: Macmillan).

MOSSBERGER, K., and STOKER, G. (1997), 'Inner-City Policy in Britain: Why It Will Not Go Away', *Urban Affairs Review*, 32: 378–402.

ORR, M., and STOKER, G. (1994), 'Urban Regimes and Leadership in Detroit', *Urban Affairs Quarterly*, 30: 48–73.

OSBORNE, D., and GAEBLER, T. (1991), *Reinventing Government* (Reading: Addison Wesley).

OVERMAN, E., and BOYD, K. (1994), 'Best Practice Research and Post Bureaucratic Reform', *Journal of Public Administration Research and Theory*, 4: 67–83.

PETERS, B. G. (1997), 'Shouldn't Row, Can't Steer: What's a Government to Do', *Public Policy and Administration*, 12: 51–61.

PIERRE, J. (1999), 'Models of Urban Governance: The Institutional Dimension of Urban Politics', *Urban Affairs Review*, 34: 372–96.

PICKVANCE, C. (1995), 'Marxist Theories of Urban Politics', in D. Judge, G. Stoker, and H. Wolman (eds.), *Theories of Urban Politics* (London: Sage).

RHODES, R. (1997), 'From Marketisation to Diplomacy: It's the Mix that Matters', *Public Policy and Administration*, 12: 31–50.

STEWART, J., and STOKER, G. (1988), *From Local Administration to Community Government* (London: Fabian Society).

STOKER, G. (1995), 'Regime Theory and Urban Politics', in D. Judge, G. Stoker, and H. Wolman (eds.), *Theories of Urban Politics* (London: Sage).

—— (1998*a*), 'Theory and Urban Politics', *International Political Science Review*, 19: 119–29.

—— (1998*b*), 'Governance as Theory: Five propositions', *International Social Science Journal*, 155:17–28.

—— (1998*c*), 'Quangos and Local Democracy', in M. Flinders and M. Smith (eds.), *Quangos, Accountability and Reform: The Politics of Quasi-Government* (London: Macmillan).

—— and MOSSBERGER, K. (1994), 'Urban Regime Theory in Comparative Perspective', *Government and Policy*, 12: 195–212.

—— and YOUNG, S. (199), *Cities in the 1990s* (Harlow: Longman).

STONE, C. (1989), *Regime Politics: Governing Atlanta 1946–1988* (Lawrence: University of Kansas Press).

—— (1993), 'Urban Regimes and the Capacity to Govern: A Political Economy Approach', *Journal of Urban Affairs*, 15:1–28.

—— (1997), 'Urban Regime Analysis: Theory, Service Provision and Cross-National Considerations' (paper to the Joint Sessions of the European Consortium for Political Research, Bern, Switzerland).

TAYLOR, A. (1997), ' "Arm's Length but Hands On" Mapping the New Governance. The Department of National Heritage and Cultural Policies in Britain', *Public Administration*.

6

Economic Governance

ANDREW GAMBLE

The idea of governance applied to the economy raises a number of fundamental issues both about the nature of the economy and of governance. Must an economy be governed, either through the state or through other institutions external to it? Or should we conceive of economies as self-governing? Is an economy best understood as a spontaneous order, a catallaxy made up of a myriad of separate individual exchanges, which does not need planning or administering from the outside, or is an economy always embedded in non-economic institutions, and to that extent governed by them?

One of the difficulties in discussing economic governance is the assumption that the economy belongs to the private sphere and governance to the public, and that economic governance is therefore concerned with the relationship between the economy and the state, how the state *governs* the economy. But governing is not the exclusive preserve of government. To govern means to influence, shape, regulate, or determine outcomes, and in this sense there are many other agencies and institutions that are involved in governing a social order.

The separation of governing as a process from government, a particular agent, explains the popularity of the term, governance. Governance denotes the steering capacities of a political system, the ways in which governing is carried out, without making any assumption as to which institutions or agents do the steering. For any social order like the economy, governance needs to be understood at two levels. First, there are the basic laws, rules, standards, and principles which provide the constitutional framework for governing. Many of these rules will not be formalized, but

This chapter is based on research conducted for the PERC political economy of the company project, funded by the Leverhulme Trust. The author wishes to thank Gavin Kelly and Jon Pierre for comments on an earlier draft.

are implicit in the process of governing. Second, there are the techniques, tools, practices, and ethos of governing, associated with particular institutions and agencies. The state is always involved in governance, but often in an enabling rather than a directing role, helping to establish and sustain the institutions in society, including crucially markets, which make steering possible.

The overemphasis on the relationship between the state and the economy, and the dichotomy which that sets up between planning and the market, has in the past led to neglect of the other ways in which economies are governed. It has produced an unhelpful fixation on the public and the private, as though these were two clearly defined spheres. The boundary between private and public is a highly significant one in modern societies, but it is a politically defined boundary, and one which changes. The public and the private do not arise as self-sufficient, free-standing spheres. They are constructed through collective choices. The private sphere does not exist prior to the state, or the state to the private sphere; both have to be constituted by acts of the state. A distinction needs to be drawn between the role of the state in constituting the rules and norms of an economic order, and its interventions as an agent within that order.

The idea of economic governance therefore implies that although the economy is *governed* it is not necessarily governed by the state. There are different modes of governance, many of them non-state. There is some disagreement about how many, but the list includes markets (of many different kinds), hierarchies (including companies and public agencies), networks/associations (private interest organizations and policy communities), and clans/communities (private, local, face-to-face relationships) (Hollingsworth and Linberg, 1985; Hollingsworth, Schmitter, and Streeck, 1994; Thompson *et al.*, 1991; Rhodes, 1996; Crouch and Streeck, 1997). All of these modes of governance have to be politically constituted in some way, but beyond that they can operate without direct involvement by the state. Once constituted an economy might be largely self-governing and the role of government minimal.

The recognition that in any actual economy not one but several modes of governance are relevant to the way in which the economy is governed requires abandonment of the stark opposition between states and markets. What is opened up is the possibility that diversity in capitalist economies around the world can be explained by the particular institutional combinations of modes of economic governance which are found in different countries. The degree of involvement of the state will vary between economies, but it is not a good guide to understanding the steering capacities of that political system. State involvement may be low, but the steering capacity may be high because of reliance on other institutions.

This perspective on governance leaves behind the old debate about spontaneous versus planned orders. It certainly suggests that the idea of the economy as a spontaneous order which has some kind of pre-political existence and legitimacy is mistaken (Hayek, 1973; Kley, 1994; Gamble, 1996). However if an economy is constituted in a particular way it may well appear as a spontaneous order, reproducing itself with little overt political or government interference. Hayek was right to argue that an economy can be governed without direct involvement by the state, but wrong to suggest that this can be achieved without prior state intervention at the constitutional level, and wrong to minimize the contribution of modes of governance other than markets. Governance arrangements are often not planned, but that does not mean they are somehow natural, rather than the outcome of a particular collective choice.

Central to economic governance, I shall argue, is the notion of an economic constitution. The existence of an economy implies a degree of order, consistency, and predictability in the way in which agents behave. That in turn implies rules, constraints, and norms which agents accept as binding upon them. Together these make up the economic constitution. In political theory constitutions have been understood in two main ways; first, as a set of principles or legally entrenched rights, which are assumed to be in some sense pre-political, and typically provide a framework for the achievements of autonomously established ends; and second, as the expression of a particular form of government rooted in specific political and social structures (Bellamy and Castiglione, 1996). I shall use economic constitution in this second sense. It denotes the rules and norms which constitute an economic order, but also the modes, the institutions, and the procedures of governance, which determine the division of powers, the representation of interests, the locus of decision-making, the limits within which power is exercised, the boundary between the public and the private, and the objectives of policy.

Understood in this way all economic governance involves an economic constitution. Key questions to consider then become how economic constitutions have evolved, why they differ, and to what level of economic activity they refer. Economic constitutions are the distillation of the practices and principles of a particular historical period, and therefore reflect particular circumstances and a specific mix of modes of governance. There

can be considerable argument, however, over whether within each historical period there can be many different economic constitutions, or whether
within each historical period there is convergence upon a single model.
This is an argument as to whether economic governance is best analysed at
the level of localities, economic sectors, nation states, or at the level of the
global economy as a single interdependent system. In theoretical terms the
argument becomes one between the institutionalism of comparative political economy which emphasizes particularity and diversity and the struc-
turalism of international political economy which emphasizes common
problems and convergence (Strange, 1997).

A governance perspective offers a means of reconciling the two
approaches. There is no single site from which the economy is governed.
An exclusive focus on the nation state as the site of economic governance
makes state/market and public/private the terms in which governance is
discussed, and gives priority to the state as the leading agent of governance.
The implication is that governance (steering) is something which states do
to markets. The emphasis is upon intervention by the state in pursuit of its
own interests and agenda. But a wider view of governance recognizes that
there are not only several different modes of economic governance but also
many different agents. Markets, hierarchies, and networks are not contain-
able within tight, territorially defined, political jurisdictions; they
frequently and perhaps increasingly go beyond them, and need to be
understood in terms of a pattern of regional and global economic governance. But national economies themselves, although extremely important
sites of economic governance, need to be disaggregated, because within
them different sectors and regions are governed in different ways. At the
local level the diversity of patterns of economic governance throughout the
global economy is what is striking. At the global level, it is the common patterns and common responses which stand out.

The complexity of economic governance is not a new phenomenon.
Recent trends towards a more interdependent global economy should not
be contrasted with a period when all governance took place within nation
states. Since its inception the global economy of modern times has always
been characterized by different modes of governance. What has changed
has been the balance between them, and the territorial and political circumstances in which they have operated. From the standpoint of the history of this global economy over the last two hundred years it is possible to
discern three successive patterns in its economic constitution—liberal,
national protectionist, and neo-liberal.

The liberal economic constitution of the nineteenth century which favoured a self-governing economy gave way in the twentieth century to an economic constitution in which the state and its various agencies were assigned a much more direct role in governing the economy, often in conjunction with business and labour associations (Streeck and Schmitter, 1985; Cawson, 1985). In the last thirty years of the twentieth century, however, the assumption that the state had a major direct role to play in economic governance was challenged, and the importance of other forms of governance, particularly self-governing markets, but also the corporate hierarchies of transnational companies as well as networks and policy communities became the focus of attention. The state has in some areas disengaged from the economy, but it remains a key player in economic governance. Its role has in some cases altered, with greater emphasis being placed on regulation than on administration. De-regulation has therefore often been a misleading term. A more accurate term is re-regulation, because the disengagement of the state from direct administrative responsibility for certain economic functions has often been accompanied by an increase in its regulatory responsibilities.

A change in the attitude towards the role of the state has also occurred. Although the state is still expected to have an active role (except in the more extreme neo-liberal and libertarian doctrines) its role is often conceived as an enabling rather than a planning one. The state's task is to support other modes of governance, such as markets and networks or corporate hierarchies in governing the economy, rather than to seek to impose its own pattern or its own agenda. Possible reasons for this shift are explored below. They include first the recognition, arising out of the many policy failures of the recent past, that the capacity of the state to perform governance functions directly is limited; second, the growing complexity of the policy-making process in relation to information and resources; and third, the impact of contemporary trends in the global economy which has made management of discrete national economic spaces more difficult.

ECONOMIC CONSTITUTIONS IN HISTORICAL PERSPECTIVE

The emergence of modern forms of economy, state, and society in the last two hundred years provides the historical context for understanding contemporary forms of economic governance. These forms included the creation of market economies and clearly defined property rights, the widening and deepening of the division of labour, the exploitation of new technologies, which made possible a cumulative advance in living standards. Associated with them were the establishment of the state as an independent public power, the elaboration of the institutions and organizations of civil society, and the breakdown of local regional self-sufficiency through the emergence of a global economy.

It is the complex structure of modern societies which makes possible several different modes through which economies can be governed, as well as several different levels (local, sectoral, sub-regional, national, regional, global) at which governance can be located (Cerny, 1990). There are pressures towards uniformity, but also at the same time significant pressures sustaining and creating diversity. As suggested above, the patterns of governance which emerge together make up the *economic constitution*, which is not a formal document, but the distillation of dominant practices and doctrines which define the parameters within which the governing of the economy takes place in a particular period. Such constitutions arise incrementally and are rationalised only after they have become established. They reflect the political purposes of particular agents as well as the distribution of political power between groups. To that extent they are politically and socially constructed rather than the spontaneous creation of markets.

This point can be illustrated with reference to the first modern economic constitution, the liberal economic constitution of the nineteenth century which reflected the practice and beliefs of a particular national economy, that of Britain, the leading economy of the time. This economic constitution not only became the model for other states throughout the global economy, but also became the constitution for that global economy itself, based on an attempt to universalize certain rules about property, finance, and trade. The liberal economic constitution was therefore both a doctrine, centred on the ideals of liberal political economy—free trade, sound finance, and laissez-faire—and a reflection of the institutional means by which the British economy and the global economy were co-ordinated and governed. The celebration of the power, productivity, and efficiency of markets as the main instrument of economic governance was the backbone of the laissez-faire vision. The state had an important role, but it was a minimal one; it had to remove the obstacles to the working of the free market, and ensure that they were not re-established. The state had specific functions to discharge—enforcement of law, maintenance of social order, safeguarding of the currency—and was much more active than the normal caricature of laissez-faire suggests, since there were a great number of obstacles to the efficient working of markets. But under this liberal economic constitution there was no requirement for the state at the national level to be responsible for the level of employment or for economic prosperity. Its responsibilities for human capital and for infrastructure were also small. What the liberal economic constitution assumed was that once the basic laws and institutions had been established the economy was in principle self-governing. The market itself provided the steering and corrective mechanisms, in particular the price system, which were required for successful economic governance. Interventions by the state risked disturbing the delicate mechanism which co-ordinated economic activity across the globe and ensured such high and rising levels of prosperity.

The policy rules for national governments contained in this economic constitution were that governments should pursue sound finance, by maintaining balanced budgets and keeping expenditure and therefore taxation to a minimum; they should adhere to the gold standard, thus imposing on themselves a severe external financial discipline which would ensure that money would be stable in value; they should support open markets and free trade, and resist the lobbying of special interests whatever the implications for particular sectors of the economy, in order to maximize wealth for the whole community; and they should confine their internal interventions to making sure that markets were as competitive as possible, and that all restraints on trade, from whatever source they came, were outlawed. The division between the public and the private was relatively clearcut. There was an important if limited public sphere and an important role for the public interest in defining and enforcing the conditions for a thriving market economy. But the dynamism emanated from the private sphere itself. Economic agency in the liberal constitution is located in private individuals. The role of the state is restricted to maintaining the conditions for the market to function.

As many of its critics pointed out, however, the very success of the liberal economic constitution obscured the foundations of that very success, by making it appear that the only mode of governance on which it relied was the market. Schumpeter argued that the liberal civilization of the nineteenth century, brilliant though it was, rested on non-market and often non-liberal institutions—such as religion and community which gave legitimacy to the social order, and in particular to existing property rights, while at the same imposing certain limits within which wealth seeking was conducted (Schumpeter, 1950). The capitalist economy was governed through pre-capitalist institutions which originated outside the processes of market exchange. It relied upon a strong civic culture and the willingness of individuals to act in the public interest and pursue public purposes, as well as trusting one another in economic exchange. Without these non-market forms of governance market relations themselves could not have been sustained.

The crucial role played by the state was emphasized by Karl Polanyi, who argued that far from being a natural, spontaneous development, the liberal economic order in important respects was created and sustained by the state (Polanyi, 1957). It was an artificial and vulnerable political creation which required continuous political support. It was successfully established in Britain and some other countries, but elsewhere key elements were resisted, and states emerged with very different economic aims, which eventually led to the creation of different national economic constitutions, which rejected some key elements of the liberal constitution, particularly in relation to the role of the state in the economy. Protection was used as a weapon to establish industries which could compete with Britain, and some countries like Germany began to develop novel policies towards human capital, welfare, and investment. So long as Britain, however, remained the world's leading industrial and financial power the liberal constitution was the one which ruled the global economy.

In the twentieth century the liberal economic constitution came under sustained assault both at the global and at the national level, and was substantially modified, and in many countries was rejected altogether as a framework for governance. This occurred in the context of an enormous expansion in the scope and scale of government, measured by the size of the public sector, the growth of public spending and taxation as a proportion of GDP, and by the extensive new responsibilities which national governments assumed. These changes were fuelled by the new pressures of democratic polities, major new technological advances, increasing military and economic competition between states, and the rise of collectivist ideologies of right and left.

The twentieth century has been notable for the fierceness of its ideological disputes. The economy and how it should be governed has often been central; two key debates have been the case for capitalism and socialism as alternative economic systems and the merits of different institutional models of capitalism. Both debates moved public discourse on political economy away from many of the assumptions of the liberal economic constitution of the nineteenth century. The economic constitutions which came to dominate the twentieth century at both global and national level have been much more collectivist, nationalist, and protectionist in their basic assumptions.

At the global level there have been three economic constitutions in the last two hundred years, the liberal economic constitution of the nineteenth and early twentieth century, the national protectionist constitution of the short twentieth century (1917–1991), and the neo-liberal constitution which has been emerging since 1971 and became fully dominant in the 1990s. The rise and fall of these different economic constitutions can be understood cyclically, as a reaction to the costs imposed on particular groups and communities by the operation of the dominant mode of economic governance (Polanyi, 1957), or as the result of the frustration of expectations (Hirschman, 1982). But they can also be analysed in terms of the particular combination of the main modes of governance—hierarchies, markets, networks, and communities—which they sanction.

CAPITALISM AND SOCIALISM

The debate about capitalism and socialism is mostly of historical interest only today, but it still leaves a powerful imprint on contemporary thinking because of the way it polarized questions about economic governance and the nature of economic order. It focused on just two modes of governance—hierarchies and markets—virtually ignoring networks and communities. Socialism was identified with public ownership and central planning and allocation of all resources, while capitalism was identified with private ownership and decentralized market allocation of resources. In their extreme forms the two were often presented as ideal types which excluded the other. Socialism was promoted as an alternative and superior economic order which could achieve not only equality but also greater efficiency by eliminating markets and using scientific central planning to co-ordinate the economy. The debate created the sharp ideological opposition between the market and planning, which obscured the actual way in which modern economies are governed.

The appeal of planning as an alternative to the market partly reflected the dominance of the market as a mode of governance in the liberal economic constitution. Socialists argued that economic governance needed to be reformed and control given to public agencies because of the failures associated with markets—particularly unemployment, waste, and poverty. Planning by the state was regarded as the natural counterpart of changes in the way capitalist economies were organized. The emergence of Fordist regimes of accumulation in many sectors was associated with growing concentration and centralization of capital, the emergence of mass production and scientific management, and the integration of mass production and mass consumption. National economic planning was put forward as the logical extension of what was increasingly occurring within the advanced sectors of the economy. Hierarchy as mode of governance was the rational and scientific means to overcome the anarchy of capitalist production and create the economic basis for a socialist society.

The claims that socialism offered a mode of economic governance for a modern economy which could dispense with markets was subjected to sustained theoretical and then practical examination. Von Mises argued that rational calculation was impossible in a socialist economy because prices were no longer determined through market exchanges but imposed centrally by the planning authorities. Modern economies based on specialization and division of labour could only be governed through decentralized markets. His views were rejected by many economists, but most of those who argued against Mises also came to accept that central planning could not replace markets; it had to use markets as a tool to ensure efficient resource allocation (Lavoie, 1985).

Central planning in practice did make use of markets, but relied more heavily on hierarchical administrative allocation as the means of governing the economy. Despite some successes in particular sectors, the centrally planned economies proved quite incapable of matching the economic performance of capitalist market economies. The experience of the Soviet bloc demonstrated that the central planning authorities could never have sufficient knowledge to plan effectively. The market as a decentralized system of knowledge and incentives was shown to be much more efficient in providing co-ordination for an economy with a complex division of labour (Kornai, 1992; Nove, 1983).

Socialism has been discredited as an alternative economic system to capitalism, and no one any longer imagines that a modern economy resting on division of labour and specialized exchange could dispense with markets as a mode of governance. But the argument at times in the last twenty years has swung too far in the other direction, with suggestions from neo-liberal thinkers that a modern economy should aim to dispense not just with the state, but with hierarchy itself as a mode of governance. But hierarchy is unlikely to go away. In the sense of bureaucratic planning it is a ubiquitous feature of modern economies, and the main method of co-ordination of all large public and private organization, including government agencies and medium and large private companies. From an economic efficiency standpoint the existence of such a large sphere of hierarchical governance within a market economy arises because in many circumstances organisation is the most efficient way to reduce transaction costs (Williamson, 1985).

MODELS OF CAPITALISM

One of the outcomes from the capitalism/socialism debate was an acceptance that modes of governance need not be mutually exclusive ideological alternatives. They can serve different purposes. What matters is how they are combined and which mode predominates at particular levels and in particular sectors. This has been the theme of the literature on models of capitalism. It has two main sources. One is the experience of those states which already in the nineteenth century in seeking to catch up and modernize rejected key aspects of the liberal economic constitution, at least at the national level. Many of these states were conservative nationalist regimes which embraced interventionist policies as part of their strategy for delivering a prosperous economy and a strong military. They were instinctively protectionist, both in terms of trade and welfare, accepting that the legitimacy of the political order and of private property rights depended on the state intervening to promote economic security for all its citizens (Barrington Moore, 1967).

   The other main source lay in the gradual accommodation of centre-left parties to the need to work within the constraints of a capitalist economy, and to accept certain key aspects of its economic constitution such as private property rights. But they remained critical of market failures including problems created by the concentration of wealth and power in market economies. This led to a perspective which argued the need to reform the institutions of capitalism and to use public power to regulate markets in the interests of the majority of workers and consumers. Capitalism had to be tamed through developing the countervailing power of democracy exercised through the state. Markets would not be abolished but they would be regulated in the public interest (Kalecki, 1943; Przeworski, 1985).

The assumption of both conservative modernizers and social demo-cratic reformers was that acceptance of the basic structure of capitalism as the form which economic order must take in the modern world did not mean that there is only one kind of capitalism possible to which all national systems must conform and will converge towards. The literature on differ-ent national models of capitalism compares the institutions, policies, and capacities, in short the governance arrangements of different national sys-tems. Much of this type of analysis can be traced back to Shonfield (Shonfield, 1965), and has been developed by many subsequent writers (Zysman, 1983; Dyson, 1980; Hall, 1986; Crouch and Streeck, 1997; Weiss, 1998). Authors vary in the emphasis which they put on different modes of governance, but there is a general recognition of the need to understand the way economies are governed institutionally, which means incorporating networks and communities alongside markets and hierarchies in the char-acterization of the different models.

One of the main themes in this literature is between national economic constitutions which give priority to the market as a mode of governance and those which give a more significant role to the state or to networks. Among the advanced industrial states the countries with the strongest attachment to liberal economic constitutions (Britain and the United States) are often contrasted with the economic constitutions of Germany, France, Sweden, and Japan (Johnson, 1982; Hall, 1986; Zysman, 1983; Albert, 1991). One of the important differences has been the readiness of the state to promote long-term economic development, whether through formal planning mechanisms, corporatist arrangements, or informal net-works to promote a consensus on national goals and to steer the economy by long-term subsidies and support to particular sectors, arranged through the state, the banks, or private interest associations. The Anglo-Saxon model by contrast has continued to put much greater emphasis on free and open markets as the main steering mechanism for a capitalist economy, because it promotes maximum efficiency, flexibility, and adapt-ability, which critics suggest means that investment decisions tend to be determined by short-term financial returns (Hutton, 1995). In contrast, the main advantages of the alternatives to the Anglo-Saxon model are argued to be their encouragement of relationship of trust which facilitate long-term investment in new capacity, new technologies and human capital, restraint of domestic consumption and incomes, while at the same time guaranteeing high employment and low inflation (Albert, 1991).

The literature on models of capitalism emphasizes the diversity in the way that national capitalisms are governed, because of their different histories and institutions. The main objection to this way of approaching economic governance is that it focuses on the national level and the different economic constitutions of individual states, rather than looking at how all states are constrained within the economic constitution which operates at the global level (Strange, 1997). The idea of national models originates in a particular period in the history of the global economy, the national protectionist era, when states and national economies appeared to have greater autonomy. The national economic constitutions which emerged had various names; the New Deal in the US, the Keynesian welfare state in Britain, the social market economy in Germany; the developmental state in Japan. There were important differences between them, but what all shared was the acceptance of a significant role for the state in governing the economy. The idea of a self-governing economy (never strong in either Germany or Japan) was abandoned, and in its place came notions of government involvement and planning. The public sector was enlarged in scope and scale, and many new tools of government policy were introduced, along with many new responsibilities and objectives for government. Governments came to accept that they had a responsibility to ensure full employment, stable prices, and economic growth. They become managers of the economy, and sought to equip themselves with the tools they needed to achieve their targets.

A further change was that the economic governance required for corporate capitalism came to be viewed as different from that required for liberal capitalism. Instead of the constitution being regarded as essentially a framework of rules to govern the exchanges of a multitude of individual agents, it was now seen as the principles needed to regulate the arrangements between the major corporate interests and corporate bodies in the economy in order to deliver an effective partnership between the state, labour, and capital. Many of the rules in the liberal economic constitution were fixed, like the rules on balanced budgets and the exchange rate; under corporatism they become variable and discretionary. The state was charged with a general responsibility to secure the best balance between the different objectives of economic policy, rather than concentrating on upholding the basic framework of rules as a set of immovable constraints (Schmitter and Lehmbruch, 1979; Cawson, 1985).

NEO-LIBERALISM

The national economic constitutions which became established in the course of the twentieth century did so in the context of a fundamental shift in the international economic constitution because of the change from an open trading order to a fragmented global economy of currency, trading, and military blocs. The re-establishment of a new framework for international economic governance at Bretton Woods in 1944 allowed the slow emergence of trends towards a more integrated global economy to become re-established, at the same time providing a favourable context for the development of diverse national capitalist models.

The collapse of the international monetary framework in 1971 and the reappearance of severe slumps, the slowdown in growth, the acceleration of inflation and the steep rise in unemployment, created major new problems of economic management for governments, and led to a reassessment in many states of the economic constitutions which had served them so well in the post-war period. The challenge to the post-war economic constitutions came from both left and right but the most cogent and successful was the neo-liberal critique, which sought to bring economic governance into line with the new realities, as it perceived them, of the global economy. In particular in the absence of any state which could underwrite a regime of fixed exchange rates for the international economy, the neo-liberals put forward monetarism and the observance of strict monetary targets as the best way to ensure macroeconomic stability. The neo-liberal economic constitution abandoned full employment and economic growth as goals to which government should be committed, and instead gave priority to the control of inflation. They accompanied this with plans to reduce public spending and taxation, eliminate public sector borrowing, privatize public sector enterprises and services, and deregulate the private sector.

The neo-liberal agenda was strongly opposed to corporatism, and sought to destroy the representative institutions which had been built up to help manage the economy in previous decades. It wanted to go back to the liberal economic constitution where the state provided just a framework within which individual economic agents acted. But it was never simply a reversion to the liberal economic constitution. One reason was that the state was now so big, and growing so fast, that at best the efforts of neo-liberal governments only succeeded in halting the growth of public spending; they did not manage to reduce it. Under the neo-liberal economic constitution states remain active states, pursuing clear macroeconomic targets and managing the economy in ways that were never true of liberal states in the nineteenth century.

The neo-liberal economic constitution was adopted as their internal constitution by a number of countries, including the US, UK, Australia, New Zealand, and Chile. It has been generally resisted in many European countries who have wanted to preserve their social model, and it has also had only limited application in some of the East Asian countries. But its success in the 1990s in apparently reviving the economics of the US and the UK while Germany has stagnated and East Asia plunged into financial crisis, has led to some speculation that it is destined to become the norm throughout the capitalist world, because it is what the financial markets and the transnational companies want as a framework for economic governance. The suggestion is increasingly made that the social model of many European countries is under serious strain, because decisions on inward investment are increasingly determined by whether national governments can demonstrate that they are pursuing policies to promote flexible labour markets and curtail government spending.

OVERLOAD AND UNGOVERNABILITY

The advent of the neo-liberal economic constitution has put the spotlight on the role of government in economic governance. Does government have the capacity any longer to be directly involved in governing economies? The questioning began following the series of policy failures and policy disasters which overtook most states in the 1970s.

The sea-change in the global economy which took place at this time tested the steering capacities of governments to the limit, and forced them into rapid adjustments and major restructuring of their economies. Many industries were found to be no longer competitive or viable and were phased out. Governments had to cope with much higher social security spending for the unemployed, while trying to find resources to invest in new industries and new technologies.

The crisis of the 1970s was however not just an economic crisis, but developed into a more general political crisis for the regulated market system which had initially emerged in response to the perceived inadequacies of the way in which markets were governed. Three key factors in the enlargement of the scope of the state in the twentieth century were the development of a normative economic policy, aimed at promoting employment and growth; the underwriting of the process of scientific discovery and technological innovation; and the development of a normative social policy, aimed at extending rights and opportunities to all citizens (Bell, 1977). The growth of state programmes in these and other areas, including the military, had seemed largely unchecked and unstoppable. But the problems of the 1970s raised large doubts about the capacity of the state to cope with the complexity of the tasks with which it was now confronted. Terms like overload and ungovernability began to be freely used.

The heart of the issue was recognized to be information and compliance. Could states ever have enough information available to them centrally to be able to make rational choices? The problem of information encouraged, on the one hand, the approach to policy and problem-solving which Lindblom called mutual adjustment, a process of trial and error, cautious experiment, and bargaining to find the best way forward in a world of complexity and uncertainty. On the other, it persuaded governments to experiment with new methods of delivery of services, including privatization, decentralization, and the creation of new public agencies at arms length from the policy makers in the central executive.

The question of compliance raises the issue of whether, given the political and economic structure of democratic market systems, governments can resist pressure and impose their own agenda, but also have the instruments at their disposal to change the behaviour of private sector actors both by inducing them to follow state policies, and (more enduringly) to change the structures of the economic environment which give actors incentives to behave in the ways states want (Ikenberry, 1986).

Governments have many incentives and sanctions which they can deploy to try to induce private actors to comply with state policies. But there is a considerable literature which points out the difficulties of achieving it. Governments find it easy to impose certain decisions, such as changes in the rates of existing taxes, but very much harder to introduce policies which require the co-operation of a large number of private actors, such as incomes policy. The really big economic questions facing governments, such as reforming the welfare state or improving the skills possessed by the long-term unemployed or enhancing competitiveness require the creation of strong partnerships between public and private sector actors which are very hard to achieve.

The central problem of economic governance is that the culture of modern democracies still tends to assign to states the leading role in governing the economy, a role which they can only imperfectly fulfil, and raises expectations which they cannot meet.

The problem is universal in the sense that all states lack the capacities to achieve their goals, but it is also particular because it raises the issue of why some states are more successful at managing their economies than others. In the period since 1945 in particular the management of national economies assumed great importance, and the relative performance of national economies against a number of indicators was keenly noted. Some states rose while others declined. The key question was whether states could do anything about it. The belief that they could, and that different policies or structural reforms of institutions could improve relative economic performance became an important factor in the politics of many states. In the 1970s and 1980s the issue was redefined as one of competitiveness. It became a staple part of political rhetoric of both left and right, although many social scientists doubted that it made any sense to talk of improving the competitiveness of entire national economies, rather than of particular sectors and firms (Krugman, 1994; Wilks and Wright, 1987).

STATE AUTONOMY AND STATE CAPACITY

Just as the failures of the market earlier in the century had created a discourse of market failure, so the problem of overload and ungovernability in the 1970s created a discourse of government failure. It put the focus firmly on the question of the viability and desirability of government seeking to govern the economy, and therefore on questions of state autonomy and state capacity. Public choice models of bureaucratic politics argue that the structure of political markets means that bureaucrats have no effective budget constraint and seek to maximize the size of their budgets (Niskanen, 1971). Politicians and civil servants are assumed to be driven by self-interest, and this leads to a series of perverse, sub-optimal outcomes, such as the steady growth in the scale and scope of government activities. The focus in this literature is on the ubiquity of government failure and the reasons for it.

Government may increasingly be hollowed out in the neo-liberal constitution, and other modes of governance—particularly networks, and hierarchies, in the shape of transnational capital—are becoming more important. But there has always been a considerable degree of variation in economic constitutions and forms of economic governance at the national level, and this seems likely to persist. The extent of diversity is limited by the institutions of international economic governance. The range of variation between national economic constitutions apparent earlier in the twentieth century had become much less by the end (particularly after the demise of the Soviet Union), but there are no signs of complete convergence. There is still considerable debate as to what determines the limits to the amount of variation that is possible, and whether the variations that are observed have consequences for economic perfomance. The role of agency and in particular state agency has been stressed in many accounts, and with reason, but it operates within particular structures which impose constraints on what agents can do. This makes the question of how much autonomy states and other agents enjoy in practice an important question for comparative analysis of economic governance.

A key literature has focused on state capacities, and therefore on strong and weak states, and the ability of states to achieve control over their environment (Skocpol, 1979; Evans *et al.*, 1985). Michael Mann has distinguished between despotic power (the exercise of arbitrary will) and infrastructural power, which extends the reach of the central state throughout a society and makes possible the co-ordination of many different agencies and the implementation of complex policies (Mann, 1986). These ideas of state capacities have been further refined in the institutionalist analysis of Peter Hall, who argues that five sets of structural variables are most important for a nation's economic policy: the organization of labour, the organization of capital, the organization of the state, the organization of the political system, and the structural position of the country within the international economy. These structures determine the organization of policy making in a state, and influence not only the degree of power which any particular agent has over policy outcomes, but also how agents define their interests (Hall, 1986). On this view the institutional variation which is derived from the way capital, labour, and the state are organized is the key to explaining differences in economic policies and economic outcomes between national economic systems. Even under a neo-liberal global economic constitution state capacities still matter (Weiss, 1998).

In functionalist accounts of the political and economic system the actions of states are explained by the functions they perform for the reproduction of the system. In classical Marxism, but also in many neo-Marxist accounts, such as the regulation school, the role of the state is to assist the reproduction of capital. The purposes of the state are derived from the structure of class interests. The state may act on behalf of capital in general or it may be conceived as acting as an instrument of particular class fractions, but the limits of its autonomy are set by the overriding need to ensure that capitalist relations of production are reproduced, and with them the conditions for profitable accumulation of capital. In the more sophisticated accounts, such as the French regulation school these conditions for profitable accumulation are extended to include legitimation and modes of social regulation which include all the political, economic, social, and cultural institutions which govern the economy (Aglietta, 1979; Lipietz, 1987; Jessop, 1995; Kenny, 1999). In another influential formulation the problem for capitalist states becomes balancing the requirements of accumulation with the requirements of legitimation (O'Connor, 1973). The problem of governance becomes reconciling the conflict between these two imperatives, the structural expression of which is the constant tendency for spending to outpace revenue. The state has to choose between cutting back public spending programmes or increasing tax burdens.

In the 1970s however there was sharp disagreement among Marxists as to whether the steering capacities which the state had acquired through the adoption of Keynesian techniques of economic management were sufficient to ensure that there would be no repeat of the 1930s slump and great depression. Some suggested that while the economic crisis might be indefinitely postponed, the steps taken to contain it would displace the crisis onto the legitimacy of the capitalist order (Habermas, 1976). In particular the deepening of corporatist arrangements in the 1970s appeared in a number of countries to threaten the prerogatives of capital. The morass into which Keynesian economic management appeared to be heading was one of the main reasons for the appeal of neo-liberalism, which offered to restore both profitability and legitimacy to the capitalist system. From a Marxist perspective neo-liberalism represented an attempt to put the clock back by restoring a balance of class forces which favoured the interests of capital rather than labour.

REGULATION

Most functionalist and state-centric perspectives accept that states have the capacity to steer the economy, but this still leaves large questions about the kind of role different state agencies, including governments, should play. Should governments seek to facilitate the operation of markets, allowing many sectors of the economy to be self-governing, and not seeking to interfere in the logic of markets? Such a policy stance, which is observable in many European economies, and also in the United States, confines governments at best to a market accelerating role, where governments intervene to allow adjustments to changed economic conditions which are required by the market to take place more quickly (Weaver, 1985). But others argue that effective economic governance also requires state agencies to be directly involved in governing the economy, either alone or in partnership with the major private interest associations (Hutton, 1995).

There is a sense that the options open to democracies have narrowed. According to Charles Lindblom the politico-economic alternatives available to humanity make up a very short list, and several of these alternatives have virtually disappeared in the twentieth century as the result of the experience with central planning. What remains are regulated market systems, leaning either to planner sovereignty or consumer sovereignty (Lindblom, 1977). But what is common to both systems is that the state does not directly control production; it only has the power to create the conditions in which profitable production is carried on. It has to rely on other agents to organize production. Yet because the state depends for its revenues on the ability of these agents to produce and enlarge the wealth of the society, this creates a structural power which gives business a privileged position in the governance arrangements of market systems. The ability of states to pursue particular objectives depends on their capacity to mobilize and co-ordinate private capital (Gourevitch, 1986).

Through steering the economy governments hope to achieve stability and development. But there can often be a conflict between them. Stability is measured in relation to full employment of resources and a currency that holds its value, while development is measured in terms of investments in social and physical capital which underpin competitiveness. Every economic constitution includes rules about how stability is to be defined and achieved, which reflect a particular conception of fiscal and monetary order. Twentieth-century economic constitutions have also contained rules which define economic development. The desire to achieve both stability and development is common to regulated market systems, but there is considerable disagreement over the most effective tools and agencies.

The argument is not a simple one of public versus private. One of the most intriguing areas of research on systems of economic governance has explored the role of private economic governance—the use of various kinds of associations in some countries to mediate between economic agents and the state. This use of networks in place of either hierarchical or market modes of governance is particularly characteristic of systems with a strong corporatist tradition such as Germany (Hollingsworth, 1994). But it is also a characteristic of certain sectors in the UK, where the principle of self-regulation by particular industries and sectors (the City of London is a particular instance) (Moran, 1986, 1991) has long been accepted as preferable to the kind of statutory regulation characteristic of the United States (Roe, 1994).

The self-regulation which characterized the UK gave a particular twist to the kind of corporatism which developed there, because it meant that the state was always relatively weak in relation to other interests, and was often reluctant to interfere. This was particularly true of industrial relations. The British system of corporate bias (Middlemas, 1979) conformed to the view of the state held by Keynes. He included within his definition of the state all those associations and organizations that defined themselves as serving the public interest rather than maximizing private profit, and placed great emphasis on the need for an expansion of a public ethos and sense of public service. Such a conception of the state saw the government as playing an indirect enabling role, with its main task being to achieve stability through its macro policy. This view of the state believed that the real issue facing economic governance was keeping the role of government limited, while increasing the role of the state, by persuading more individuals, groups, and associations to act in the public interest (Keynes, 1972).

The British system of self-regulation largely survived the central planning regime devised for the wartime economy, and was fairly successful in delivering stability in the 1950s and 1960s, but failed to deliver development. The steps taken to remedy this in the 1960s and 1970s were not successful, and the ability to achieve stability was lost as well. This prompted increasing attacks on the British system of self-regulation first in a more etatiste corporatist direction, then in a neo-liberal direction. The self-regulation of many sectors in the economy, including the trade unions, education, and the City, was severely weakened, and in its place Britain edged unmistakably towards a regulatory state, in which the state withdrew from attempting to intervene directly in particular sectors, and instead chose to rely upon a regulatory regime to enforce new rules to promote competition and monitor compliance with them.

Many observers of the British case therefore describe the process of deregulation which occurred in the 1980s and 1990s not as deregulation but as reregulation. What was dismantled were often the protections afforded by self-regulation, and the introduction of stricter regimes of market competition. But many of these markets could not be expected to sustain themselves without assistance, which was why new regulatory agencies had to be set up. Britain is a very good example of how the dismantling of large parts of its public sector and the desire of successive governments to avoid either corporatism or planning, did not result in a system of economic governance dominated entirely by markets, but a much more developed regulatory system, which in some respects was more intrusive and certainly more transparent than what it replaced (Loughlin and Scott, 1997; Grant, 1993).

This move to a regulatory state was also a feature of other countries. In other European countries it was in part a reflection of the moves for deeper integration in the European Union (Majone, 1994). The single market and the plans for the single currency involved the promulgation of rules which were binding on all member states and were aimed at defining a unified European economic space. Such a regulatory state naturally has implications for particular national systems, although whether it threatens the maintenance of private governance through private interest associations remains to be seen.

What it does appear to do is to highlight the difference between the economic constitutions of for example the UK and Germany. Both embrace the regulatory state, but whereas the British believe that this means all markets, meaning all prices, should become flexible within the European Union, to facilitate trade and economic development, the Germans are reluctant to abandon the governance arrangements which have served them so well in the past. These arrangements have relied more heavily on associations as a mode of governance than either hierarchies or markets. The associative mode of governance has been most important not at the national level of bargaining between peak associations and the state, but at the micro level of negotiations among business firms. On the basis of mutual recognition of their status and entitlements, firms seek to reach formal, long-term agreements to protect their interests, while at the same time being influenced in their calculations and behaviour by a conception of the public interest. This kind of self-government or private interest government has become characteristic of particular sectors in the German economy (Streeck, 1985; Hollingsworth, Schmitter, and Streeck, 1994).

The extent to which sectors in an economy are self-governing, and the extent to which the state intervenes in them, varies considerably between national systems, and also between types of sectors. The size of firms in a sector and the technological complexity of the production process are crucial factors. In the United States self-government of the German kind as well as state intervention have been relatively weak, and the importance of market and hierarchical (corporate) modes of governance have been more significant in most sectors. But it is interesting that even in the United States there are some sectors in which clan governance and associative governance are powerful (Hollingsworth and Linberg, 1985; Hollingsworth, Schmitter, and Streeck, 1994). The willingness and the ability of the state to intervene directly in particular sectors depends on how different modes of governance perform. All modes of governance are subject to failure, including of course government. States have to decide what degree of failure and instability is acceptable before intervening and trying to change the mode of governance in a particular sector.

GLOBALIZATION

Globalization has in many ways become the central debate in contemporary discussion of economic governance, because it goes directly to the heart of the issue about state autonomy and state capacity. In its more extreme forms globalization is a typical example of a functionalist explanation which treats the state not just as a cipher but as an irrelevance. This is because it argues that the growth of the global economy means that nation states have lost their ability to manage their economies, or to steer them in any direction. The important forces shaping what happens to economies are made by the financial markets and by transnational companies. It is these networks which are now decisive for the governance of the world economy. National economies and nation states have become anachronistic. Nation states can obstruct the processes of globalization, but only temporarily, and the main effect is the relative impoverishment of their citizens. They can choose to act as facilitators, which means adopting the agenda of the big players in the financial markets and among transnational companies. But the argument is that they are powerless to shape a different course (Ohmae, 1995).

  If the hyper-globalization thesis was true, it would still not mean the end of governance, only that governance had now become organized entirely through the leading private agents in global markets. The attempt to steer the economy, using international institutions like the IMF and the World Bank, and drawing on transnational networks like the Trilateral Commission, would still be present. What would have changed would be the virtual exclusion of states and their agents from a central role. Instead the global economy would become a self-governing spontaneous order, in which economic outcomes would be shaped by the logic of producer and consumer choices within markets.

This thesis has been much criticized both as an accurate account of what is happening to economic governance in the contemporary global economy, and also as a prediction of future trends (Hirst and Thompson 1996; Weiss 1998). The globalization literature exaggerates the extent to which a global economy as distinct from an international economy really exists, and also exaggerates the capacities of nation states in the past compared to what they are now. According to the critics there are very few instances where nation-states have lost their ability to steer economies, and in some instances it has been enhanced. Globalization it is argued is frequently used by domestic governments as an excuse for policies they wish to pursue on other grounds. One version of this argues that in the 1980s and 1990s neo-liberal governments in many countries have attempted to reshape their economic constitution and weaken the influence of organized labour and other domestic lobby groups on economic policy by seeking to re-establish the principle of sound money through the external discipline of the international financial markets (Gill, 1998).

There is however a version of the globalization thesis which is more sustainable than the hyper-globalization one (Perraton *et al.*, 1997). All sides of the debate accept that there have been some significant changes, particularly in the financial markets, since the break-up of the Bretton Woods system and the floating of the major currencies. Financial crises which have forced governments to change course are not new in the history of the global economy, but the vulnerability of governments to them has increased since 1971. Evidence for a global economy which is defined as meaning global production systems and global labour markets is extremely thin. The global economy remains, as it has always been, part of a world system which combines a unified economic space with fragmented political authority (Wallerstein, 1973). The tensions between these two principles of the world system have always been the source of the dynamism and the conflicts within it.

In thinking about the governance of this world economy what is interesting about the present time is that the global economy has emerged from a long period in which the state system was particularly strong, following the breakdown of the liberal world order of the nineteenth century and the Russian Revolution. In the 1930s and 1940s in particular, national protectionism in different forms became dominant, and shaped the thinking of many domestic elites. It accounts for the importance that was given to the national economy and its management. With the gradual rebuilding of a liberal economic order after 1945 new forms of governance at international level began to be established, and policies to make national economies more open and to encourage regional integration (as in Europe), as well as broader international integration (such as through GATT), became prominent. A much more complex economic governance structure has emerged as a result, in which the capacities of governments to steer their national economies is only one aspect, although still undoubtedly a crucial one in understanding how economies are governed. Economic governance under the neo-liberal economic constitution of this stage of the development of the global economy will continue to be varied. Different national economies will not conform to a single pattern, and different combinations of markets, hierarchies, networks, and communities will continue to be found. There are powerful pressures towards greater conformity, some of which are being expressed through the new regional arrangements which are emerging in different parts of the world. Within this complex pattern of governance states still have some autonomy and some capacity to shape how the economy is governed. But they are only one player within an increasingly diversified world.

REFERENCES

AGLIETTA, M. (1979), *A Theory of Capitalist Regulation* (London: Verso).

ALBERT, M. (1991), *Capitalisme contre Capitalisme* (Paris: Seuil).

BARRINGTON MOORE JR. (1967), *Social Origins of Dictatorship and Democracy* (London: Allen Lane).

BELL, D. (1977), *The Cultural Contradictions of Capitalism* (New York: Basic Books).

BELLAMY, R., and CASTIGLIONE, D. (1996) (eds.), 'Constitutionalism in Transformation: European and Theoretical Perspectives', *Political Studies*, 44: 3.

CAWSON, A. (1985) (ed.), *Organised Interests and the State: Studies in Meso Corporatism* (London: Sage).

CERNY, P. (1990), *The Changing Architecture of Politics* (London: Sage).

CROUCH, C., and STREECK, W. (1997) (eds.), *Political Economy of Modern Capitalism* (London: Sage).

DYSON, K. (1980), *The State Tradition in Western Europe* (Oxford: Martin Robertson).

EVANS, P., REUSCHMEYER, D., and SKOCPOL, T. (1985), *Bringing the State Back In* (Cambridge: Cambridge University Press).

GAMBLE, A. (1996), *Hayek: the iron cage of liberty* (Cambridge: Polity).

GILL, S. (1998), 'European Governance and New Constitutionalism: Economic and Monetary Union and Alternatives to Disciplinary NeoLiberalism in Europe', *New Political Economy*, 3: 1, 5–26.

GOUREVITCH, P. (1986), *Politics in Hard Times* (Ithaca, NY: Cornell University Press).

GRANT, W. (1993), *The Politics of Economic Policy* (Hemel Hempstead: Harvester Wheatsheaf).

HABERMAS, J. (1976), *Legitimation crisis* (London: Heinemann).

HALL, P. (1986), *Governing the Economy* (Cambridge: Cambridge University Press).

HAYEK, F. (1973), *Law, Legislation, and Liberty* (London: Routledge).

HAYWARD, J., and BERKI, R. (1979), *State and Society in Contemporary Europe* (Oxford: Martin Robertson).

HIRSCHMAN, A. (1982), *Shifting Involvements* (Princeton: Princeton University Press).

HIRST, P., and THOMPSON, G. (1996), *Globalisation in Question* (Cambridge: Polity).

HOLLINGSWORTH, J., and LINBERG, L. (1985), 'The Governance of the American Economy: The Role of Markets, Clans, Hierarchies, and Associative Behaviour', in Streeck and Schmitter, (eds.), *Private Interest Government: Beyond Market and State* (London: Sage).

—— SCHMITTER, P., and STREECK, W. (1994) (eds.), *Governing Market Economies* (New York: Oxford University Press).

HUTTON, W. (1995), *The State We're In* (London: Cape).

IKENBERRY, J. (1986), 'The Irony of State Strength: Comparative Responses to the Oil Shocks in the 1970s', *International Organization*, 40: 1, 105–37.

JESSOP, R. (1995), 'The Regulation Approach, Governance and Post-Fordism: Alternative Perspectives on Economic and Political Change', *Economy and Society*, 24: 3, 307–33.

JOHNSON, C. (1982), *MITI and the Japanese Miracle* (Stanford: Stanford University Press).

KALECKI, M. (1943), 'Political Aspects of Full Employment', *Political Quarterly*, 14: 322–31.

KENNY, M. (1999), 'Regulation Theory', in A. Gamble, D. Marsh, and T. Tant (eds.), *Marxism and Social Science* (London: Macmillan).

KEYNES, J. M. (1972), 'The End of Laissez-faire', in *Essays in Persuasion*, Collected Writings, vol. 9 (London: Macmillan).

KLEY, R. (1994), *Hayek's Social and Political Thought* (Oxford: Oxford University Press).

KORNAI, J. (1992), *The Socialist System* (Oxford: Oxford University Press).

KRUGMAN, P. (1994), *Peddling Prosperity* (New York: Norton).

LAVOIE, D. (1985), *Rivalry and Central Planning: the Socialist Calculation Debate* (Cambridge: Cambridge University Press).

LINDBLOM, C. (1977), *Politics and Markets* (New York: Basic Books).

LIPIETZ, A. (1987), *Mirages and Miracles: the Crises of Global Fordism* (London: Verso).

LOUGHLIN, M., and SCOTT, C. (1997), 'The Regulatory State', in P. Dunleavy *et al.* (eds.), *Developments in British Politics* 5 (London: Macmillan), 205–19.

MAJONE, G. (1994), 'The Rise of the Regulatory State in Europe', *West European Politics* 17: 77–101.

MANN, M. (1986), 'The Autonomous Power of the State', in J. Hall (ed.), *States in History* (Oxford: Blackwell), 109–36.

MIDDLEMAS, K. (1979), *Politics in Industrial Society* (London: Andre Deutsch).

MORAN, M.(1986), *The Politics of Banking* (London: Macmillan).

—— (1991), *The Politics of the Financial Sectors Revolution: the USA, UK, and Japan* (London: Macmillan).

NISKANEN, W. (1971), *Bureaucracy and Representative Government* (Chicago: Aldine).

NOVE, A. (1983), *The Economics of Feasible Socialism* (London: Allen & Unwin).

O'CONNOR, J. (1973), *The Fiscal Crisis of the State* (New York: St Martins Press).

OHMAE, K. (1995), *The End of the Nation-State* (London: Harper Collins).

PERRATON, J., GOLDBLATT, D., HELD, D., and MCGREW, A. (1997), 'The Globalisation of Economic Activity', *New Political Economy*, 2/2: 257–77.

POLANYI, K. (1957), *The Great Transformation* (New York: Rinehart).

PRZEWORSKI, A. (1985), *Capitalism and Social Democracy* (Cambridge: Cambridge University Press).

RHODES, R. (1996), 'The New Governance: Governing Without Consensus', *Political Studies*, 44/4: 652–67.

ROE, M. (1994), *Strong Managers Weak Owners: The Political Roots of American Corporate Finance* (Princeton: Princeton University Press).

SCHMITTER, P., and LEHMBRUCH, G. (1979) (eds.), *Trends Towards Corporatist Intermediation* (London: Sage).

SCHUMPETER, J. (1950), *Captialism, Socialism, and Democracy* (London: Allen & Unwin).

SHONFIELD, A. (1965), *Modern Capitalism: The Changing Balance of Public and Private Power* (Oxford: Oxford University Press).

Skocpol, T. (1979), *States and Social Revolutions* (Cambridge: Cambridge University Press).

Strange, S. (1997), 'The Future of Global Capitalism, or Will Divergence Persist Forever?', in Crouch and Streeck (eds.), *Political Economy of Modern Capitalism*.

Streeck, W., and Schmitter, P. (1985), *Private Interest Government: Beyond Market and State* (London: Sage).

Thompson, G., Frances, J., Levacic, R., and Mitchell, J. (eds.) (1991), *Markets, Hierarachies, & Networks* (London: Sage).

Wallerstein, I. (1973), *The Modern World System* (New York: Academic Press).

Weaver, R. (1985), *The Politics of Industrial Change* (Washington: Brookings).

Weiss, L. (1998), *The Myth of the Powerless State* (Cambridge: Polity).

Wilks, S., and Wright, M. (1987) (eds.), *Comparative Government-Industry Relations: Western Europe, the United States, Japan* (Oxford: Oxford University Press).

Williamson, O. (1985), *The Economic Institutions of Capitalism* (Glencoe: The Free Press).

Zysman, J. (1983), *Governments, Markets, and Growth: Financial Systems and the Politics of Industrial Change* (Ithaca, NY: Cornell University Press).

7

Societal Governance: Levels, Modes, and Orders of Social–Political Interaction

JAN KOOIMAN

In today's shared-power, no-one-in-charge, interdependent world, public problems and issues spill over organizational and institutional boundaries. Many people are affected by problems like global warming, AIDS, homelessness, drug abuse, crime, growing poverty among children, and teen pregnancy, but no one person, group or organization has the necessary power or authority to solve these problems. Instead, organizations and institutions must share objectives, resources, activities, power, or some of their authority in order to achieve collective gains or minimize losses.

J. M. Bryson and B. C. Crosby (1993: 323)

GOVERNANCE AND SOCIETAL DEVELOPMENTS

This chapter advances the conceptual ideas presented in *Modern Governance: Government-Society Interactions* (1993). In that book, attention was drawn to recent developments in those interactions with a 'co-', public–private character, offset against a 'go-it-alone' government perspective. In the past few years the literature on 'governance' has almost 'exploded' in many different areas and disciplines. My own explorations in this field have also continued. The present chapter presents the main outlines of one aspect of this continued effort: the question of different levels, modes, and orders of governance as patterns of societal governance. While

I would like to thank Guy Peters and Jeroen Warner for their editorial comments on this chapter, and many of my former PhD-students and other colleagues of the Public Management group at the Erasmus University for their inspiration in my work on the Governance concept.

the earlier work was still strongly 'government-oriented', this chapter broadens the perspective in the sense that it looks at governance as societal, with public as well as private 'governors' participating. While their roles may differ between societal levels and from sector to sector, the essence of the argument is that governance of modern societies is a mix of all kinds of governing levels, modes and orders. These mixes can be seen as 'answers' of those societies to changing governing demands. While this point of view is partly in line with other recent theorizing on governance (Rhodes, 1997), it also differs in important aspects. The approach pursued here may be phrased in the form of a working definition, the elements of which will be made clear in the chapter itself, social–political governance will be considered to be *arrangements in which public as well as private actors aim at solving societal problems or create societal opportunities, and aim at the care for the societal institutions within which these governing activities take place.*

Societal Trends and Changing Governing Relations

Governance as a growth industry must have its basis in societal developments, is particularly attributable to growing or changing societal interdependencies. Most governance concepts in use highlight this awareness. One might say that this common element expresses itself quite well in the notion of long-term societal trends such as differentiation and integration. These processes result in lengthening chains of interdependence, or phrased more dynamically in lengthening chains of interaction (Kaufmann *et al.*, 1986). These chains become increasingly institutionalized with multilevel and multisectorial dimensions. These lengthening chains of interaction cause and require a multiplication of the number of parties participating in them, while the number of interactions among these parties also multiplies.

The dividing lines between public and private sectors are blurring, and interests generally are not just public or private, they frequently are shared. Hence, it is generally more appropriate to speak of *shifting* roles of government than of *shrinking* roles of government as part of such changing relationships. A reshuffling of government tasks and a greater awareness of the need to co-operate with other societal actors does not render traditional government interventions obsolete. It merely implies a growing awareness, not only of the limitations of traditional public command-and-control as a governing mechanism, but also as responses to societal problems which require broader sets of approaches and instruments. Related developments take place in the third sector and/or civil society (Perrault *et al.*, 1997). This is expressed in the new and expanding roles of Non-Governmental Organizations (NGOs) in many parts of the world, in special interest groups becoming involved in governance issues, and in local community initiatives in many forms and areas of governance. Private enterprise too increasingly acknowledges (or is made to acknowledge) its societal responsibilities in areas such as environmental protection, consumer participation and in issues such as employment creation.

Coping with the Diversity, Dynamics and Complexity of Societal Situations

My conceptualization of these societal tendencies uses three characteristics, which form a basis for further theoretical refinement (see also Rosenau, this volume). My claim—and I am aware of the ambition underlying this effort—is that to understand what is going on in modern societal governance, in particular on the borderline between 'the' social and 'the' political, one must confront head-on issues connected with their diversity, complexity, and dynamics.

To clarify what I mean by diversity, dynamics, and complexity I shall draw on systems thinking; a system being a whole of entities which display more interrelations among themselves than with other entities. *Diversity*, from that perspective, is a characteristic of the entities that form the system and points to the nature and degree in which they differ. *Complexity* is an indicator for the architecture of the relations among the parts of a system, among the parts and the whole and between the system and its environment. *Dynamics* applies to the tensions within a system and between systems. The concept of diversity calls attention to the actors in social–political systems; to aspects of the entitities themselves, such as goals, intentions and powers. The concept of complexity invites examination of structures, interdependencies and interrelations at and between different levels. By introducing the dynamics of social-political systems, their problems and their opportunities, I call attention to the irregularity with which developments within and around such systems take place; and how to deal with them—mainly cast in cybernetic terms.

It is important to distinguish among those three characteristics, because each separately specifies particular and special aspects of societal phenomena and social-political governance. But the relation among them is also important, because they can become richer in substance and meaning in their mutual interrelation; and because they can, separately and in conjunction, serve as basic elements for theory development.[1] The starting point of this governance conceptualization is that social-political phenomena and their governing—in terms of interactions should be placed in the context of the diversity, dynamics and complexity of modern societies. These societies derive their strength from these characteristics, in other words, they continually present these societies with opportunities. But they also present them with problems. These opportunities and problems themselves are also complex, dynamic, and diverse. After all, they reflect the strong and the weak sides of these societies. This also applies without a doubt to the conditions under which opportunities are created and used and problems formulated and solved.

As a result, we formulate two presuppositions. First, the empirical/analytical assumption that diversity, dynamics, and complexity of modern societies are important for description, analysis, and comprehension. Second, the more normative assumption is that by taking social dynamics, diversity, and complexity seriously we shall be better placed to apply fruitfully this knowledge to creating opportunities or solving problems, than if we see them as simple, uniform and static. Separately, but especially in their interrelatedness, these three aspects are the key building blocks of my theorizing on social–political governing and governability. Only if we take these three basic characteristics of modern societies seriously can we begin to conceptualize how they can be used in governing those societies in a 'cross-modern' way. I will return to this theme. But first we need to take a closer look at the conceptualization of interactions as a central concept in which diversity, complexity, and dynamics can be related to each other.

---

[1] Recent developments in physics indicate that the systematic realisation of the dynamics, complexity and diversity of phenomena to be studied and of subjects to be handled can bring about fundamental discussions as to the nature of science itself (Prigogine and Strengers, 1984). Everything in nature is liable to forces of conservation and change; in other words nature is basically dynamic. Even the smallest physical and biological particles consist of even smaller elements which cohere in many ways; that is to say, they are complex. And all phenomena in biological and social life display an immense and fundamentally incomprehensible scope of differentiation and variability. In other words: they are basically diverse.

The difficulties we have in coping with these qualities might have to do with these qualities themselves, with our methods of coping with them or with the lack of position to observe them. This means that fundamental aspects of the physical, natural and social world we live in and which we make use of are not only 'in the eye of the beholder' but also belong to the reality 'out there', whatever our theoretical or applied capacity to understand or to handle them may be.

LEVELS OF GOVERNING: INTERACTIONS AS A
CENTRAL CONCEPT

Interactions and Governance

There seems to be a shift away from more traditional patterns, in which governing was basically regarded as 'one-way traffic' from those governing to those governed, towards a 'two-way traffic' model in which aspects, problems, and opportunities of both the governing system and the system to be governed are taken into consideration. This is what I call *social–political governance*, based upon broad and systematic interactions between those who are governing and those who are governed, and this applies to public–public as well as public–private interactions. In addition to varieties such as shifts from the public to the private sphere in terms of deregulation and privatization, other forms of more systemic interaction are being tried. These new forms can be put under headings such as managing, steering and guiding but the emphasis is on the bilateral or even multilateral aspects of governing. This means that not only the locus of boundaries between state and society change, but also that the boundaries themselves change in character and become increasingly permeable. Where government begins and society ends, becomes more diffuse. The borderline between public and private responsibilities itself becomes an object of interaction. Often, these interactions are themselves based on the recognition of (inter)dependencies. No single actor, public or private, has the knowledge and information required to solve complex, dynamic, and diversified problems; no actor has an overview sufficient to make the needed instruments effective; no single actor has sufficient action potential to dominate unilaterally. These are basically matters of the relation between governance and governing.

Chandler's advice for 'structure to follow strategy' now seems to be followed at last: it appears that contrary to the usual neo-corporatist formalization and structuring gives way to a central focus on problems or opportunities. In doing so, the structural components become part of the outcome of interactions. The idea is to start working on something together first (e.g. approaching a complex problem situation), and defer worries about the form. These are basically matters of governing.

I term such approaches *interactive social–political forms of governing*. This chapter will develop the theoretical foundations for these forms, models, and modes of interaction by conceptualizing the concept of interaction as a general social phenomenon. This stresses the point that my conceptualization considers governing interactions as specific types of social–political interactions, I start conceptualizing governance by developing some general conceptual ideas *on interactions as social phenomena.*

Societal developments are seen as continuous processes of differentiation and integration of knowledge, actions, organizations etc. Differentiation and integration cannot be considered in isolation from each other. This means that the concept of interaction is conceptualized to make apparent that actions relate to each other (intentional or action level) and that under such influences structures in which those actions are embedded also develop (structural or conditional level). And it should be clear that many entities are involved in the mutual influence of action and structural level in interactions. Only when such an approach is accepted can governing questions be given the recognition they deserve. In this perspective, each interaction consists of processes and structures. This becomes clear if we realize that interactions among systems themselves can be considered as systems.

The *process* element refers to the action aspect of interactions; processes are the outcome of the capacity of social actors to act. The action or intentional level of interactions means social interaction. This holds good for goal-oriented action as well as all manner of non-goal oriented activities. The concrete (individual, but also organizational or group) values, goals, interests and purposes are expressed in action, and need to be included in the action level of interactions as well.

The *structural* aspect of interactions indicates the material, social–structural, and cultural frames and contexts in which interactions come about. This structural level can be considered as those circumstances that are limiting, broadening and at the same time conditional for the action level. It consists of institutions, general social structures, rules and behavioural norms, patterns of communication, material and technological possibilities, and limitations with conditional importance. With the aid of the structure and process elements, an interaction can be broken down into constituent elements, such that it can be conceptualized as an object of governing.

However, a governing theory which only considered structures and processes, without considering the actors that form part and parcel of governing, would seem at odds with my endeavour to design a highly democratic social–political governance theory. Governing in an interaction perspective will, wherever possible, try to break through the (apparently) sharply defined boundaries between separate entities (such as those between the governors and the governed) by focusing on trans-boundary interactions between them. These considerations and distinctions in themselves contribute to the analytical power of interactions as I conceptualize them. But next to this analysis, the relations between these elements also merit attention; in other words, interaction is a concept for synthesis.

Interaction as I conceptualize it provides insight in the mutual relationships within and between social–political problems and opportunities. It points at movements of tension, at the dynamics among entities. It shows that the course and effects of actions and processes also depend on what others are doing or what occurs in other processes. With the help of the interactions concept, social–political reality can be observed in terms of its differentiation, as well as its integration. Its analytical strength also lies in the fact that it can zoom in on interactions, and in doing so, detect the multiplicity of those involved in a particular problem or opportunity. Finally, interactions are important in that they can be deliberately used, initiating interactions where they had not been used as such. In sum, an interaction can be considered a mutually influential relation between two or more entities. In an interaction I distinguish an action (or intentional) and a structural level. Between and within these levels, forces are at work to maintain existing relations or to change them. In these tensions the dynamics of an interaction are implied. In the characteristics of the entities between which the interactions occur, the diversity of the social–political reality comes into being. In the mutual connection between the many interactions, the complexity of the governing world is realized.

Diversity, Complexity and Dynamics in the Framework of Interactions

Since governance theory emphasizes interactions and, particularly, governing-as-interaction(s), it is essential not to lose sight of the *actors*. In fact they cannot be separated from the interactions among them. Actors and interactions mutually determine each other. We are used to considering individuals and organizations as rather independent from the interactions they participate in. They interact and, seemingly, can stop them at will. But basically actors are continuously formed by (and in) the interactions in which they relate to each other. They constitute, as it were, *intersections* in interaction processes. Taking a closer view, the actors themselves consist of interactions and the boundaries from which they derive their identities are relative and often fuzzy. This applies to social systems, but also to organizations, groups and individuals. Insight in the diversity of participants in social–political interactions can only be gained by involving them in the governing process, giving them the opportunity to act out their identities.

In the development of the interaction concept for the sake of governing, the tension between the action and the structural level of each interaction can be considered the main source of dynamics. This tension is decisive for the nature and direction of the interactions involved, of the tensions within interactions and within the structural level. The proposition imposes itself that the choice between change and conservation is a central issue characterizing social–political interactions. At the action (or intentional) level of interactions, the tension between change and conservation shapes the most central aspirations of actors in serving special and joint interests and also satisfies the system-internal and system-external needs.

The more space an interaction creates, the more freedom for actors to select the values, goals, and interests they want to strive after. A space-creating interaction is characterized by a large action space and a large degree of flexibility. Conversely, the more controlling an interaction, the more it will influence contrary aspirations of actors. Controlling interactions leave little action space for actors. In strongly controlling interactions, the values, goals, and interests of actors and the level to which they can aspire, are influenced by structural components of the interactions rather than by the actors exerting influence on these interactions. The more space-creating an interaction, the more open is the structure. An open structure is less sensitive to entropy than a closed one. New impulses can enter and countervail the tendency for entropy.

The complexity of social–political systems is primarily expressed in the fact that a multitude of interactions take place in many different forms and intensities. Such interactions can only be influenced if these aspects of complexity are sufficiently understood. To govern socio-political problems and opportunities requires clarity about the nature of interactions involved in a problem to be tackled or an opportunity to be created, the way these interactions hang together and their characteristic patterns. The basic relation between complexity and interactions exists in that interactions as such are an indication of the complexity of the social–political world. Interactions should be considered relational elements of systems and the relational elements between parts of systems and systems as wholes.

MODES OF GOVERNING

To get a handle on the complexity of governing interactions (from the perspective of designing a social–political theory of governing and governance) I shall group governing interactions into three different modes of governing: self-governing, co-governing and hierarchical governing.

The most 'chaotic' and fluid forms of social–political interactions are clearly of a *self-governing* character. In modern societies, certainly, the sectors govern themselves up to a point—they could not do otherwise. An interesting debate in this respect concerns the 'autopoietic' character of sectors in societies. A key issue in this debate, especially in German social science is, if and to what extent this 'autopoietic' or self-organizing character of such systems prevents them being influenced or governed from the outside. 'Showcases' in this discussion are law-as-a-system and economics-as-a-system.

'Co' forms of governing centres on heterarchical forms of governing. Heterarchy is to say that different forms of horizontal and vertical relations are mixed, and can follow each other in time; horizontal structures however dominate (Lagas, 1997). There is a certain degree of equality in the structure within which participating entities relate to each other. Autonomy of those entities remains an important characteristic of interplays; relinquishing autonomy is always only partial and contains mutual agreements, rights, and obligations. *Hierarchical* modes of governance are the most formalized forms of governing interactions, but yet interactions. Rights and obligations are organized according to superordinate and subordinate responsibilities and tasks. In particular, positive and negative sanctions attached to interventions have a highly formalized character and are surrounded by political and juridical guarantees.

For the purpose of gaining insight in modes of governing we can ask analytic questions along the following lines: what can self-governing interactions *as systems* do? What effects can they be expected to have and what problems may arise in what situations? The same applies to 'co' modes of governing and hierachical governing. There may also be social–political considerations in terms of certain 'ideological' or 'methodological' preferences. In the late 1980s and in the early 1990s, self-governing became 'ideologically popular', while interactive governing became popular from a methodological point of view. In the mid-1990s there seems to be a comeback of hierarchical forms in view of a perceived need for a 'strong state'.

From a governing perspective, the special characteristics of the three modes as systems or their mixes are the main object of analysis. The next three sections provide a preliminary survey of the characteristics of the three modes. These sections have a somewhat different character, and should be considered as first efforts in discussing self-governing, 'co' governing, and hierarchical governing more systematically.

Self-Governing

From a theoretical point of view, thinking about the self-governing needs and capacities of social or social–political systems almost naturally starts from *autopoiesis* (see for recent surveys in English: Dunsire, 1996; Brans and Rossbach, 1997). This concept, originating from biology, is controversial, nevertheless it offers several entries into the way social and social–political systems govern themselves. There is a growing body of literature applying autopoietic concepts such as self-reference, self-organization, and self-steering (*Selbststeuerung*) to substantive areas such as law, economics, technology, politics, and even Sunday rest. The original model characterizes why a system is 'living'. 'Living' refers to the reproduction of the organization; it is autonomous, in the sense that the interactive components recursively generate the same network of processes; such a system is operationally closed with no apparent inputs and outputs. The most controversial of these 'original' characteristics is operational or organizational closure. This is so because this closure is a central argument in explaining the failure of 'external' governing of systems such as law and economics.

The autopoietic character of social systems is interesting in the context of governing. Systems 'see' only what they can interpret in their own terms, including communications from outside. This also applies to interactions with and interventions by other systems. The 'objective' qualities of governing acts are not of primary importance; their only effect can be whatever 'meaning' social systems themselves attribute to them. If this meaning fits into what governing is about, it may produce effects. Otherwise it will either be ignored, limited, or exaggerated. Autopoietic systems can only be governed by their internal self-referential modes of organization and operation.

Autopoiesis, especially in the broader sense of self-referentiality and related concepts, can be viewed as a starting point for theorizing on self-governing in modern societies. There are three important aspects to this:

- self-governing principles in modern societies: what are the strengths and weakenesses of existing self-governing principles;
- what are the consequences of continuing societal differentiation for the 'closure' tendencies to external influences connected with this;
- the search for alternative governing modes in the light of the (apparent) limitations of traditional 'command-and-control systems, and the way which self-governing can be part of these modes of governance mixes.

Co-Governing

Co-governing denotes utilizing organized forms of interactions for governing purposes. In social–political governing, these are key forms of 'horizontal' governing: actors co-operate, co-ordinate, communicate without a central or dominating governing actor. It is especially these forms of governing which in my theorizing appear better equipped than other modes of governing in diverse, dynamic, and complex situations.

Conceptualizing 'co-governing' as a mode of governing is best started with an attempt to define concepts such as co-ordination, co-operation, collaboration. There is an abundance of literature that utilizes these concepts at different levels of societal organization, varying from inter-individual collaboration to co-ordination at the level of markets, networks, and hierarchies as general social mechanisms. For the purpose of my argument—that is to say, to look at 'co' forms of societal interaction as modes of governing—it is important to establish a theoretical link between forms of 'co' as identified in the literature and my own conceptualization of types and qualities of interactions, and the way in which diversity, dynamics, and complexity of governing situations can be expressed in those terms.

A simple way of approaching such a link is first to identify 'co' modes at different levels of societal organization: a micro, meso, and macro societal level. For micro forms of 'co' I will—analogous with the relevant literature—adopt the concept of *collaboration*, which is an interaction taking place between actors, where actors at the intentional level are individuals and the structural level (in general) can be considered to be some kind of formal organizational arrangement, such as a working group or project. I reserve the word *co-ordination* for the meso level of societal interaction, in which the actors are organizations: the intentional level of 'doing things together' is expressed in bi-, or multiple intra- and inter-organizational arrangements and the structural level of those interactions occurs in sectors or subsectors of societal differentiation. A third level of societal 'co'

interactions can be identified in terms of macro mechanisms or arrangements where there is a question of co-ordination within and between 'the'
state, 'the' market, hierarchies, networks, etc. Here the intentional level of
interactions is the broader societal institutions where market actors (such
as whole industries) deal with governments (such as government departments or EU Directorates); the structural level of those interactions
encompasses the national, but in particular supra- or international contexts such as treaties, global agreements, and the processes these are
embedded in, such as globalization and international competition.

These distinctions are no more than the beginning of conceptualizing
'co' modes of governance, but they help in 'ordering' the relevant literature
in terms of their potential contribution to further theorizing on 'co' modes
of governance. From literature on public–private *collaboration*, for example, we gain insights from the 'rationales and contexts' of such collaboration, obstacles to such collaboration and ideas how to overcome those and
interventions and facilitating roles in such collaboration (Huxham, 1996).
Literature on intra-and inter-organisational *coordination* is abundant and
gives insights into aspects such as rules, goals, linkages, autonomy, and
processes such as mutual adjustment and alliances (Rogers *et al.*, 1982) and
questions about the what, how and why of certain types of co-ordination
(Dijkzeul, 1997). Third, literature on the more macro forms of 'co' says
something about aspects of public–private interactions which concern
broader societal impacts such as the willingness, abilities and capacities of
societies to 'guide', 'control' and 'evaluate' differentiation and integration
processes against the background of growing interdependencies between
public and private parts of these societies (Kaufmann *et al.*, 1986).

For my purpose, these distinctions are a first step in linking those levels
of 'co' with the analysis of the interdependence between those levels as 'lib-
erating' or 'controlling' constraints for governing interactions at those
levels. Certain 'co' arrangements such as forms of collaboration or co-
ordination between public and private are stimulated or hindered by certain varieties of 'co' arrangements at the macro level. Only a integrated look
at the qualities of such arrangements in their mutual influences can lend
insight gained in the different forms of 'co' between public and private as I
will mention hereafter.

Fortunately the recent interest in the 'new institutionalism' helps in dis-
covering many of these mutual forms of influence of different types of
interactions at different societal levels, and can contribute to our knowledge about the intentional and structural characteristics of different

modes of 'co' governance in different societal contexts. Four of those will be briefly discussed next.

Networks as patterns of interplays. The emergence of mixed networks of public and private actors has to do with broad social developments. Growing social differentiation engenders increasing dependencies. In this context, the emergence of policy networks is an important change in the political decision-making structure. Concepts like 'Negotiation by governments' in the context of networks as 'a new model of social ordening' between 'market' and 'state' are bandied about; or 'as governance in a centreless society with complex configurations of horizontal co-ordination and synchronization'. Others such as ourselves consider the development of mixed public–private networks in terms of the need to solve social–political problems.

Public–private partnerships. The public–private partnership (PPP), a specific form of social–political governance, has been at the centre of interest for some years (Kouwenhoven, 1993). The growing interest in co-operation between public and private parties has been at least partially influenced by economic, social, political and cultural changes. As a consequence, the question is increasingly voiced whether certain issues could not be dealt with more effectively and efficiently by joint action of public and private parties, rather than their acting in isolation. Such co-operation is often referred to as a public–private partnership (PPP).

Essential to this is the synergetic effect actors expect in interactions, thus enabling greater effectiveness and/or efficiency than separate acting would, given that their objectives are not incompatible. It is only then that private means can contribute to the solution of public problems, or can public means be used to react to commercial opportunities and threats. Likewise, PPPs set themselves apart from similar organizations by the preservation of the identities of the parties involved. It will be obvious, then, that PPPs are considered specific governing interplays.

Communicative governing. New patterns of governance stimulate learning processes that will lead to co-operative behaviour and mutual adjustment, so that responsibily for managing structural changes is shared by all or most involved actors. One such alternative form of governance, described as communicative governing is based on the image of complex problems in which problem-resolving capacities are distributed across autonomous but interdependent actors. In this type of governing a form of rationality is presented in which social actors are considered 'reasonable citizens' (Van Vliet, 1993). This is another kind of rationality than the selfish, opportunistic profit- or benefit-maximizing kind used in economic or public-choice theory. This call upon the 'reasonable citizen' corresponds with the concept of *communicative rationality* which is considered appropriate in complex problem-solving as a substitution for instrumental, functional or strategic forms of rationality.

Responsive regulation. In this concept the basic idea is that 'regulation should respond to industry conduct, to how effectively industry is making private regulation work'. It builds upon the 'responsive law' concept, but treats it more as an innovative effort than an evolutionary stage in legal development. It is more in line with the idea of 'interactive corporate compliance'. Responsive regulation should not be seen as an optimum solution, but as a solution 'that responds better than others to the plural configurations of support and opposition that exist at a particular moment in history' (Ayres and Braithwaite, 1992). Responsive regulation should be seen in the context of the shifting balance between the key institutions for securing social order—the community, the market, the state, and the societal associations. These four are important in both constituing and challenging each other's powers. But they are more in the 'republican' tradition than in the corporatist, because they emphasize direct participation and communitarian sources of order in the regulatory arena.

Hierarchical Governing

Intervention systems are the most classical and characteristic mode of governing interaction between the state and its individual citizens, groups, or organizations. The most common and widely practised instruments are either laws or policies. There is hardly any area of societal activity not governed at least partly by either one or more laws, or one or more policies. For almost any broader subject on almost every level of public involvement in social affairs, policy is standard practice. Often this involvement is closely linked with one or more forms of legal or administrative regulation. In special situations, in particular the governing of socio-economic sectors, there is also the usage of organizational frameworks. These have come to be known as (neo)corporatist arrangements. Because of their specific interactional qualities between public and private they deserve special attention.

These hierarchical forms of governing have long historical roots, heavily influenced by Max Weber, and especially his studies on bureaucracy that set the stage for almost all theorizing on hierarchical/bureaucratic forms of 'co-ordination of social life' (Thompson *et al.*, 1991). Yet most theorizing of hierarchical modes of governance is directed at organizations internally. For some systematic thinking about hierarchy as an important form of 'rational social action' we would have to go back to Dahl and Lindblom's classic *Politics, Economics and Welfare* (1963) or more recent studies like Kaufmann *et al.* (1986). For Dahl and Lindblom hierarchy is next to polyarchy, the price system and bargaining one of the four major 'processes for calculation and control involving leaders and non-leaders'. 'Hierarchy is the processs in which leaders control non-leaders.' (1963: 23). Hierarchy is not seen as a pure unilateral control and is considered to be a continuum (pp. 227–30) and its bureaucratic mode extensively conceptualized in terms of its contribution to rational social action, and its costs. And also its role in the distribution of claims, its contribution to stability and processes of resource output and development are discussed thoroughly.

Somewhat in the same line of thinking, *Guidance, Control and Evaluation in the Public Sector* (Kaufmann *et al.*, 1986) distinguishes between 'co-ordinating mechanisms and institutional arrangements like solidarity, hierarchy and market-exchange' (pp. 407 ff.) Here hierarchy is especially positioned in terms of institutionalized redistribution mechanisms. Hierarchy is conceptualized in terms of redistributive transactions (one-way transfers), legalized short-term imbalances of benefits and obligations, social assymetry of 'distributors' and receivers, and the exposition of a common set of defined rules and obligations (p. 416). Hierarchies are considered to work well as long as they accomodate a limited variety of wants and means of wants satisfaction. Failures of hierarchy can be counteracted by institutionalizing a minimum of solidarity or other co-ordinating mechanisms (p. 416).

It is important to build upon the above conceptualizations to enable theorizing on hierarchical governance to develop coherent insights about the qualities and limitations of that mode of governance in different societal problem-solving and opportunity-creating settings. Against this background the following short introductions to three important varieties of instruments/techniques of hierarchical governance need to be examined.

Policies as interventionist systems. Policy aims at intervening in social–political situations in a rational manner on the basis of knowledge of causal relations, but at the same time these situations are context.

Recent developments in policy theorizing emphasize the institutional framework in which policies are prepared, developed, and implemented. This development can be characterized as the addition of the social to the political. In older theories, attention was focused on the governmental side of these processes. In more recent ones the social, interactional, private aspects have received more attention. One can call this a change from more 'closed' to more 'open' approaches towards policy-making.

Legal interventions. The state is factually and legally bounded in the choice, form, and application of the means it uses. The constitutional state requires the relations between state and citizens to be dominated by legal principles and rules. The more the state intervenes in the private sphere, the more formal demands and guarantees are. Consequently, design and applications of interventions are also based on principles such as equality before the law, legal security, unity of the law, and due care. Interventions by the state are subject to political scrutiny, which means consultation of social partners, which usually presents limitations to the scope of potential juridical interventions. And there is the growing interconnection of interventions by law on different levels of sub-national, national and supra-national regulation. The grip of the state on social conditions seems to have become almost a handicap. In the course of extending intervention by legal means, the limitations and disadvantages have come into view. This is one of the reasons why legal intervention is coming under scrutiny—deregulation is one of the outcomes thereof.

Corporatist and affiliated arrangements. From the state perspective there are advantages in organising interventions in a corporatist setting: it enhances the efficacy of regulation, it helps overcome implementation problems, it can prevent erosion of legitimacy, etc. But there are costs. In particular it limits scope and intensity of direct intervention and can only be applied to sectors where these arrangements can be reached, relations often acquire a complex and reciprocal character and a loss of flexibility may appear. This can also have problematic effects on the interest representation itself in terms of 'inarticulation'.

Mixed-Mode Governing

Social–political (collective) problem solving and collective opportunity creation in complex, dynamic, and diverse situations are public as well as a private, governmental as well as a market challenges. At one time one party takes the lead, in another situation it is another. A growing number of social–political challenges evoke shared responsibilities and 'co-arrangements'. Insight in the diversity, dynamics, and complexity of social–political questions and the conditions in which these questions arise is indispensable for solving social–political problems and creating social–political opportunities (preferably) in thorough and combined public and private action. To state this simply it is the private (market) part of a sector that usually carries the responsibility for the governing of the primary interactions taking place in it. It is the task of private non-market parties to take care of governing the more organized interactions which accompany these primary processes. And it is the task/responsibility of public organizations to take care that problems and opportunities within and around the primary and secondary processes and structures of these sectors take place according to principles and rules that reflect common and broader system/society-wide interests connected with these processes.

All this expresses itself in different mixes of public, public–private and private interactions, organized in the three modes. Little is known about their qualities. In the context of this chapter I can just say that on the basis of analyses so far the mix of self- and co-governing is hardly explored; the mix of co- and hierarchical somewhat more; and the same can be said of the mix between self- and hierarchical governing. However an analytical grip on the mix of all three is still in an exploratory stage.

GOVERNING ORDERS

I will link different levels of aggregation with different levels of analysis in terms of the action-structure level of governing interactions with the distinction between *first-order* and *second-order* governing. First-order governing aims to solve problems directly, at a particular level. Second-order governing attempts to influence the conditions under which first-order problem-solving or opportunity creation takes place; second-order governing applies to the structural conditions of first-order governing. To these two orders a third one is added: *meta*. Basically, 'meta' inquires: who or what—ultimately—governs the governors? In itself, this is a simple question, but in practice the answer to this question is far from simple. I shall look into the question and its answers in more detail later, but here, a few words are apt to make the ideas around these three levels or orders of governing more accessible.

Problem-Solving and Opportunity Creation: First-Order Governing

Here I set out to develop a problem and opportunity theory-in-practice, an analytical framework to describe and to cope with the diversity, complexity, and dynamics of social–political questions or challenges. Such a problem and opportunity theory is needed as we need an instrument to make the diversity, dynamics and complexity of social–political issues accessible and visible. I speak of a problem and opportunity theory, because the great challenges in modern societies are not only finding solutions to collective problems, but also creating collective opportunities. I think the 'classical' distinction of turning to government for problem-solving, and to the private sector for creating opportunities is an inappropriate and ineffective point of view in modern societies. Collective problem-solving and collective opportunity creation in complex, dynamic, and diverse situations is a public as well as a private challenge. At one time one party takes the lead, in another situation it is another, and there seem to be a growing number of social–political challenges that call for shared responsibilities and 'co-arrangements'.

For solving social–political problems and creating social–political opportunities a thorough and combined public and private insight in the diversity, dynamics, and complexity of social–political questions and the conditions in which these questions arise is indispensable. It is not the pretension of this chapter to develop a comprehensive theory of problem-solving and opportunity creation, but simply to show that problem-solving and opportunity creating processes are different and have different governance needs.

Problem-solving can be carved up into four different stages: recognizing diversity of interests and aspects, deciding on the complexity of the relation among different parts of the problem 'as a system', located sources of tensions (dynamics) and back to where these can be located. Depending on the situation, these steps must be made more than once; the process is cyclical. In the process of image formation the cycle runs from identification of those who experience problems, through stocktaking of the interactions taking part in terms of partial problems or problem aspects, to the localisation of pockets of tensions in interactions which can be identified as problem sources. If necessary, a new inventory of those experiencing problems can be made, new part-problems defined and now sources of problems localized after the last phase. This process ends, in principle, only when no new discoveries are made. Then the solution space can be defined (this part of the total process can also start earlier and run parallel to the problem aspect) and the *problem–solution system* can be defined.

The process of opportunity creation runs just the other way around. There are no experiences to be taken stock of and identified yet. Here it is the governor him or herself who has the experience of an opportunity. Opportunities do not start from the diversity of those participating in a situation, but rather from the dynamics within a certain situation. An opportunity can be said to be a 'positively' experienced tension evaluated from a future-oriented perspective, while a problem is more a 'negatively' experienced tension within a past-oriented perspective.

The governor tries to analyse systematically what this potential opportunity looks like. What are the relevant tensions which bring on the opportunity experience? Thereafter he, she, or they try to trace the potential area effected by the opportunity: which kinds of interactions are potentially involved in the opportunity? Then the entities participating in those interactions are identified. From this more profound opportunity expectation the perspective of opportunity-creating and opportunity-exploiting strategies can be developed. In this process it is important to make an inventory of the perceptions and opinions that the identified entities have on the strategies. If this inventory is made, the governor can start the cycle all over again, as was the case for problem identification. If image formation is satisfied and the strategic space defined, the opportunity-strategy system can be defined and its boundaries drawn. The defining process as such is ended, and it is time for the instrumental and action phases. As said earlier these phases can also start earlier and run (partially) in parallel with the process of image formation of the opportunity as such.

Institution Building: Second-Order Governing

Social-political problem-solving and opportunity creation (first-order governing) does not take place in a void: not only theoretically but also in practice both are embedded in institutional settings, which can be looked upon as frameworks which have to cope with the diversity, dynamics, and complexity of (parts of) modern societies—second-order governing. Can we say that in conceptual terms most coping with these characteristics in problem-solving and opportunity creation was on the processual aspects of governing, in second-order governing the attention is more on the structural aspects of governing interactions. This is not only a question of analytical distinction and attention, I am inclined to think that taking care of these institutional settings for first-order governing is a governing order by itself, with its own character and taste.

Fortunately recent scholarly interest in the role of institutions in influencing behaviour of actors (and therefore in their willingness or ability to enter in interactions) in different disciplines under the heading of 'new' institutionalism, has given insight in many factors of importance in this context (Hall and Taylor, 1996; Lowndes, 1996; Scott, 1995; DiMaggio and Powell, 1991; March and Olsen, 1989; Goodin, 1996). These insights may serve as a first step into a more coherent theorizing of second-order governing in my own terms and concepts.

First, it is becoming clear that one can identify institutional influences on 'calculating' behaviour of actors. Governing actors trying to maximize the attainment of certain goals will be influenced by institutions in the way these help or hinder them. Information plays a crucial role here, such as in enforcement mechanisms for agreements and in penalties for defection. In terms of interactions one line of neo-institutional thinking (the more political–economic one) provides insights in the way interactions based upon principles of rational behaviour can be institutionalized and how such institutional arrangements constrain, control, or enable goal-maximizing actors to interact. If one wants an 'efficient' institution one tends to stress formal institutional arrangements such as contracts, administrative hierarchies, legislative and decision-making procedures, budget mechanisms, and bureau types. One might think in terms of the institutionalization of the interaction between basically 'self-governing' entities or actors, which carry on these interactions within the confines of formalized rules, because out of the 'substance' of the interaction parties will want the maximum possible result.

A second normative type of institution has received attention in recent literature. In the opinion of those stressing these normative aspects, institutions are particularly important because they focus on rights and obligations, neglected in much of the more behavioural-oriented literature. Here it is important from a governing perspective that attention is called to prescriptive, evaluative, and obligatory dimensions of institutions (Scott, 1995) in the form of values, these are broad indicators of what is preferred or unacceptable, and norms which specify how things should be done. These 'logics of appropriateness' also structure institutions. These normative aspects of governing institutions are extremely important at the 'borderline' between the social and the political, and between public and private in whatever capacity. The contribution to the development of this governance theorizing is summarized quite well as follows (adapted from Goodin, 1996):

- actors interact in contexts which are collectively constrained;
- some of these interactional constraints take the form of institutions (organised patterns of socially constructed norms and roles);
- institutions shape interests of those interacting and are at the same time shaped by them.

Distinctions and observations such as these, about second-order governing are important, because they show that in second-order governing we indeed deal with phenomena of another 'order', and with other governing dimensions which ask for other sorts of governing activities. Somewhat analogous to social–political problem-solving and opportunity creation as first-order governing actions, we deal with the 'maintenance' and 'design' and 'renewal' of social–political institutions as a second-order governing activity. And it is certainly conceivable to develop quite systematic ideas on such 'maintenance' or 'renewal' of the institutionalization of social–political governing such as in the way 'efficient' 'appropriate' institutions control or enable problem-solving or opportunity creation in modern societies.

One approach to this could be to look at their capacity for stabilization or change. Stability is a defining feature of institutions, as they stabilize expectations and structure social, economic, and political life. However different emphases may be attributed to the relative stability of institutions. As Lowndes (1996, 193) points out: 'proponents of "efficient" . . . institutions argue that existing institutional arrangements will persist only as long as they serve the interests of utility-seeking rational actors'. By contrast, she shows that others emphasize that 'appropriate' institutional arrangements are 'never "closed" or "complete", but always ambiguous and in flux', underlining 'the power of competing "modes of rationality" or "belief systems" to shape and reshape institutional arrangements'. Lowndes (1996, 194) concludes that: 'there is an institutional "life cycle", whereby rules and norms develop, become recognized and adhered to, and then fall into disuse, to be replaced by new arrangements'. Cultural aspects (symbols, meanings) but also structural aspects of institutions (such as power and authority relations) add to this institutional influence. This also applies to individual behaviour expressed in the role behaviour of actors and which is expected from them. Lowndes argues that:

an emphasis on *norms and obligations* implies consensus and continuity, and makes it hard to understand the sources of institutional change . . . An emphasis on *rational action* implies a selfish free-for-all and makes it hard to understand institutional stability and 'robustness' . . . Both rational action and norm-driven behaviour play important roles in an institutional life cycle; both conflict and continuity are central to institutional life. (Lowndes 1996, 194–5)

Many of the insights from these kinds of theorizing on institutions highlight different aspects of second-order governing, and can be of considerable help in identifying aspects of relationships between intentional and structural levels of social–political interaction and their governing.

Meta: Third-Order Governing

I have produced several building blocks for social–political governing, but a proper building has not yet been fabricated. This I hope to do by developing 'mortar' between the building blocks to keep the whole construction together. This mortar consists of two elements: political and managerial norms and criteria. In other words, what has yet to be developed is a norm-oriented framework which 'binds together' what the analysis has 'taken apart'.

The perceived lack of normative elements is not completely true. At all kinds of places and moments normative preconceptions have crept into the analysis, explicitly but certainly implicitly as well, e.g. the systems concept. This can hardly can be avoided in the treatment of a theme like social–political governing, which is value-drenched, top to bottom and inside and out. In fact, the concept of 'social–political governing' as such is much more than just an analytical concept. It is a highly normatively charged concept and the entire development of the conceptualization can be seen as a normative exercise. Governing as such is needed, and is phrased in terms of the social–political. In other words: the underlying normative presumption is that social–political governing is a sensible thing to do in 'cross-modern' times. It is not something 'professional' or 'formal' governors are wont to do, but something that can and should be seen as a 'systems quality'.

In so doing, I argue that governing is an aspect of a system to be governed, its governing system and its environment *together*. Here the governing rabbit is conjured out of the systems-theoretical hat. And to continue the image: the magic is more than adding the rabbit to the hat. The whole is more than the sum of the constituent parts, which again is one of the foundations of the systems paradigm. Governing is not just things governors do or do not do, or things the governed do or do not do. This systems quality is best phrased in the term *governability*. The governability of a system expresses not only how the system governs itself as a whole but also how it wants to govern itself as a whole. Somewhere in the conception, matching the empirical and the normative must take place, and here, governability is done most explicitly. To adapt President Truman's phrase: 'the—normative—buck stops here'.

Governability in particular matches the three 'orders' with normative content. In first-order governing day-to-day problems are tackled; in second-order governing the conditions for first-order governing are formulated. But a lot of differences, clashes, conflicts, risks, and uncertainties remain unsolved. What to do then? These are the kinds of dilemmas that belong to the domain of 'meta'. Basically these have to do with normative qualities of 'governability': how legitimately do we handle problems we seem unable to solve, what kinds of effectiveness conditions for governing we find acceptable or unacceptable? The combination of the analytical with the more normative aspects of governing, and in particular, the governing of the 'whole', is thus expressed in terms of *governance* and *governability*. Governance can be seen as the total effort of a system to govern itself; governability is the outcome of this process. Of course this is not an 'end state', but a kind of stock-taking of complex, diverse, and especially dynamic processes at one particular moment in time. In their combination, these processes at the different levels of governing constitute the analytical body of governance; the normative elements at these levels together are their quality standards. Body and standards are the building blocks and mortar of governance and time and again determine the 'state of governability' of a system. The more 'balanced' these elements, the more 'governable' is the system. This balance as a process is to be considered in terms of dynamic equilibria; In other words: never a dull moment.

If governance and governability have such a high political value content, political visions on this subject are necessary and possible. From a political position, debates should take place on the nature and appropriate forms of social–political governance and governability. Such discussions and debates on broader governance visions, however, are not commonplace. Countries differ in their traditions on this point. The French tradition has discussions on these broader issues. In a country like the Netherlands, debates concerning the interface between state, market, and civil society are a rare occurrence. In this tradition, boundaries tend to change because of 'technical' debates. This makes compromises easier, but the discussion of broader implications are often blurred and after-the-fact.

In the normative part of our conception, a high value is attached to the explication of normative issues involving issues of first-order, but especially second-order and, most explicitly, meta-governance. From a governance point of view there should be much more social–political and political–philosophical debate on the consequences of influence of the diversity, dynamics and complexity of our societies on 'cross-modernity'. In our opinion, a good way to order such discussions is to look into the relevance of the 'governing mix' of the three modes of governing for the overall governance quality. These are not 'freewheeling' and 'up-in-the-clouds' types of issues, but issues that have their roots and outcomes in the continuous governing interactions in sectors of social–political life, on a national and supra-national scale. After all, 'governance' is a systems quality; and all parts of those systems should be part of those governance discussions. And argued from the presupposition (Section 1) that the analysis needs to be based on the requirements of the diversity, complexity, and dynamics of 'cross-modern' societies, the debate should especially concentrate on tensions between modes and orders of governance and at the interface of state, market, and civil society.

CONCLUSION: A 'CROSS-MODERN' POSITION

This chapter has explored the utility of the governance concept as an instrument to conceptualize problems and opportunities and their contexts on the borderline between the social and the political—in current terminology: the borderline between state, market and civil society. These issues cannot be handled by each of these realms in isolation. Their character and nature is such that they 'trespass' the traditional boundaries separating them. This means that governing them requires the images, instruments and action potential of all three to try to solve them (if they can be solved at all) or at least, not to let them run out of control on account of their own complexities, diversities, and dynamics.

The governance approach, then, focuses on the interactions taking place between social systems. By starting from the continuous interaction processes which human actions give their irreversible and unpredictable character, it is attempted to get a grip on the diversity, complexity, and dynamics of social–political governing situations. In doing so, there is also scope for influencing these characteristics of our societies which are somewhere on the crossroads between the 'modern' and the 'post-modern'. We might call this 'cross-modern'. In this respect I find a kindred spirit in Toulmin (1990), who has identified two philosophical traditions which contributed to modernity: one based upon the principle of rationality, the other based upon principles of humanism. A combination of elements taken from these two traditions I shall call cross-modern. Basing my theory on elements of both traditions, then, may lead towards the improved governability of 'cross-modern' (western) democracies. It is necessary in this context for governments and their social partners to mark out their mutual responsibilities, jointly and continuously. This implies a growing awareness and acceptance of different modes of governing, including 'self-governing' capacities of social systems, 'co-governing' arrangements and authoritative top-down governing; each contributing in single and mixed modes to questions of governability in a broader sense.

Pragmatic (meta) principles such as openness to difference, the willingness to communicate, and the willingness to learn are important criteria in coping with diversity, dynamics, and complexity. But they are not sufficient to bring about the necessary integration among social systems. We need also substantive criteria on the basis of which these systems are willing and able to interact with each other and accept each other's boundaries. Because of the lack of an overall and overarching social–political ideal, the only other way to establish such criteria is to accept the 'cross-modern' character of western democracies. That is to say, not only to accept the 'rational' and the 'humanistic' roots of our societies, but to develop new substantive criteria on the basis of the juxtaposition and combination of both. This is the inherent richness on which our democratic societies are built, a wellspring that has not yet dried up.

To pursue scientific endeavours is to put one foot in the past and one in the future. This is what my governance theory does. It is about to leave familiar terrain, but not quite sure what the new land to be charted should be called. Therefore I use terms with which we are familiar (cybernetics, problems) and some that we do not know so well but look promising (emergence, opportunities). In 'cross-modern' situations it seems preferable to apply useful concepts from more than one tradition. Many things in life are not either–or, but and–and. Global standardization may be useful and needed but the same applies to local variety and autonomy.

To accept that insights and truths are always intersubjective is not to deny that—intersubjectively—some insights are more useful than others, and some truths seem better than others. Replacing a 'this is true' statement by 'this could be truer than that' makes diversity of opinion the lifeblood of social–political science and of social–political governance. If insight and truth is in the eye of the beholder, then what we need are social–political governing processes (and structures) that take both interactions and actors seriously. Interactions shape actors and actors shape interactions as well. They are 'equal' as basic units of analysis and theory development in terms of 'and-and', not of 'either-or'.

By taking diversity, dynamics and complexity in their mutual 'cross-modern' relations as a starting point, a governance model emerges which social systems and the entities shaping them can be consciously, explicitly and purposefully interrelated. Governance theory starts from diversity, dynamics and complexity of the societies to be governed—and governing themselves. These societies need order, but nothing can change without dynamics. They need similarity to enable communication, but diversity to gain new insights. They need standards to reduce uncertainty and risk, but complexity to solve problems and create opportunities. So we aim our theorizing on governance to be diverse but consistent, complex but elegant, and dynamic but orderly. The 'both–and', not the 'either–or', is a key characteristic of this exploration and I hope a stimulating one.

REFERENCES

Ayres, I., and Braithwaite, J. (1992), *Responsive Regulation* (Oxford and New York: Oxford University Press).

Brans, M., and Rossbach, S. (1997), 'The Autopoiesis of Administrative Systems: Niklas Luhmann on Public Administration and Public Policy', *Public Administration*, 75: 417–39.

Bryson, J. M., and Crosby, B. C. (1993), 'Policy Planning and the Design of Forums, Arenas and Courts', in B. Bozeman (ed.), *Public Management* (San Francisco: Jossey Bass).

Dahl, R. A., and Lindblom, C. E. (1963), *Politics, Economics and Welfare* (New York: Harper Torchbooks).

Dijkzeul, D. (1997), *The Management of Multilateral Organisations* (Deventer: Kluwer).

DiMaggio, P. J., and Powell, W. W. (1991), *The New Institutionalism in Organizational Analysis* (Chicago: Chicago University Press).

Dunsire, A. (1996), 'Tipping the Balance: Autopoiesis and Governance', *Administration and Society*, 26: 299–334.

Goodin, R. E. (ed.) (1996), *The Theory of Institutional Design* (Cambridge: Cambridge University Press).

Hall, P. A., and Taylor, R. C. R. (1996), 'Political Science and the Three New Institutionalisms', *Political Studies*, 44: 936–57.

Huxham, C. (ed.) (1996), *Creating Collaborative Advantage* (London: Sage).

Kaufmann, X. F., *et al.* (eds.) (1986), *Guidance, Control, and Evaluation in the Public Sector* (Berlin: De Gruyter).

Kooiman, J. (ed.) (1993), *Modern Governance: Government-Society Interactions* (London: Sage).

Kouwenhoven, V. (1993), 'Public–Private Partnertships', in J. Kooiman (ed.), *Modern Governance* (London: Sage), 119–30.

Lagas, P. (1997) 'Heterarchy as Trigger for Public Governing andGovernance' in J. Kooiman *et al.*, *Social-political Governance and Management* (Management Report No. 34 [13] 3 vol. Rotterdam School of Management, Erasmus University Rotterdam), 144–50.

Lowndes, V. (1996), 'Varieties of New Institutionalism: A Critical Appraisal', *Public Administration*, 181–97.

March, J. G., and Olsen, J. P. (1989), *Rediscovering Institutions: The Organizational Basis of Politics* (New York: The Free Press).

Perrault, P. H., Hobbes, H., and Dijkzeul, D. (1997) *Governance: Responding to Pluralist Societies* (The Hague: ISNAR, internal paper).

Prigogine, I., and Stengers, I. (1984), *Order out of Chaos* (New York: Bantam).

Rhodes, R. A. W. (1997), *Understanding Governance* (Buckingham: Open University Press).

Rogers, D. L., Whetten, D. A., and Associates (1982), *Interorganisational Co-ordination* (Ames: Iowa State University Press).

Scott, W. R. (1995), *Institutions and Organizations* (Thousand Oaks, Calif.: Sage).

Thompson, G., *et al.* (eds.) (1991), *Markets, Hierarchies and Networks* (London: Sage).

Toulmin, S. (1990), *Cosmopolis* (Chicago: Chicago University Press).

Vliet, M. van (1993), 'Environmental Regulation of Business: Options and Constraints for Communicative Governance', in J. Kooiman (ed.), *Modern Governance* (London: Sage), 105–14.

PART II
Emerging Forms of International Governance

8

Change, Complexity, and Governance in Globalizing Space

JAMES N. ROSENAU

> Now that we have a global world with global institutions, the question
> of institutional reform takes on a larger meaning. We know very little
> and understand next to nothing about 'globalization'. All we have so
> far is slogans and anecdotes. But we do know that the supra-national
> question is alarming from the point of view of democratic theory. We
> have these bodies that are not accountable to anybody, anywhere. This
> is the sort of thing we are going to be thinking about.
>
> (Przeworski, 1997: 11)

Well, yes and no. Yes, the world is globalizing and yes, the lack of accountability at the global level is alarming; but no, our knowledge of globalization is not inconspicuous. And yes, the question of institutional reform is
urgent; but no, our comprehension is not confined to slogans and anec-
dotes. Before the question of institutional reform can be faced, however,
the challenges globalization poses for democratic governance need to be
identified and the variety of ways in which the challenges are addressed
need to be clarified. Such is the purpose of this inquiry. I am less interested
in suggesting institutional reforms than in clarifying the problems reformers will have to confront. I assume that the tasks of reformers will be greatly
eased if the obstacles they must surmount are better understood.

A prime obstacle is the prevailing premises and paradigms through
which international relations (IR) is probed. In political science the IR subfield is rooted in the assumption that states and the anarchical system they
sustain constitute both the boundaries and the dynamics of the subfield.
There is no lack of contestation among the champions of the subfield's
main paradigms—variants of realism and liberalism—but all the contes-
tants proceed from the unarticulated given that the authority of states and
national governments is so predominant that inquiry must begin and end

I am grateful to David Johnson and Hongying Wang for their assistance and comments.

with assessments of how that authority is exercised. To be sure, some IR analysts acknowledge that state authority may be frayed and ineffective under certain circumstances, and increasing numbers are ready to allow that the community of non-governmental organizations (NGOs) is playing an ever more active role in the course of world affairs. Despite such concessions, however, the mainstream of IR analysts—or at least the mainstream in the US—have no hesitation in treating the fraying of authority and the activation of NGOs as essentially peripheral to the centrality and pervasiveness of the state system. Such a perspective has the consequence of simplifying the IR subfield. It means that the calculations, decisions, and actions of state leaders can be subjected to empirical or game theoretical analyses without undue concern for any confounding factors external to the processes of governmental policy making and intergovernmental diplomacy. They may concentrate on a country or region, an international organization, or an issue regime, but they almost always do so in the context of authority that is state-based. Put differently, for a preponderance of IR scholars governance refers to the activities of national governments.

Many of the studies and findings that emanate from these mainstream orientations are provocative, clarifying, and otherwise valuable. Cumulatively they offer a great deal about the nature, underpinnings, and conduct of governance in the world of states. Enriched by analyses of international regimes comprised of intergovernmental agreements on the rules, norms, and practices that govern activities in particular issue areas (Krasner, 1983: 2), it amounts to a literature that is vastly more nuanced and diverse than was the case only a few decades ago, and it continues to progress with virtually every book and journal issue that is published. But for those who move outside the mainstream and treat the acceleration of globalizing processes as the precursor of a new epoch—as I do—the problem with the subfield and its literature is that it is increasingly obsolete as a source of understanding either world politics or international governance. So let the reader be forewarned: what follows is a bit radical, or at least expressive of a minority perspective by a long-time practitioner in the IR subfield who feels increasingly marginalized—not silenced nor mistreated, but none the less marginalized—by a pervasive sense that the study of world affairs is ever more out of touch with the dynamics that are driving the course of events.

THE LIMITS OF IR THEORIZING

It follows that comprehension of the issues raised by the above epigraph is not easily developed. The dynamics of globalization are complex and the pace of change renders them all the more elusive. As indicated, political scientists in the United States who probe the IR subfield, unlike many (though not all) counterparts elsewhere in the world, tend either to ignore the dynamics of globalization or to treat them as secondary to the behaviour of states. Consequently, they are for the most part ill-equipped to focus on the forces and dialectics of change and complexity through which globalizing processes unfold. Rather, often unwilling to acknowledge the diverse ways in which the authority and power of states have been undermined by the transforming and de-territorializing processes wrought by globalization, the IR mainstream tends to focus on the activities of governments and, in so doing, to investigate the sources of war as the central interstate phenomenon or otherwise to posit states as rational actors and presume that their choices underlie the continued viability of the international system and its ability to maintain control over the pace and direction of change. Whether they adhere to realist or liberal theory, IR scholars are thus disinclined to attach relevance to restless publics, to ignore the deleterious potential of income disparities and poverty conditions, to assess the consequences of dynamic microelectronic technologies, or to allow for the possibility that non-governmental actors shoulder some of the crucial tasks of governance—to mention only a few of the glaring gaps in IR studies (Durfee and Rosenau, 1996). Thus it is not far-fetched to observe that the concepts of change, complexity, and dialectics lie beyond the concern of numerous IR scholars, that such concepts do not pervade their literature, formulations, or footnotes.[1] It is as if constancy and not change is the world's primary pattern, as if history knows no breakpoints, no reorganization of the values and priorities through which peoples ponder their circumstances, frame their aspirations, and conduct their lives.

Not surprisingly, it follows that most IR scholars have not developed broad-gauged approaches to the concept of governance, much less

[1] And even when the underpinnings of change in world affairs do seem worthy of investigation, such inquiries tends to focus exclusively on states and to ignore the complexities of globalization. Indeed, in one recent case 'globalization' is not an entry in the index and the author's concern with global change turns out to be a preoccupation with changes in the international system (cf. Maoz, 1996).

schemata and data linked to theories of governance. Persuaded that the world is anarchical in the sense that it is dominated by sovereign states who answer to no higher authority, most practitioners in the field are disposed not to posit authority as located outside the reach of states and their international system. For them governance in globalized space tends to connote world government, an arrangement that they dismiss as so naive and far-fetched that they seem unable to envision the possibility of governance outside the domestic realm. Consequently, most IR practitioners view governance as what governments do, whereas transnational processes and actors tend to be seen as relevant only as they make inputs into the work of governments. To be sure, theories about international organizations and regimes mark the IR literature, but such actors are seen as engaging in co-operation rather than governance, in co-operative acts to which authority may be attached but which can also be withdrawn if states so wish. Thus, convinced that the only authority that exists in the international realm is possessed or delegated by states and that it can readily be retrieved by states, a vast majority of IR scholars have had no need to develop or use the concept of governance in the analysis of world affairs.[2] For them 'a new world order' would rest not on processes of governance but on little more than a realignment of the pecking order among states. Hence, they tend to scoff at the notion that a global civil society may eventually emerge as the basis for global governance.[3]

   [2] Lately, however, there are signs of movement in this direction. In addition to conferences such as the one for which this paper was prepared, a new journal, *Global Governance*, was founded in 1995, and several books organized around the concept of governance on a global scale are now available. See, for example, the report of the Commission on Global Governance (1995); Desai and Redfern (1995); Diehl (1997); Falk (1995); Held (1995a); Hewson and Sinclair (1999); and Simai (1994). Still, this literature is not yet so voluminous that clarity on the obstacles to such forms of governance has been achieved. There remains plenty of room for what the above epigraph calls this 'sort of thing we are going to be thinking about'.
   [3] Nor are those who scoff at such formulations confined to scholars who perceive constancy as the central tendency of world affairs. Calling them 'semantic euphemisms', for example, a vigorous advocate of looking 'seriously at the power exercised by authorities other than states', Susan Strange, derisively dismisses such concepts as globalization, interdependence, and global governance as deceptive means for depicting and analysing the dynamics of change and the advent of political and economic processes that extend beyond the competence of states. Even those outside the IR mainstream, in other words, are having difficulty moving beyond the long-established terminology. Or at least the dismissal of these newer labels seems in conflict with the Strange's ensuing comment that 'I have at last reached the final parting of the ways from the discipline of international relations. . . . I can no longer profess a special concern with international politics if that is defined as a study different from other kinds of politics and which takes the state as the unit of analysis and

Hardly more surprising, this narrow perspective explains why the politics of the field are still called 'international' rather than by some more encompassing label. Indeed, while one can only applaud the focus of this book on how theories of governance may differ from one political science subfield to another, my assignment here has been cast as that of approaching the topic from the perspective of the IR subfield. For reasons already indicated, however, I have reformulated the assignment. Convinced that the word 'international' no longer embraces much of what transpires across national boundaries, my comfort zone no longer tolerates use of the word. Rather, I have become habituated to the notion that once one moves beyond national boundaries one's focus turns to global politics or, perhaps more accurately, to politics on a global scale. As will be seen, moreover, based on the presumption that politics on either side of national boundaries have become so inextricably linked as to render domestic and foreign affairs largely indistinguishable from each other, I am inclined to view all politics as global in scale (Rosenau, 1997a).

Given a perspective that allows for governance occurring apart from what governments do, here governance is conceived as systems of rule, as the purposive activities of any collectivity that sustain mechanisms designed to insure its safety, prosperity, coherence, stability, and continuance.[4] Governments specialize in such mechanisms, but they are also to be found in a variety of other types of collectivities, from states that form issue regimes to crime syndicates that circumvent national boundaries, from groups who seek to promote a new world order to those concerned with particular issue areas, from formal international organizations or informal coalitions of the willing that intervene to prevent or end domestic violence to debt-rating agencies that monitor financial markets, from NGOs that highlight the failings of governments to social movements that launch protests against corporate practices, from organized ethnic groups to corporations, from non-profit associations to epistemic communities, from economic zones to professional societies, and so on across the vast array of organizations that people form to protect their interests and enhance their

the international society of states as the main problematic' (Strange, 1996: xiii, xv). For a cogent discussion of the terminological problems that follow from the dynamics of change, see Mesjasz (1997).

[4] The conception of governance as systems of rule that embrace mechanisms of control is developed in Rosenau (1995b). So as to insure a focus on nongovernmental as well as governmental rule systems, I use the label 'collectivity' to refer to any group of people—be it a state, a corporation, a non-profit organization, a social movement, etc.—who have a common affiliation but who are so numerous that they cannot interact on a face-to-face basis.

well being. It is possible, in short, to conceive of governance without government (Rosenau and Czempiel, 1992).

The focus here on global governance is not in any way to imply a concern with some form of world government. Quite the contrary, I, too, assume that the prospects for a world government in the foreseeable future are nil, but at the same time I conceive of governance as occurring on a global scale in the sense that there are worldwide problems—e.g. environmental pollution, currency crises, corruption, AIDS, terrorism, mass migrations, and the drug trade—crying out for amelioration, and that while these problems cannot be addressed by states alone or by any single agency of governance, they will be confronted piecemeal and incrementally by diverse types of collectivities. In other words, governance occurs on a global scale through both the co-ordination of states and the activities of a vast array of rule systems that exercise authority in the pursuit of goals and that function outside national jurisdictions. Some of the systems are formalized, many consist essentially of informal structures, and some are still largely inchoate, but taken together they cumulate to governance on a global scale.

In short, my conception of global governance is a broad one. The analysis focuses on governance in—and not of—the world. It posits authority on a global scale as highly disaggregated, as dispersed across a densely populated globalized space in which territoriality has been supplemented—and in some instances replaced—by autonomy as a pillar of governance processes. As indicated, it is a formulation that encompasses a variety of rule systems that frame their goals, accumulate their authority, generate their resources, recruit their personnel, and mobilize their followers through diverse procedures across every sphere of human endeavour in every part of the world.

Stated differently, I treat the world not as national and international arenas, but as a globalized space—a space that is not disaggregated in terms of specified geographic territories so much as it consists of a wide range of fast-moving, boundary-spanning actors whose activities cascade erratically across amorphous ethnoscapes, mediascapes, ideoscapes, technoscapes, and financescapes (Appadurai, 1996: 34–40).[5] For the foreseeable future, therefore, I view this disaggregated system of diverse transnational collectivities as a multi-centric world that competes, cooper-

---

[5] These diverse 'scapes' are the formulation of Appadurai (1996: 33). One observer characterizes financescapes as a 'space without rules' wherein a 'several trillion-dollar pool . . . sloshes around in what is effectively a supranational cyberspace' (Mathews, 1995: A19).

ates, or otherwise interacts with the state-centric world and, as such, constitutes the new world order, an order that is so decentralized that it does not lend itself either to hierarchy or coordination under hegemonic leadership (Rosenau, 1990: ch. 10).

KEEPING THE STATE IN AND PREDOMINANT

Compelling as such a perspective may be, it is easily misunderstood. For all the emphasis on the coexistence of the state-centric and multi-centric worlds and the insistence that thus the state continues to play a vital role in the course of events, many observers somehow manage to misinterpret this nuanced formulation and regard it as consigning the state to the dustbin of history. It is almost as if their analytic habits are such that they need to insist on the commanding position of the state before they will begin to consider the activities of other collectivities. More than that, they need to insist that when 'push comes to shove' (Waltz, 1979:94) the state will prevail, as if the fact that push rarely comes to shove is analytically irrelevant. The analytic insight that states are pressed by the course of events to reflect the larger, more powerful forces inherent in the dynamics of fragmegration[6] is, consequently, not considered and states are thus elevated to levels of competence that the post-international model treats as empirically exaggerated. In effect, many analysts not only want to 'bring the state back in'—to cite an oft-quoted phrase[7]—but they want to keep it in as the predominant and pre-eminent global actor. Usually the litany goes like this: only the state sets the rules; only the state provides sufficient resources; only the state can enforce the rules; only the state can alter the rules; and so on through an endless array of competencies that appear to leave little room for outcomes other than those imposed by the state. Yes, this line of reasoning concludes, NGOs make inputs into policy-making processes; yes, epistemic communities may help shape deliberations; yes, different state officials may represent antagonistic interests; yes, external circumstances may narrow policy alternatives or even dictate the decisions made; yes, there are issues where the state appears peripheral; yes, public pressures can be intense; and yes, forthcoming elections can further narrow the

---

[6] See the section 'Dialectical Processes', below, for an explanation of this concept.

[7] See the various essays in Evans, Rueschemeyer, and Skocpol (1985).

range of choices available to state officials; but no matter, the state is autonomous and has the ultimate authority to resort to force and exercise its right to use shove when situations need a push.

My experience tells me that the ensuing analysis is not likely to moderate or counter this line of reasoning. Efforts to introduce nuances that more adequately reflect the complexities of global life invariably seem to fall on deaf ears when the nuances involve a possible erosion in the role of the state. The result is a stark choice: either one concedes that states are important and facilitates an ensuing discussion in which other actors are presumed to be secondary, or one clings to a nuanced formulation and facilitates self-doubt that perhaps a mainstream revision of the formulation is in order. Here I shall adhere to the latter strategy even though it may well be that some readers will be more attentive to what follows if the predominance of the state is exaggerated before any qualifications, ambiguities, contradictions, or nuances are introduced.

THE DYNAMICS OF CHANGE AND COMPLEXITY

Whatever level and forms of governance analysts seek to clarify, they must confront two underlying forces at work in human affairs as the century ends and a new millennium begins: one is the dynamics of change and the other concerns the ever greater complexity that the changes are fostering. Whether it involves a local community, a national state, a developing society, a geographic region, or the global system, comprehension of the goals, processes, and institutions of governance cannot be advanced unless they are assessed in a transformative context marked by increasingly complex actions and interactions among public and private organizations. This is no easy task inasmuch as governance, however defined, is centrally concerned with the management of change and the reduction of complexity.

And the task is made all the more difficult by the ambiguities and controversies that surround the concepts of change and complexity. Not only has the literature of political science yet to focus on the concepts in any meaningful or consensual way, but their relevance has been subjected to serious challenges. Some observers, for example, contend that key changes in the world have come to an end and settled into predictable regularities, just as others argue that the presence of complexity has been exaggerated and that simplicity is the more dominant characteristic of the human condition.

If governance is about the maintenance of collective order, the achieve-ment of collective goals, and the collective processes of rule through which order and goals are sought—as the ensuing inquiry presumes—then ana-lysts need to be clear about their use of the concepts of change and com-plexity before proceeding to explore the substantive problems posed by governance. It matters, for example, whether one views the transforma-tions that underlay and accompanied the end of the Cold War as continu-ing to unfold or as having settled into routinized arrangements. As one observer put it with respect to eastern Europe:

barring some sort of extraordinary, and probably violent, upheaval, the time of fundamental change is substantially over: further developments will take place in environments that are essentially democratic and capitalistic. The societies may become more or less efficient, humane, responsive, productive, corrupt, civil, or effective, but these changes probably will have to come about within (or despite) the present political and economic framework, not through further fundamental institutional transformation. In consequence, it may be sensible now to decrease the talk of 'transition' and to put a quiet, dignified end to the new field of transi-tology (Mueller, 1996: 103).

Likewise, substantial analytic consequences follow from whether one regards the pervasive processes of globalization as heightening the inter-dependence of peoples, economies, and societies and thus deepening the complexity of modern life, or whether the course of events is seen as increasingly founded on a bumper-sticker logic. In the words of another analyst, it may be erroneous to conceive of the present era as one of unpar-alleled complexity because:

We live in an age of sound bites, from voice mail and E-mail to television adver-tising and news stories. Complex business and government issues—from work-place reorganization to the megacity—are throttled down to a catchy slogan, symbol, mission statement or stereotype in order to be communicated to, and be accepted by, an ill-informed but information-besieged citizenry. We succumb to fads and false messiahs, eroding our faith in our leaders and our very system of government (Schacter, 1997).

As previously implied, the pages that follow derive from unequivocal premises that reject these quoted observations. Stated most succinctly, the degrees of change and complexity unfolding throughout the world are considered to be so great as to lie beyond our full comprehension. Indeed, not only is the age of transitology conceived to be far from over, but it seems likely that only decades from now will the extent of the present transformations be clearly discernible. More than that, the numerous and diverse changes are seen to be adding to the complexities with which communities and societies must contend. Whether or not linearity was ever the central tendency of human affairs, it is now clear that we live in a non-linear world in which causes and effects are so inextricably intertwined as to underlie central tendencies consisting of feedback loops, contradictory patterns, anomalous developments, and punctuated equilibria.

A qualification of these premises is in order: the links between change and constancy and between complexity and simplicity are seen as dialectic processes, with the dynamics of change fostering impulses to cling to the constants and with the advances of complexity generating aspirations to simplicity. There are, in other words, times and places when inertia and continuities prevail and when bumper sticker logic seems compelling, but such reversions are regarded not as new patterns, but as reactions against the ever greater changes and complexities. Stasis and simplicity feed off change and complexity, but it is the latter that are the dominant dynamics. Where they are taking the world is not at all evident, but it is clear that they enormously complicate the tasks of governance.

Inasmuch as whole chapters and books have been written on the subjects of change, complexity, and the dialectic processes they encompass, this is not the place to elaborate at length on the conceptual nuances that attach to each of the three.[8] Yet, as the foregoing discussion suggests, the concepts are sufficiently controversial to require at least a brief delineation of how they are used in the ensuing analysis. Much of the controversy stems, I have long been convinced, from temperamental differences among analysts that cannot be bridged no matter how extensive and compelling a conceptual formulation may be. These temperamental differences underlie our paradigmatic orientations and are thus central to our intellectual stances. Where one observer sees change, another sees the recurrence of age-old patterns; where one discerns complex processes, another discerns regression toward a long-standing mean; where one perceives the operation of a dialectic, another perceives independent processes. These fundamental temperamental differences can readily be cast in terms of governance issues: where one analyst cites evidence of the emergence of new institutions, another demonstrates that the evidence merely reflects the adapta-

---

[8] For an extensive formulation of the change concept, see Rosenau (1990: ch. 4). My understanding of the nature of complexity is developed in Rosenau (1997b). The notion that change and stasis are linked dialectically through the process of globalization and localization is advanced in Rosenau (1994; 1995a).

tion of old institutions; where one treats governments as paralysed by the growing complexity of globalized societies, another points to the stalemates as products of classic bureaucratic in-fighting; where one regards globalizing and localizing dynamics inextricably linked in deep dialectic processes, another presumes that localization derives from cultural origins unique to those who share a common locale.

The recognition of these inherently unbridgeable differences, however, cannot serve as an excuse for using the concepts loosely. Rather, misunderstanding is best minimized through clarity as to how change, complexity, and their dialectic links are conceived to underlie governance on a global level. The temperament of readers may differ from my own, but at least they will be able to evaluate what follows in the context of explicit premises.

Dialectic Processes

It is in the nature of change and complexity that neither unfolds in a linear way. Rather, as already indicated, both evolve along paths marked by reversals, sideward movements, feedback loops, and a variety of other non-linear dynamics that make it difficult to both practice and trace the exercise of governance. Perhaps most notable in this regard are the worldwide tensions that derive from the simultaneity of dynamics promoting integration, centralization, and globalization on the one hand, and those generating disintegration, decentralization, and localization on the other hand. Not only do the two sets of dynamics unfold simultaneously, but they are also causally linked, with increments of the one often giving rise to increments of the other. The tensions thereby created strike me as so essential that they define the era into which the world is moving as it leaves the post-Cold War era behind. I call the new epoch one of 'fragmegration', a label that nicely captures the interactive causal links between fragmentation and integration even though it may at first seem grating to the ear and difficult to pronounce.[9]

Fragmegrative dynamics derive their impetus from the many process of globalization that have come to mark the course of events. Localizing and fragmenting reactions to globalization may often seem in the ascendancy in the politics of particular locales, and there may well be periods of time when localizing forces predominate on a global scale, but in the long run it is the globalizing dynamics that are presumed to underlie the nature and

---

[9] Development of the fragmegration approach has occurred in fits and starts. See Rosenau (1983; 1995*a*); and Rosenau (1997*a*: ch. 6).

processes of change as they erode the capabilities of states, undermine the meaning of territory, and collapse the distances that separate peoples, economies, cultures, and societies.

Change

Whether they result from slow, evolutionary processes or sharp historical breakpoints, the changes of concern here are those which involve differences in kind, rather than in degree, compared to previous decades.[10] The distinction between the two kinds of change are conceived to reflect differences in the number, scale, scope, and rapidity of the processes through which the affairs of collectivities are conducted and with respect to which governance must contend. Where the differences along these dimensions are regarded as huge and unmistakable, transformative changes in kind are deemed to have taken place. Lesser shifts along these dimensions—differences in degree—may eventually cumulate to differences in kind, but until they do the tasks of governance can be carried out in familiar ways. It is the differences in kind that pose the most severe challenges to those responsible for governance as well as to those who seek to develop adequate theories of governance on a global scale.

For present purposes, four differences in kind require notation. One concerns the structures that sustain the structures of global politics; another involves the structures of the globalized world economy, the third focuses on the time frame within which events and trends unfold, and the fourth pertains to what I call the skill revolution and its consequences for collective action. The first of these differences has been well summarized by David Held:

[T]here is a fundamental difference between, on the one hand, the development of particular trade routes, and the global reach of nineteenth-century empires, and, on the other hand, an international order involving the conjuncture of a global system of production and exchange which is beyond the control of any single nation-state (even of the most powerful); extensive networks of transnational interaction and communication which transcend national societies and evade most forms of national regulation; the power and activities of a vast array of international regimes and organizations, many of which reduce the scope for action of

---

[10] It should be noted that I do not take the measurement problems associated with the differences in kind and degree lightly even though I assume they are solvable. Here, however, my concern is analytic clarity rather than empirical precision and thus no attempt is made to elaborate on how the differences might be measured.

even leading states; and the internationalization of security structures which limit the scope for the independent use of military force by states. While in the eighteenth and nineteenth centuries trade routes and empires linked distant populations together through quite simple networks of interaction, the contemporary global order is defined by multiple systems of transaction and coordination which link people, communities and societies in highly complex ways and which, given the nature of modern communications, virtually annihilate territorial boundaries as barriers to socio-economic activity and relations, and create new political uncertainties (Held, 1995*b*: 101).

As for the second point, the structure of the global economy, the differences have been argued in terms of whether it consists of an 'extension of the modern international economy into somewhat unfamiliar territory or a systemic transformation which entails both changes in quantity (breadth and depth) and quality, defining new structures and new modes of financing'. Having identified this basis for addressing the kind-or-degree question, Korbin has no difficulty answering it:

[W]e are in the midst of a qualitative transformation of the international world economy. Our argument is based on three related propositions. First, dramatic increases in the scale of technology in many industries—in its cost, risk and complexity—have rendered even the largest national markets too small to be meaningful economic units; they are no longer the 'principal entities' of the world economy. National markets are fused transnationally rather than linked across borders. Second, the recent explosion of transnational strategic alliances is a manifestation of a fundamental change in the mode of organization of international economic transactions from markets and/or hierarchies (i.e., trade and MNEs) to *post-modern* global networks. Last, and related to the second point, the emerging global economy is integrated through information systems and information technology rather than hierarchical organizational structures (Korbin, 1996: 3–4 in xerox version, italics in the original).

Third, the elapse of time in the current period is distinguished by processes of aggregation and disaggregation that are occurring and interacting so rapidly—more often than not instantaneously to the point of being simultaneous—that this difference can readily be viewed as one of kind rather than of degree. One need only compare the dynamics of organizational decision-making, societal mobilization, and inter-societal relationships in the present and previous eras to appreciate that the differences are not trivial, that they are so substantial as to be far more than merely updated repetitions of earlier patterns. Or, to use a more specific example, a comparison of the collapse of the Roman empire across centuries and of the British empire across decades with that of the Soviet empire across weeks and months will highlight how modern technologies have fostered differences in kind rather than degree.[11] In addition, with the pace of politics at all levels of community having accelerated to the extent that reactions to events occur roughly at the same time as the events themselves, actors are perpetually in a mode of seeking to catch up with the decisions to which they are also parties.

The fourth set of changes involve a change in the skill level of citizens everywhere in the world. As elaborated at length elsewhere (Rosenau and Fagen, 1997), people are considered to have become so much more adept at both emotionally and analytically locating themselves in world affairs than earlier generations that their capacities for collective action amount to a difference in kind than simply one of degree.[12] The implications of this skill revolution for the conduct of public affairs are enormous, highlighting as they do the greater obstacles and opportunities involved in mobilizing public support by those charged with the responsibilities of governance. No longer can leaders rely on the unthinking compliance of their followers when they engage in governance. In effect, traditional criteria of legitimacy have given way to performance criteria, a transformation that can significantly alter the balance of forces that sustain the dynamics of governance.

Complexity

Faced with all these differences in kind, world affairs today are conceived to be ever more complex. They have never been simple, of course, but the extent of their complexity has reached a point where political analysts are increasingly attentive to a growing body of literature known as 'complexity theory' (Lewin, 1992; Waldrop, 1992).

As I understand it, at the core of complexity theory is the complex adaptive system: not a cluster of unrelated activities, but a system; not a simple

[11] For an amusing fantasy that captures these differences by imagining King George III in 1776 tuned into CNN and possessing fibre optic phone lines, a pocket beeper, and access to the World Wide Web as he copes with a rebellious colony in America—with the result that 'had the communications miracle been granted us earlier, there would be no Washington, DC, for our politicians to blame for everything that annoys their constituents' (Baker, 1996).

[12] For diverse indicators pointing to the skill revolution, see Rosenau (1990: ch. 13). An effort to more directly and systematically test the skill revolution hypothesis can be found in Rosenau and Fagen (1997).

system, but a complex one; and not a static, unchanging set of arrangements, but a complex adaptive system. Such a system is distinguished by a
set of interrelated parts, each one of which is potentially capable of being
an autonomous agent that, through acting autonomously, can impact on
the others, and all of which either engage in patterned behaviour as they
sustain day-to-day routines or break with the routines when new challenges require new responses and new patterns. The interrelationships of
the agents is what makes them a system. The capacity of the agents to break
with routines and thus initiate unfamiliar feedback processes is what makes
the system complex (since in a simple system all the agents consistently act
in prescribed ways.) The capacity of the agents to cope collectively with the
new challenges is what makes them adaptive systems. Such, then, is the
modern urban community, the nation state, and the international system.
Like any complex adaptive system in the natural world, the agents that
comprise world affairs are brought together into systemic wholes that consist of patterned structures ever subject to transformation as a result of
feedback processes from their external environments or from internal
stimuli that provoke the agents to break with their established routines.
There may have been long periods of stasis in history where, relatively
speaking, each period in the life of a human system was like the one before
it; but for a variety of reasons elaborated elsewhere (Rosenau, 1990: chs. 1,
5), the present period is one of turbulence, of social systems and their polities undergoing profound transformations that exhibit all the characteristics of complex adaptive systems.

   Among the many insights into the nature of complex adaptive systems,
four stand out as offering especially useful insights into world affairs even
as they also highlight enormous challenges to modern governance at all
levels that political scientists cannot ignore. First, such systems co-evolve
with their environments as they adapt;[13] second, being adaptive, they are
able to self-organize into an orderly whole and, as they do, they begin to
acquire new attributes (what complexity theorists call 'emergent properties'); third, their complexity is such that they are vulnerable to small events
resulting in large outcomes (the so-called 'butterfly effect'); and fourth,
slight changes in their initial conditions can lead to very different outcomes
(Rosenau, 1997b).

---

[13] As one complexity theorist put it, referring to self-organization as a natural property
of complex genetic systems, 'There is "order for free" out there' (Stuart Kauffman, quoted
in Lewin, 1992: 25).

UNIQUE CHALLENGES TO IR THEORIZING

Although rapid change and great complexity are dynamics with which governance at every level of human organization must contend, the challenges they pose for students of IR are arguably more acute and puzzling than for those who focus on local, urban, regional, and national communities. Why? Because the whole world with its far-reaching globalizing processes defines the theoretical scope and serves as the data base for inquiry, thus compelling the investigator to focus on tasks of governance that perforce must span diverse cultures, confront contradictory authority structures, and cope with interaction patterns in which some actors cling to narrow jurisdictional boundaries while others have long since abandoned notions of territoriality. To assess governance on a global scale is to search for collective order and movement toward collective goals among both firmly bounded polities and transnational entities whose activities are not limited by geographic boundaries.

More than that, since authority in a globalized world is highly decentralized and exercised by a wide variety of collectivities, the processes of governance are necessarily more vulnerable to the dynamics of change and complexity than is the case for formally established local, urban, regional, and national governments.[14] Global politics, in other words, are likely to be more susceptible to the power of small events and the distortive potential of initial conditions than are local or domestic politics.[15] An election, a recession, or a *coup d'état* can redirect a polity, but the onset and outcomes of such events are more readily anticipated than is case when an embassy is seized, a currency collapses, a migration surges, an Okinawan school girl is raped by American soldiers, or a Philippine maid is hung at the order of a Singaporean court. Controls are in place with which to address the domestic events, but their absence is often conspicuous insofar as governance in globalized space is concerned.

[14] This is not to imply, of course, that formally established governments are invulnerable to the dynamics of change and complexity. As can be seen in other chapters of this volume, governments of all kinds are subject to the dislocations fostered by the swift-moving processes of globalization. Comparatively, however, the vulnerabilities of rule systems in globalized space is likely to be greater by virtue of their greater number and diversity.

[15] It should be noted, moreover, that the characteristics of complex adaptive systems pose substantial methodological problems. A major implication of the distortive potential of initial conditions, for instance, is that situations are content-dependent, thus rendering it extremely difficult to generalize from one situation to another. This is not the place, however, to address the methodological challenges that attend the presumption of complexity.

Indeed, in some instances the unexpected cascades precipitated by a small event can career out of control erratically across months and years. Consider, for instance, the cascades that followed the shooting down of the airplane carrying the president of Rwanda in 1994:

The Rwandan leader was a Hutu, and his death set off the Hutu massacre of Tutsi in Rwanda. A subsequent Tutsi takeover in Rwanda led to an exodus of more than a million Hutu into Zaire. And it was partly to hound these refugees, and to stop Hutu attacks on Rwanda and Burundi from Zairian territory, that the Tutsi-led Government in Rwanda lent critical support to the Zairian rebellion that is now about to topple Mr. Mobuto (French, 1997).

Control over market forces provides another insightful illustration of the large difference between the exercise of controls in domestic and globalized space. A number of interdependence issues—e.g. migration, monetary flows, and drug trafficking—are driven by supply and demand, by the actions of millions of discrete individuals which, when summed, can pose substantial problems that endlessly criss-cross established national boundaries and thus exacerbate the tasks of rule systems. Market forces within countries can be regulated with relative ease, but the demand of huge numbers of people for drugs, for jobs or safety across borders, and for foreign currencies, along with the supplies that these demands evoke, are not readily controlled by states. Consequently, the persistence of such patterns as global challenges configure analytic problems that most subfields of political science never need confront. For students of governance on a global scale, however, these varied market forces are unavoidable. Analysts are compelled to trace and assess whatever rule systems, if any, may be operative as mechanisms of governance when the flows of people, money, or drugs reach crisis proportions.

Of course, not all interdependence issues are founded on the laws of supply and demand. Environmental pollution, human rights, terrorism, and crime are no less boundary-spanning and no less resistant to regulation, but their roots lie not so much in the dynamics of the workplace as in normative concerns. These norm-driven interdependence issues are so potentially capable of causing individual and societal damage that, like migration, currency crises and the drug trade, their governance is necessarily preoccupying for students of world affairs. Unlike the supply-and-demand issues, however, those deriving from global norms are relatively subject to controls because those who violate the norms are relatively few in number and their identity is readily identifiable. Indeed, each norm-driven issue has become the focus of a large literature that focuses on the clash between the resistance to regulation and the various control mechanisms that NGOs, international regimes, the United Nations, and sub-national groups have evolved to overcome the resistance.[16] In two of these issue areas—the environment and human rights—moderate records of successful governance have been recorded, whereas the resistances to control are still dominant with respect to transnational crime and terrorism, and in all of the areas there remains much to be done if the normative concerns are to be fully met.

The variability of control mechanisms suggests another, equally crucial reason why the tasks of IR analysts are considerably more difficult than those facing their non-IR counterparts. The distinction can be summarized as a difference in pattern recognition. National and sub-national spaces, while hardly less subject to the dynamics of change and complexity than globalized space, are nonetheless pervaded with recognizable and long-standing patterns. They encompass patterns marked by authority structures that are in place rather than in flux, by deep-seated habits of compliance, by well-worn techniques for mobilizing support, and by established mechanisms for ensuring that officials are accountable. To be sure, the patterns that sustain national and subnational processes are not so firmly rooted as to be immune to the dynamics at work in globalized space; and it is also the case, as previously noted, that the demarcation between domestic and foreign affairs has become increasingly porous; but relative to globalized space, the patterns through which governance is sustained in national and sub-national spaces are clearly discernible and tied to easily traced territorial boundaries. In globalized space, however, discernible patterns are still very much in formation. The changes initiated by the acceleration of globalization in the last several decades have yet to settle into apparent regularities, thus leaving IR specialists with the difficult challenge of seeking to grasp unfamiliar patterns and elusive structures.

Finally, and relatedly, IR analysts are at a disadvantage relative to their non-IR colleagues because of a bewildering array of agents whose actions are consequential for the course of events. The identities of the relevant actors in other subfields of political science present no analytic problems. They are governments and the groups and parties that seek to affect the policies of the officials, bureaucracies, legislatures, or courts that act on behalf of governments. To be sure, both the governments and the groups seeking to affect their policies divide into supporters and adversaries in

---

[16] See e.g. the various essays in Princen and Finger (1994), and Willetts (1996).

ways that may sometimes obscure the loci of control, but such factional obscurities are models of clarity compared to those created by the agents vying for control in globalized space. In the absence of any centralized authorities that can serve as focal points around which conflicting actors can converge, students of IR must not only confront diverse collectivities, but they are also endlessly faced with the perplexing problem of how to classify the various agents so that their conduct can be cogently analysed and explained. There is no established actor typology around which the IR subfield has formed a widely shared consensus. Rather, a multiplicity of collectivities varyingly and contradictorily serve to organize inquiry.

Furthermore, although the need for more adequate classsificatory schemes has been fully appreciated,[17] most efforts at classifying actors tend to slip back into framing categories that reflect the very distinction the new typologies are intended to avoid, namely, the distinction between states and their intergovernmental organizations (IGOs) on the one hand and all types of NGOs on the other hand. Not only does the NGO category embrace numerous unalike organizations, but it also privileges states by being a residual category for any agent that is not a state. No matter that the boundary between foreign and domestic affairs is porous and eroding. No matter that states are increasingly unable to exercise control over increasing numbers of complex and changing dynamics unfolding in globalized space. No matter that a wide variety of rule systems have evolved in globalized space independently of the interstate system. Such developments tend to be downplayed, if not ignored, by the unremitting tendency to differentiate between states and an amorphous cluster of agents grouped together as NGOs.

The tendency to cluster and classify in this way is, of course, not surprising. In the absence of an agreed upon nomenclature for all the diversity that marks the agents occupying one or another part of globalized space, it is perhaps natural to fall back on an overly simple dichotomy. Consider, for example, the challenge of framing a more elaborate and viable typology for the following: states; insurgents ('aspiring states'); warring factions ('failed states'); diaspora; terrorists (state-, insurgent-, and crime-sponsored); non-profit interest groups such as political parties, unions, and religious organizations; IGOs; domestic political and administrative entities

---

[17] By the Union of International Associations, which for more than three decades has published a series of annual compilations—known as the *Yearbook of International Organizations*—of established governmental and nongovernmental organizations active in the global arena.

(DGOs?); firms and corporations; crime and drug syndicates; non-profit advocacy groups; for-profit service groups such as media organizations; transnational regimes comprised of both public and private participants; donor communities; coalitions of the willing; civil associations; business alliances; and private voluntary organizations (PVOs).[18]

If governance on a global scale involves the norms and practices that constrain and empower social, economic, and political entities engaged in collective behaviour in globalized space, then all of these agents—and many more too numerous to list here[19]—need to be sorted out. IR analysts have yet to take on this task not only because of their state/non-state orientations, but also because none among us has been able to frame a theory of globalized space amenable to the generation of an appropriate actor typology. Obviously, an understanding of governance on a global scale is bound to be hampered until it yields an incisive conception of the agents that sustain it.

While change and complexity dynamics render the challenges confronting students of IR especially difficult, none of the foregoing is to suggest that globalized space is a jungle, an arena in which collectivities compete so ferociously for influence, market shares, or mere survival that the result is an unrestrained free-for-all. Conflict is a recurrent pattern, but complexity theory tells us that there are other, equally important patterns through which conflicts get ameliorated. That is, while the collectivities in globalized space are not responsive to a common authority, they all are complex adaptive systems, which means that they tend to adjust to each other in ways that allow for movement toward their respective goals and to co-evolve as the movement occurs. Thus has it become commonplace and acceptable for competitive multinational corporations to form alliances (Bleeke and Ernst, 1993) even though in earlier times they would have been condemned for engaging in collusion. And thus has it become customary for non-profit transnational organizations with, say, similar environmental or human rights concerns to join together to press for progress on their

---

[18] The difference between NGOs and PVOs is that the former may be partially or fully funded by governments, whereas the latter rely exclusively on private sources for funding.

[19] The 1992/1993 edition of its *Yearbook of International Organizations* has no fewer than 32 pages of appendices (all with two columns of fine print) that elaborate the definitions and classification rules used to generate, compile and classify the thousands of diverse organizations it identifies. For a summary of the main outlines of the data presented in tthe 1992/1993 edition of the *Yearbook*; as well as for a discussion of the methodological problems that attach to gathering materials on a variety of types of NGOs, see Rosenau (1995c).

issues.[20] And thus too, have states and their international organization(s) joined with humanitarian agencies to form coalitions of the willing to intervene in collapsed societies such as Albania, Rwanda, or El Salvador.[21] Viewed from the perspective of complexity theory, arrangements such as these are not as ad hoc as they may seem. Rather they reflect the shared need to address common problems in the absence of higher authorities. More than that, since globalized space is a dense and still uncharted political landscape, it is hardly surprising that innovative mechanisms for developing rule systems have become so pronounced in so many different fields of endeavor. Authority remains highly disaggregated in globalized space, but it is by no means in sheer disarray; rather, it has congealed in a variety of ways and in disparate locales.

GOVERNANCE IN GLOBALIZED SPACE

How, then, to comprehend the order and disorder, the stabilities and instabilities, that mark world affairs? Given the pervasive changes, the deepening complexities, the perplexing dialectics, and the innumerable collectivities that sustain the dynamics of fragmegration, how do we go about constructing viable theoretical perspectives that will infuse meaning into the course of events? And, to revert to the opening epigraph, how do we begin to lay the bases for thinking creatively about institutional reforms which can reduce the lack of transparency and democratic deficit that mark so many collectivities in globalized space?

Full responses to these questions require more time and space than is available, but a few lines of theoretical development are plainly suggested by the foregoing analysis. First and foremost perhaps, it seems clear that we need to abandon the long-standing and conventional approaches to IR that locate states at the analytic epicentre of our inquiries. States remain important agents of both change and constancy in world affairs, but so many new collectivities and structures have emerged as equally important that keeping states exclusively at the epicentre tends to blind us to the underlying forces and processes that sustain the evolution of global politics. Put differently, while states continue to be vital and active participants

[20] These processes are amply described in Lipschutz and Mayer (1996); Sikkink (1993); Taylor (1995); and Wapner (1996).
[21] See e.g. Bohlen (1997); Cervenak (1997); and Seybolt (1997).

at the core of public affairs, they are no longer the only actors who initiate and dominate the cascades which radiate out from the epicentre.

Second, theory needs to be developed that treats globalized space as the locale of the epicentre, as a vast arena composed of actors and processes that are not limited by territorial boundaries or sovereign rights, as a bifurcated system composed of both state-centric and multi-centric worlds. But how to approach this emergent space in a systematic way that can trace its underlying patterns? The answer lies in the concept of governance. It is not in opposition to the state-centric perspective; rather it encompasses and extends beyond the governance sustained by states. By locating rule systems at the heart of our theoretical formulations, we can trace and assess the processes of governance wherever they may occur. That is, through focusing on rule systems we will not be confined to the world of states and will be empowered to explore issues and processes in terms of the way in which authority is created, dispersed, consolidated, or otherwise employed to exercise control with respect to the numerous issues and processes that states are unable or unwilling to address. Put differently, a governance perspective will enable us to observe and compare the situations within and between the multi-centric and state-centric worlds, thereby allowing us to probe the challenges embedded in globalization and its corollary, localization, and to be sensitive to the fragmegrative dialectics whereby globalizing and localizing forces are inextricably linked.

Third, it follows that a governance perspective necessitates an elaboration of the concept of authority in such a way that it is not confined to vertical hierarchical structures in which subordinates comply with the directives of superiors. Rather, allowance must be made for authority that is embedded in horizontal networks and non-governmental collectivities.

Fourth, if globalized space is as heterogeneous as it appears to be, innovative ways of theorizing about accountability are needed. The democratic deficit that marks the multi-centric world needs to be approached in terms of rule systems that are not constrained by the domestic–foreign dichotomy. Having already touched on the changing relevance of states, the nature of globalized space, and the concept of governance, let us conclude by looking briefly at the third and fourth of these theoretical necessities.

The Creation and Exercise of Authority Structures

At the core of rule systems are authority structures that enable them to generate compliance on the part of persons and organizations in their domains. Often collectivities establish their authority structures through a legal enactment, be it a constitution, a law, a court decision, by-laws, or any other authority-granting mechanism that conveys legitimacy upon the roles or offices occupied by the authorities. But the key to the effectiveness of an authority structure does not lie in its formal documents. It is to be found, rather, in the readiness of those toward whom authority is directed to comply with the rules and policies promulgated by the authorities. Formal authority is vacuous if it does not evoke compliance, whereas informal authority not backed by formal documentation can be stable and effective if its exercise produces compliance. This is especially so for rule systems in the multi-centric world where hierarchy is less important than non-linear feedback processes as the basis for coherence among those who make and implement decisions. Where hierarchy is minimal, as is the case for numerous collectivities in globalized space, compliance derives more from shared aspirations and co-operative practices than from felt obligations or coercive threats that foster an unthinking acceptance of directives.

In short, authority structures are essentially and profoundly relational in character. The recurrent patterns that sustain them are continuously fashioned by the interactions between the holders and the targets of authority. The more habitual the participation of the latter in authority relationships, of course, the stronger and the more enduring is the structure likely to be. Contrariwise, the more the authorities fail to adhere to minimal performance criteria of legitimacy, the more are the targets likely to question and challenge the authorities and thus the less viable will be their compliance habits and the greater will be the fragility and vulnerability of the structured relationship. Put differently, any authority structure derives from underlying (and often unrecognized) bargaining processes between those who preside over it and those who are subject to its directives.

Authority structures can thus be viewed as located on a compliance–defiance continuum in which at the compliance extreme the relational patterns that link authorities to their followers are recurrent and stable, while at the defiance extreme the performance of the authorities and/or the consent of their followers is problematic and unstable. The more a particular authority structure moves toward the defiance extreme, and the longer its patterns of interaction are ensconced in unstable circumstances, the more is the existence of such a structure jeopardized.

Conceiving of authority structures in a compliance–defiance context serves well the task of tracing authority in globalized space. For it is a conception that can be applied equally to states and to collectivities in globalized space as diverse as crime syndicates, financial markets, non-profit organizations, multinational corporations, coalitions of the willing, issue regimes, and so on. In the case of sovereign states, most possess both the formal and informal authority that enables them to compel compliance in their domains, but in the case of some states authority is fragile as developments undermine the habitual readiness of their citizens to comply. Likewise, the collectivities active in globalized space are located at various points along the compliance–defiance continuum, with a few (such as the European Union) having successfully created both formal and informal authority that can be effectively exercised, while some (such as Greenpeace) have evolved informal authority that evokes compliance on the part of their members and still others (such as crime syndicates) that are located more towards the defiance extreme of the continuum insofar as the reliability of their members is concerned. In short, wherever collectivities persist in globalized space, they have authority structures that enable them to mobilize and give direction to their memberships on behalf of their policies (Cutler, Haufler, and Porter, 1999).

It should be emphasized that since the authority of most of the collectivities in globalized space derives from informal rather than formal sources, the nature of their capacity to evoke compliance can vary substantially. For some collectivities—say, epistemic environmental communities or credit-rating agencies—their capacity to evoke compliance is rooted in knowledge that appears to be so authoritative that defying it entails undue risks (Litfin, 1994; Sinclair, 1994). Consider, for example, this assessment of one credit-rating agency:

Moody's is the credit rating agency that signals the electronic herd of global investors where to plunk down their money, by telling them which countries' bonds are blue-chip and which are junk. That makes Moody's one powerful agency. In fact, you could almost say that we live again in a two-superpower world. There is the U.S. and there is Moody's. The U.S. can destroy a country by leveling it with bombs; Moody's can destroy a country by downgrading its bonds (Friedman, 1995).

For other collectivities—such as coalitions of the willing that intervene in the domestic affairs of collapsing countries—their authority derives from the moral imperatives and self-interest claims that are served by coalescing for humanitarian purposes (Weiss, 1990). For still others—such as NGOs and social movements held together by common ideals—their authority derives from a shared recognition that goals can only be achieved through cohesive policies and collective actions.²² Then there are many profit-making corporations wherein authority tends to be hierarchically arrayed and chief executive officers accorded the right to make final decisions that shape their organizations and frame policy directions; on the other hand, there are also increasing numbers of corporations that have decentralized their authority structures to the point where networks serve as the channels through which compliance flows (see below).

Networks

As a consequence of the Internet and other products of the microelectronic revolution as well as the requirements imposed by the rapidity of change on social movements, transnational corporations, business alliances, and a host of other collectivities that need to adapt to fast-moving situations, horizontal networks have become increasingly salient as organizational forms endowed with authority that can be effectively exercised in ways that appear to defy conventional notions about hierarchical sources of control. The story of Visa International's evolution as a company without central authority or a pyramidal structure is illustrative in this regard. The company has expanded its operations and profits enormously in the last thirty years and has done so by eschewing conventional organizational arrangements in favour of loose networks that maintain standards and co-operative practices without resort to top-down directives. Nor does it rely on bottom-up procedures. Rather horizontality has become its operative mode of conduct, with authority being embedded in the informal rules through which its networks conduct their affairs (Hocks, 1994). In effect, networks have taken on the nature of rule systems. And Visa International is now being replicated in a variety of lines of endeavor (Waldrop, 1996). 'A group of fishermen and environmentalists in New England, an association of community colleges, and the National 4-H Council are all looking into changing their organizations to be, well, disorganized' (Webber, 1997).

And where is the authority located in networks? As the chief scientist of a major computer company, Sun Microsystems, put it, 'Your e-mail flow determines whether you're really part of the organization', that is, 'The people who get the most messages and who participate in the most

²² See, for example, Eyerman and Jamison (1991); Laraña, Johnston, and Gusfield (1994); Tarrow (1994); Willetts (1996); Keck and Sikkink (1998); and Meyer and Tarrow (1998).

important exchanges are the people [in the organization] with the most power, regardless of what the official chart may say' (Webber, 1997).

When it is appreciated that the world is experiencing an organizational explosion (Salamon, 1994:109) that, in turn, is proliferating networks as major organizational structures, and when these developments are viewed as prime consequences of the rapidity of the fragmegrative dynamics that sustain globalization, it becomes clear that students of IR will have to rethink their grasp of the nature of the authority and the relevance of hierarchy in the conduct of world affairs (Powell, 1990). And it won't be easy. We are so accustomed to thinking in terms of pyramidal organizations with clear lines of command, that it may be very difficult to adjust our conceptual perspectives to a world in which rules systems rule in the absence of conventional mechanisms for exercising authority.[23]

The Accountability Deficit

Notwithstanding the important ways NGOs have created authority for themselves and thereby served as a check on the activities of states as well as each other, most collectivities in globalized space are not accountable for their actions in the sense required by even a minimalist theory of democratic governance. Indeed, from this perspective the prevailing practices whereby authority is exercised is 'alarming' (to quote the foregoing epigraph). Quite aside from the fact that international organizations are responsible to their states rather than to publics, the lack of accountability is conspicuous. Many NGOs do not expose their decision-making processes to their members or maintain procedures for electing their leaders. Some do not even have members. And for many, especially multinational corporations, the electoral procedures they do maintain are largely ritualistic formalities in the sense that stockholders are too numerous and too unorganized for their votes to have any consequence.

Yet it can be misleading to treat the domestic analogy of open and representative procedures as a minimalist theory applicable to globalized space. The theoretical need is to focus on functional equivalents of domestic procedures, and in this respect the present circumstances, while surely a matter worthy of intense concern, may not be as alarming as they seem at first glance. In the first place, there is at least one NGO—

---

[23] For a cogent example of the understanding that can be developed if a conceptual adjustment to a networking perspective is accomplished, see Thorup (1993) and Sikkink (1993).

Transparency International (TI)—that seeks to expose and contest the widespread corruption that undermines governments and corporations as well as fosters alienation among citizenries. Its programmes have been extensive, ranging from the formation of more than fifty-eight national TI chapters to the publication and wide distribution of an annual Corruption Perception Index to support for international anti-corruption conferences (*TI Report* 1996). Uninhibited by the constraints that limit the anti-corruption efforts of governments, TI has increasingly acquired an authoritative voice in this arena of globalized space. It can even be regarded as a nascent rule system in the sense that its activities and publicity have exposed corruptive practices in all parts of the world.

Second, the very dynamics of fragmegration have embedded within them one major functional equivalent of democracy. By decentralizing authority in disparate and localized sites, fragmegration has greatly inhibited the coalescence of hierarchical and autocratic centres of power. It is as if the politics of globalized space, through having both integrative and fragmented components, mimics the global market with its shifting loci of limited decision-making authority and its subservience to macro tides of inflation, currency swings, and productivity breakthroughs (Agnew and Corbridge, 1995: 207). In globalized space no collectivity can exercise extensive control over people and policies outside their own limited jurisdictions. To be sure, many collectivities still maintain authoritarian structures in which individuals' rights are denied. And certainly it is the case that numerous transnational corporations still cling to hierarchical forms of organization and make decisions without concern for whether they disempower people or do ecological harm.[24] It has been estimated, for example, that the number of transnational corporations exceed 35,000 and that, in turn, these have over 200,000 subsidiaries (Boyer and Drache, 1996: 7). While these figures indicate that sizable areas of global life rest on a form of governance that lacks democratic accountability, they also suggest that the dispersal of authority in globalized space is so widespread that severe violations of democratic values cannot be readily concentrated in hegemonic hands.

Moreover, in some cases public pressure and boycotts do get corporations to alter their practices (Sikkink, 1986); and in the case of South Africa, the disinvestment campaign against corporations contributed to

---

[24] The role of corporations is essayed in Cutler, Haufler, and Porter (1996) and Korten (1995).

the abandonment of apartheid (Minter, 1986–7). Equally important, some NGOs and social movements do exert pressure in globalized space for greater transparency and access on the part of hierarchical organizations, pressures that are in some respects functional equivalents of the various electoral, legislative, and journalistic checks that sustain a modicum of democracy in territorial polities. Indeed, some NGOs face the danger of too much democracy, of multiple accountabilities—'downward' to their partners, beneficiaries, staff, and supporters; and 'upward' to their trustees, donors, and host governments' (Edwards and Hulme, 1996: 8)—that foster indecisive policy making and stalemate. Put differently, just as markets are not democratic in their functioning, and just as they are impervious to any damage they may do, so are they not systematic in any harm they cause, all of which can also be said about the fragmegrative dynamics that underlie the disaggregation of globalized space.

Although a stretch of the imagination is required to appreciate its functional equivalency, the widespread growth of the Internet, the World Wide Web, and the other electronic technologies that are shrinking the world offers considerable potential as a source of democracy to the extent wiring for such technologies is available. More accurately, by facilitating the continued proliferation of networks that know no boundaries, these technologies have introduced a horizontal dimension to the politics of globalized space. They enable like-minded people in distant places to converge, share perspectives, protest abuses, provide information, and mobilize resources—dynamics that seem bound to constrain the vertical structures that sustain governments, corporations, and any other hierarchical organizations. As one observer put it, 'Anyone with a modem is potentially a global pamphleteer' (Markoff, 1995), while another admitted finding 'electrons more fascinating than elections' (Glassman, 1995). In other words, since these technologies have the potential 'of bringing information directly into our homes any time we want it', they could render:

political institutions (*all institutions*) . . . far less important. . . . Computers could displace schools, offices, newspapers, scheduled television and banks . . . Government's regulatory functions could weaken, or vanish. It's already a cinch on the Internet to get around the rules; censorship, telecommunications restrictions and patent laws are easily evaded (Glassman, 1995, italics in the original).

Nor can it be argued that this line of reasoning is misguided because the computer is available only to a relative small stratum of the world's population. To be sure, huge numbers of people still do not have access to computer networks, but this circumstance seems likely to undergo alteration as '[c]omputers keep getting faster, cheaper, and smaller' (Glassman, 1995). Indeed, the decline in the cost of computer equipment is matched only by the acceleration of its power to process information: 'The number of components that engineers could squeeze onto a microchip has doubled every year since 1959, [with the result that t]wenty years from now, a computer will do in 30 seconds what one of today's computers takes a year to do' (Glassman, 1995). Accordingly, it is hardly surprising—to cite but two of myriad examples—that geographically remote Mongolia is now wired into the Internet (Corcoran, 1996) and that its use is spreading so rapidly in China that the Internet 'can be accessed in 700 cities via local dial-up calls' (*Eastern Express* 1995).

In short, as it continues to decentralize into a 'pluralism of authorities' (Bauman, 1992:160), the multi-centric world of diverse non-governmental actors is increasingly pervaded with checks and balances. These constraints are not formalized as they are in territorial polities, and they operate unevenly in various segments of the multi-centric world, but more often than not they tend to inhibit unrestrained exercises of power and to subject unfair or criminal practices to the glare of publicity. The lack of accountability remains an alarming problem—even TI does not focus on the transparency of NGOs—but at the same time it can be said that nascent forms of democratic governance can be discerned in the labyrinths of globalized space.

CONCLUSION

In sum, the contradictions and dialectics of today's world need to be taken far more seriously than they have been if the challenges of governance on a global scale are to be rendered more comprehensible. The complexity and pervasiveness of cascading sequences of interaction that spill across national and issue boundaries need theoretical attention rather than being dismissed as too erratic to be understood. Governance of these sequences may prove to be minimal as they run their course, but a deeper understanding of their dynamics as complex adaptive systems will surely enhance the prospects for coping with the new circumstances created when the cascades begin to peter out.

In addition, given the variability of authority structures in globalized space, it follows that attempts to achieve governance over worldwide problems are likely to be piecemeal and partial. Co-ordination among rule systems does occur, but more often than not the differences in authority structures, and especially the scarcity of central authorities with whom agreements can be made, limit the extent to which collectivities can concert their efforts. On the other hand, since complex adaptive systems tend to acquire emergent properties, it may just be that at least some collectivities will be able to converge around common endeavours.

But to recognize the obstacles to governance on a global scale is not to say that the concept of governance lacks utility and is no more useful than a state-centric perspective. Quite to the contrary, by focusing on the presence of rule systems wherever and however they may come into being, the concept of governance provides an opportunity for discerning trend-lines indicative of whether the dynamics of change and complexity are leading the world along paths that may culminate in greater degrees of order or whether they are fostering ever wider pockets of disorder.

REFERENCES

AGNEW, J., and CORBRIDGE, S. (1995), *Mastering Space: Hegemony, Territory and International Political Economy* (New York: Routledge).
APPADURAI, A. (1996), *Modernity at Large: Cultural Dimensions of Globalization* (Minnesota: University of Minnesota Press).
BAKER, R. (1996), 'Beep Beep King', *New York Times*, 2 July, A15.
BAUMAN, Z. (1992), 'A Sociological Theory of Postmodernity', in P. Beilharz, G. Robinson, and J. Rundell (eds.), *Between Totalitarianism and Postmodernity: A Thesis Eleven Reader* (Cambridge: MIT Press).
BLEEKE, J., and ERNST, D. (eds.) (1993), *Collaborating to Compete: Using Strategic Alliances and Acquisitions in the Global Marketplace* (New York: John Wiley & Sons).
BOHLEN, C. (1997), 'First Troops in Peace Force Get a Fanfare From Albania', *New York Times*, 16 April, A7.
BOYER, R., and DRACHE, D. (1996), 'Introduction', in R. Boyer and D. Drache (eds.), *States Against Markets: The Limits of Globalization* (London: Routledge).
CERVENAK, C. M. (1997), *Learning on the Job: Organizational Interaction in El Salvador, 1991–1995* (Cambridge: Working Paper Series, Conflict Management Group).
COMMISSION ON GLOBAL GOVERNANCE (1995), *Our Global Neighborhood* (New York: Oxford University Press).

CORCORAN, E. (1996), 'How the "Butter Fund" Spread the Internet to Mongolia', *Washington Post*, 1 March, A1.

CUTLER, C., HAUFLER V., and PORTER, T. (eds.) (1999), *Private Authority and International Affairs* (Albany, NY: State Univeristy of New York Press).

DESAI, M., and REDFERN, P. (eds.) (1995), *Global Governance: Ethics and Economics of the World Order* (New York: Pinter).

DIEHL, P. (ed.), (1997) *The Politics of Global Governance: International Organizations in an Interdependent World* (Boulder, Colo.: Lynne Rienner Publishers).

DURFEE, M., and ROSENAU, J. N. (1996), 'Playing Catch-Up: IR Theory and Poverty', *Millennium*, 25: 521–45.

Eastern Express (Hong Kong) (1995), 'Internet Thrives in Nation Starved of Information,' 6 April, 9

EDWARDS, M., and HULME, D. (eds.) (1996), *Beyond the Magic Bullet: GO Performance and Accountability in the Post-Cold War World* (West Hartford: Kumanrian Press).

EVANS, P. B., RUESCHEMEYER, D., and SKOCPOL T. (eds.) (1985), *Bringing the State Back In* (Cambridge: Cambridge University Press).

EYERMAN, R., and JAMISON, A. (1991), *Social Movements: A Cognitive Approach* (Cambridge: Polity Press).

FALK, R. (1995), *On Humane Governance: Toward a New Global Politics* (Pennsylvania: Pennsylvania State University Press).

FRENCH, H. W. (1997), 'Ending a Chapter, Mobotu Cremates Rwanda Ally', *New York Times*, 16 May, A4.

FRIEDMAN, T. L. (1995), 'Don't Mess With Moody's', *New York Times*, 22 February, A19.

GLASSMAN, J. K. (1995), 'Brave New Cyberworld', *Washington Post*, 29 August, A19.

HELD, D. (1995a), *Democracy and the Global Order: From the Modern State to Cosmopolitan Governance* (Stanford: Stanford University Press).

—— (1995b) 'Democracy and the New International Order', in D. Archibugi and D. Held (eds.), *Cosmopolitan Democracy: An Agenda for a New World Order* (Cambridge: Polity Press).

HEWSON M., and SINCLAIR T. J. (eds.) (1999), *Approaches to Global Governance Theory* (Albany, NY: State University of New York Press).

HOCKS, D. W. (1994), 'Institutions in the Age of Mindcrafting', a paper presented at the Bionomics Annual Conference (San Francisco), 22 October.

KECK, M. E., and SIKKINK, K. (1998), *Activists Beyond Borders: Advocacy Networks in International Politics* (Ithaca, NY: Cornell University Press).

KORBIN, S. J. (1996), 'The Architecture of Globalization: State Sovereignty in a Networked Global Economy', in J. H. Dunning (ed.), *Globalization, Governments and Competition* (Oxford: Oxford University Press).

KORTEN, D. C. (1995), *When Corporations Rule the World* (West Hartford, Conn.: Kumarian Press).

KRASNER, S. D. (ed.) (1983), *International Regimes* (Ithaca, NY: Cornell University Press).

LARAÑA, E., JOHNSTON, H., and GUSFIELD, J. R. (eds.) (1994), *New Social Movements: From Ideology to Identity* (Philadelphia: Temple University Press).

LEWIN, R. (1992), *Complexity: Life at the Edge of Chaos* (New York: Macmillan).

LIPSCHUTZ, R. D. and MAYER, J. (1996), *Global Civil Society and Global Environmental Governance* (Albany: State University of New York Press).

LITFIN, K. T. (1994), *Ozone Discourses: Science and Politics in Global Environmental Cooperation* (New York: Columbia University Press).

MAOZ, Z. (1996), *Domestic Sources of Global Change* (Ann Arbor: University of Michigan Press).

MARKOFF, J. (1995), 'If Medium Is the Message, the Message Is the Web', *New York Times*, 20 November, A1.

MATHEWS, J. (1995), 'We Live in a Dangerous Neighborhood', *Washington Post*, 24 April.

MESJASZ, C. (1997), 'Stability, Turbulence or Chaos? System Analogies and Metaphors in the Language of Theory and Practice of International Security', a paper presented at the Annual Meeting of the International Studies Association (Toronto), 18–22 March.

MEYER, D. S., and TARROW, S. (eds.) (1998), *The Social Movement Society: Contentious Politics for a New Century* (Lanham, Md.: Rowman & Littlefield Publishers).

MINTER, W. (1986–87), 'South Africa: Straight Talk on Sanctions', *Foreign Policy*, 65: 43–63.

MUELLER, J. (1996), 'Democracy, Capitalism, and the End of Transition', in M. Mandelbaum (ed.), *Postcommunism: Four Perspectives* (New York: Council on Foreign Relations).

POWELL, W. W. (1990), 'Neither Market Nor Hierarchy: Network Forms of Organization', in B. M. Staw and L. L. Cummings (eds.), *Research in Organizational Behavior* (Conn.: JAI Press), vol. 12.

PRINCEN, T., and FINGER, M. (1994), *Environmental NGOs in World Politics* (London: Routledge).

PRZEWORSKI, A. (1997), 'Democratization Revisited', *Items* 51.

ROSENAU, J. N. (1983), ' "Fragmegrative" Challenges to National Security', in T. Heyns (ed.), *Understanding U.S. Strategy: A Reader* (Washington, DC: National Defense University).

—— (1990), *Turbulence in World Politics: A Theory of Change and Continuity* (Princeton: Princeton University Press).

—— (1994), 'New Dimensions of Security: The Interaction of Globalizing and Localizing Dynamics', *Security Dialogue*, 25: 255–81.

—— (1995*a*), 'Distant Proximities: The Dynamics and Dialectics of Globalization', in Hettne (ed.), *International Political Economy: Understanding Global Disorder* (London: Zed Books), 46–64.

—— (1995*b*), 'Governance in the 21st Century', *Global Governance*, 1: 13–43.

—— (1995*c*), 'Organizational Proliferation in a Changing World', in *Commission on Global Governance, Issues in Global Governance* (London: Kluwer Law International), 265–94.

—— (1997*a*), *Along the Domestic-Foreign Frontier: Exploring Governance in a Turbulent World* (Cambridge: Cambridge University Press).

—— (1997*b*), 'Many Damn Things Simultaneously: Complexity Theory and World Affairs', in Alberts and Czerwinski (eds.), *Complexity, Global Politics, and National Security* (Washington D.C.: National Defense University Press), 73–100.

—— and CZEMPIEL, E. (eds.) (1992), *Governance Without Government: Order and Change in World Politics* (Cambridge: Cambridge University Press).

—— and FAGEN, W. M. (1997), 'A New Dynamism in World Politics: Increasingly Skillful Citizens?', *International Studies Quarterly*, 41: 655–86.

SALAMON, L. M. (1994), 'The Global Associational Revolution: The Rise of the Third Sector on the World Scene', *Foreign Affairs* 73, July/August.

SCHACTER, H. (1997), 'Simplicity', *Globe and Mail*, 8 March, D1, D3.

SEYBOLT, T. B. (1997), *Coordination in Rwanda: The Humanitarian Response to Genocide and Civil War* (Cambridge: Working Paper Series, Conflict Management Group), February.

SIKKINK, K. (1986), 'Codes of Conduct: The WHO/UNICEF Case', *International Organization*, 40: 815–40.

—— (1993), 'Human Rights, Principled Issue-Networks, and Sovereignty in Latin America', *International Organization*, 47: 411–42.

SIMAI, M. (1994), *The Future of Global Governance: Managing Risk and Change in the International System* (United States Institute of Peace Press).

SINCLAIR, T. J. (1994), 'Passing Judgment: Credit Rating Processes as Regulatory Mechanisms of Governance in the Emerging World Order', *Review of International Political Economy* 1: 133–59.

STRANGE, S. (1996), *The Retreat of the State: The Diffusion of Power in the World Economy* (Cambridge: Cambridge University Press).

TARROW, S. (1994), *Power in Movement: Social Movements, Collective Action and Politics* (Cambridge: Cambridge University Press).

TAYLOR, B. R. (ed.) (1995), *Ecological Resistance Movements: The Global Emergence of Radical and Popular Environmentalism* (Albany, NY: State University of New York Press).

THORUP, C. L. (1993), *Redefining Governance in North America: The Impact of Cross-Border Networks and the Coalitions on Mexican Immigration into the United States* (Santa Monica: The Rand Corporation).

TI *Report* (1996), *Sharpening the Responses Against Global Corruption: Transparency International* (Berlin), March.

WALDROP, M. (1992), *Complexity: The Emerging Science at the Edge of Order and Chaos* (New York: Simon and Schuster).

—— (1996), 'The Trillion-Dollar Vision of Dee Hocks,' *Fast Company* (October–November), 75–86.

WALTZ, K. N. (1979), *Theory of International Politics* (Massachusetts: Addison-Wesley).

WAPNER, P. (1996), *Environmentalism Activism and World Civic Politics* (Albany, NY: State University of New York Press).

WEBBER, A. (1997), 'The Best Organization Is No Organization', *USA Today*, 6 March, 13a.

WEISS, T. G. (1990), *Humanitarian Emergencies and Military Help in Africa* (London: Macmillan).

WILLETTS, P. (ed.) (1996), *The Conscience of the World: The Influence of Non-Governmental Organizations in the U.N. System* (Washington, DC: The Brookings Institution).

Yearbook of International Organizations (1992), (Munich: K.G. Saur Verlag).

9

Globalization and Modes of Regionalist Governance

ANTHONY PAYNE

INTRODUCTION

This chapter constitutes an attempt to link the concept of globalization to that of governance via the notion of regionalism. As will be seen, the argument grows out of the deliberations of a research group that has been working on the political economy of regionalism at the University of Sheffield for the past three or four years. Accordingly, it defines regionalism in the manner advocated by that group, namely as 'a state-led or states-led project designed to reorganise a particular regional space along defined economic and political lines' (Payne and Gamble, 1996: 2). The leading current examples of such projects are the European Union (EU), the North American Free Trade Agreement (NAFTA) and Asia-Pacific Economic Co-operation (APEC). The adjective 'regionalist' used in the title thus derives from the noun regionalism, as defined above and as used in relation to the three cases identified, and is to be distinguished from the adjective 'regional' which derives from the noun 'region' (incidentally, a much more difficult category to define). This is no doubt an obvious distinction, but it is nevertheless one that is often not made in these sorts of discussions.

More importantly, the chapter argues that, in seeking to make an analytical link between globalization and governance at the intellectual level, a coalescence of literatures or sub-fields within political analysis is required. The starting-point of my argument is to be found in the field of international political economy (IPE), in particular the discourse of so-called 'new' IPE. This school of analysis grew up in the late 1980s on the basis of its critique of the positivist epistemology and narrow substantive agenda of mainstream IPE which it saw as trapped in a narrow debate between competing, although ultimately converging, neo-realist and neo-liberal expositions of the limits of interstate cooperation in conditions of anarchy (Leaver, 1994). By contrast, 'new' IPE offers a critical theory of the global political economy articulated initially by Robert Cox and based on a method of historical structures, defined as configurations of forces (material capabilities, ideas and institutions) which do not determine actions but nevertheless create opportunities and impose constraints (Cox, 1981). The college of scholars which identifies with this broad approach has in effect taken the process of globalization as its core research question and many overarching analyses already exist which serve effectively to establish the new structural context of a globalizing political economy. What they do not as yet do so well is disaggregate the behaviour of different agents inside the process of globalization. The concept of governance, on the other hand, has always been primarily deployed by comparative politics and public policy specialists and these fields of study have conventionally been dominated by theories that are predominantly agency-based. In good part for this reason, they have generally been ignored by many IPE specialists—evidence of the constricting divisions of labour which cause many of the problems of professional social science analysis. In my view, the worlds of study of IPE and comparative politics/policy analysis are now ripe for creative interaction, offering in conjunction precisely the means needed to dissect the impact of globalization on governance. Indeed, it is only by such 'trespassing across boundaries', to use Albert Hirschman's famous phrase, that a proper and much needed dialectic between structure and agency can be achieved in our accounts of political change. The next three sections of the chapter thus offer a modest intellectual tour through these two broad fields of study before I then try to forge some categories for the future comparative analysis of different modes of regionalist governance.

GLOBALIZATION, REGIONALISM AND
THE STATE WITHIN IPE

The first task is to establish a position on the relationship between globalization and the state and to link that in turn to an interpretation of the rise of regionalism. The first part of this exercise is in fact trickier than it sounds since, from the perspective of political analysis, there is the problem that the terrain of the political has too often been lost in this first, perhaps rather overexcited, phase of the globalization debate. Within IPE, global-ization has been framed for the most part in essentialistic fashion—seen as determined by technological change, as permitting no escape or even any alternative courses of reaction than espousal, as imposing inevitable con-vergence on cultures, economies and societies, and so on. What is either omitted or underemphasized in much of the literature, whether or not it celebrates all of this from the right or bemoans it from the left, is any sense that the process of globalization has been socially and politically con-structed by actors operating within particular historically embedded situ-ations and, further, that, so far from being transparent or obvious, the details of this process actually need a lot of research, which has not yet been done, before they can be brought properly to light.

As might be expected, though, the one issue on which political analysis has forcefully inserted itself into the globalization debate has concerned the relationship between the state and the various processes of global restruc-turing. This discussion will be explored in greater detail in a moment, but let me note straight away that here too the argument has generally been couched in too crude a manner—as either the 'retreat or return' of the state, as Amoore et al. have put it in a useful recent review of this literature (Amoore *et al.*, 1997: 184). As they suggest, the dominant conceptualization has unquestionably viewed globalization as 'seriously undermining the basis of the nation-state as a territorially bounded economic, political and social unit' (Amoore *et al.*, 1997: 185). State authority is seen to have been vari-ously diffused: 'upwards' to international institutions and transnational corporations, 'sideways' to global financial markets and global social move-ments, and 'downwards' to sub-national bodies of all shapes and sizes. In particular, states are deemed to have lost their old economic policy-making sovereignty and to have been reduced to competing with each other in the provision of the human and physical infrastructure that is presently needed to attract footloose global capital. In the strongest form in which this is put, the nation state has become irrelevant and is no longer, post-globalization, an appropriate unit of political analysis (Ohmae, 1995).

Against this interpretation, others have insisted that the decline of the state has been hugely exaggerated. They base their reading on the prior claim that a 'globalized' economy cannot yet be said to have replaced an 'inter-national' economy. In Hirst and Thompson's formulation, the former would require as a matter of definition that distinct national economies be subsumed and rearticulated into the global system by international processes and transactions, whereas in the latter 'processes that are determined at the level of national economies still dominate and international phenomena are outcomes that emerge from the distinct and differential performance of the national economies' (Hirst and Thompson, 1996: 10). Thus, in this view, such global restructuring as has taken place has been driven by the interaction of national capitalisms. Moreover, these national capitalisms, rather than necessarily converging in type, are marked, as they always have been, by different institutions, processes, and cultures (Zysman, 1996). As a consequence, states are held to continue to exercise considerable authority over their respective national economies and to contribute substantially still to the overall management of what remains in essence an 'inter-national' economy.

However, the problem is that neither of these sets of arguments is very convincing, not least because they purport to apply equally to all states at all levels of development in all parts of the world. As Michael Mann has lately observed, it would be remarkable if any political trend was so sweeping (Mann, 1997). Fortunately, a third, more nuanced, position is now beginning to be sketched out. In the words of Amoore *et al.* again, this suggests that 'the usual understanding of a dichotomy between the state and globalisation is an illusion, as the processes of global restructuring are largely embedded within state structures and institutions, politically contingent on state policies and actions, and primarily about the reorganisation of the state' (Amoore *et al.*, 1997: 186). The last phrase is the most significant, for the point being made here is precisely that the changing nature of the state is at the very heart of the process of globalization. *The state is neither transcended nor unaltered in some overarching, all-encompassing fashion: instead each state is finding that its relationship to key social forces both inside and outside of its national space is being restructured as part and parcel of all the other shifts to which globalization as a concept draws attention. In other words, the roles (not role) that can now be played by states (not the state) will vary with their history, their leadership, their location in the world order and so on. This means, for example, that states in western Europe, say, can indeed discover that many of the old social democratic forms of intervention once open to them are now no longer available and states in east Asia, say, can simultaneously find that various 'strong state' techniques of economic management can still work satisfactorily enough even in the face of the pressures of globalization. In short, one of the key research agendas in globalization studies from now on must be the comparative analysis of state forms and the way they are being reorganised in different ways in different parts of the globe.

I now turn to the second part of this preliminary mapping of our field of enquiry and ask: how, then, does regionalism fit in to this kind of thinking? At first sight, the trend towards globalization seems to be contradicted by the emergence of regionalist projects such as the EU, NAFTA, and APEC. In conventional readings these diverse initiatives have been typically constructed into a prevailing 'regional bloc scenario' which is then used to stoke fears of 'trade wars' between the blocs leading in time to 'real wars'. The problem with this line of interpretation, which is admittedly quite arresting as a 'headline' reading of some current international trends, is that it is grounded intellectually in particular body of mainstream IPE theory which is itself seriously flawed. The so-called 'hegemonic stability thesis', which is at the core of neo-realist and neo-liberal IPE, does indeed argue that, in the absence of an effective hegemon to keep order, the world will degenerate into conflict which in the present era is most likely to be manifested between regional blocs of states. But such arguments are derived from narrow presumptions about the systemic tendency for interstate relations to be governed by the problematic of anarchy and they certainly make no allowance for the various changes in the nature of the world economy highlighted by the process of globalization. As Andrew Gamble and I suggested at the outset of the Sheffield group's initial research project, a more sensible organizing claim was that 'the relationship between these two apparently competing tendencies in the contemporary world political economy— regionalism as a statist project and globalisation as a social process— appears still to be in the balance and indeed there is no reason to assume that one must necessarily triumph over the other' (Payne and Gamble, 1996: 2). By its conclusion, we were prepared to go further and claim that 'state projects like regionalism typically seek to accelerate, to modify, or occasionally to reverse the direction of social change' associated with globalization (Gamble and Payne, 1996: 250). In other words, the argument was that regionalism, far from being in contradiction with globalization, was in fact an essential part of the phenomenon. 'In practice', as we put it, 'regionalism as a set of state projects intersects with globalisation' (Gamble and Payne, 1996: 250). There is not the space here to set out the various ways in which this has occurred in relation to the EU, NAFTA, and APEC. However, the two points to insist on are: first, that the analysis of regionalist projects has to be undertaken in the context of an awareness of globalization (for, if this is not done, they will be misunderstood); and, second, that the various projects are all, albeit in different ways, centrally concerned with the reorganization of the dominant form of state operative in their region.

So far, so good, perhaps. As explained at the outset, the argument has been advanced thus far within the discourse of 'new' IPE and it has been suggested that this approach has great analytical advantages compared to mainstream IPE. Yet—on its own—even 'new' IPE is not able to capture fully all the complexities of the new political processes which have been generated by globalization and which now shape the politics of the new world order. To do this, I shall suggest that it is necessary to turn towards other literatures. But, before making that claim, it should at least be acknowledged that IPE specialists have made their own attempt—albeit less than wholly satisfactory—to come to terms with the new politics of globalization.

'NEW MEDIEVALISM' AND THE TURN TOWARDS GOVERNANCE

The main concept that IPE has come up with to characterize the new global scene is the 'new medievalism'. This was a phrase first used by the late Hedley Bull as long ago as 1977 in suggesting that one alternative to the modern state system (the others were world government or an ideologically homogeneous cosmopolitan society) might be 'a modern and secular equivalent of the kind of universal political organization that existed in Western Christendom in the Middle Ages' (Bull, 1977: 254). Bull grounded his speculation on an insightful appreciation of five major trends which, in his view, gave rise to the possible emergence of a 'new medievalism'. The first was the trend towards regional integration, as best exemplified by the European Community, in respect of which Bull anticipated the likelihood, now more prominent in the literature, that the Community was pioneering a new, hybrid form of political organization. The second was the disintegration of existing states as a result of secessionism, although he noted that this would only be of significance for 'new medievalism' if the disintegration stopped short of the creation of new states. The third trend was the revival of private international violence, specifically terrorism, which potentially challenged the claim to the legitimate monopoly of the means of coercion conventionally associated with state sovereignty. The fourth was the growth of transnational organizations with which states were increasingly being forced to share power and authority, and the fifth was the technological unification of the world, particularly in respect of communications, transport, and cultural networks, a theme which, as we have seen, has been amply highlighted in the much more recent globalization discourse.

Nevertheless, as intriguing as his analysis undoubtedly was, Bull himself ultimately remained sceptical as to how far any of these trends would actually lead to permanent changes, as opposed to marginal adjustments, in the international state system. Accordingly, his exploration of the notion of a 'new medievalism' was largely forgotten for several years until it was picked up in the early 1990s by a number of writers to highlight both the variegated nature of the political actors currently operational in international politics and the apparently common ideological discourse of a liberal democratic political economy (à la Fukuyama) within which they have now to act. For example, Robert Cox, the founding figure of 'new' IPE, drew attention to a number of features of what he called 'global *perestroika*'. The old state system, he suggested, was resolving itself into a complex of political–economic entities, including micro-regions, traditional states and macro-regions with institutions of greater or lesser functional scope; world cities were emerging as the 'keyboards' of the global economy; and multilateral processes were providing regulation and service in an increasing number of areas of policy. All in all, he went on, specifically citing Bull in the associated endnote, 'the whole picture resembles the multi-level order of medieval Europe more than the Westphalian model of a system of sovereign independent states that has heretofore been the paradigm of international relations' (Cox, 1996: 308).

This argument was then taken even further by John Ruggie, who argued that the term 'new medievalism' was useful precisely because it highlighted the fact that the world is moving through a transition as significant as that between the medieval and modern eras. He accepted the arguments of such as Jameson (1984) and Harvey (1989) that it was not just that the Westphalian state system was in crisis, but rather that modernity itself was being reconfigured by the spatial and temporal implosion of the globe (the key theme in the new sociology of globalization). Ruggie's complaint was that most of this analysis was silent on the future of the state and the state-system. In his view, the old mode of differentiation of the international political system, namely territorial sovereignty, is being 'unbundled' by globalization. It is not adequate any longer to view political relations from the single-point perspective characteristic of the age of modernity; instead political and other forms of analysis must open up the 'multiperspectival' nature of reality and appreciate, for example, that the EU 'may constitute nothing less than the emergence of the first truly postmodern international political form' (Ruggie, 1993: 140). In this sense the intellectual approach required is actually closer to that of medieval times in Europe than of the modern period. At any rate, the implied association with the sort of distinctions drawn by Hirst and Thompson in relation to economic issues is clear. The 'inter-national' economy coexisted with Westphalian states; a 'globalized' or 'globalizing' economy is consistent with 'new medievalist' political structures.

As will be apparent, the 'new medievalist' analogy is above all a metaphor and, as such, it works well enough. However, viewed as prospective political analysis, it remains no more than an hypothesis and, even as that, it needs considerable fleshing out. Simon Bromley, for one, has rightly referred to much of the talk of 'new medievalism' as 'jejune' (Bromley, 1996: 132). Its great merit, though, is that it does recognize that there is a pressing need to analyse how the globalizing economy affects political structures and the political behaviour that goes on within them. As Andrew Gamble has said, 'the advantage of new medievalism is that it does focus attention on systems of rule, which globalisation does not' (Gamble, 1997: 14). In short, the concept raises the very matter of the *governance* of a globalizing economy and thus begins to demand of us precisely the shift from the IPE to the comparative politics and public policy literature which I believe to be necessary. As many have pointed out, there has already been an extensive debate in these fields of study about the meaning of the concept of governance—ranging from 'old' notions of governance understood as the 'steering' done by governments to the 'new governance' defined by Rhodes as 'governing without government' via 'self-organizing, interorganizational networks' (Rhodes, 1996: 660). Although these formulations are not without their interest, the exercise in hand here needs to adopt a significantly broader (and possibly therefore also admittedly looser) notion of governance than this specialist literature allows. The best formal conceptualization is provided by James Rosenau who uses the term to refer to 'spheres of authority . . . at all levels of human activity . . . that amount to systems of rule in which goals are pursued through the exercise of control' (Rosenau, 1997: 145).

Conceived in this fashion, the question before us can be reformulated very straightforwardly as follows: what are the systems of rule by which globalization is enabled to go about its business? Entry into this debate can obviously be made in a variety of ways and at a number of levels. Indeed, it is a central part of the 'new medievalist' hypothesis that this must be so.

There is, for example, an important literature just now emerging on forms of global governance and there is also a huge amount being said also on local and other sub-national forms of governance in the context of globalization. I choose to continue to focus for the moment on the regionalist level and in the rest of the chapter I concern myself therefore with the question of 'regionalist governance'.

THEORIES OF REGIONALIST GOVERNANCE

The immediate problem to be faced is that the theoretical discussion of governance at the regionalist level has—until very recently—been remarkably sterile and unhelpful. The main source is the long-running debate conducted between the neo-functionalists and the intergovernmentalists in the context of attempts to explain the dynamics of post-war European integration (Caporaso and Keeler, 1995). Neo-functionalists emphasize an incremental and gradual process of change driven fundamentally by the logic of self-sustaining processes which cause integration in one sector to 'spill over' into others. They privilege social and political elites acting across state boundaries but are generally less interested in specifying the key agents than in identifying the political process involved. Intergovernmentalists focus on the outcomes of interstate bargains. They see national governments as the principal agents advancing or blocking regional integration but incorporate the influence of domestic politics by conceiving of regionalist politics as a series of 'two-level games' where national governments serve as the crucial link between the domestic and international levels. The trouble is that neither camp can escape from the conventional concept of a Westphalian state which is able to enjoy both internal and external sovereignty. The intergovernmentalists self-evidently assert their attachment to such a view, whilst the neo-functionalists fall into the same trap by failing to conceive of the 'supra-nationalism', which is the supposed end-result of the spillover process, in any fundamentally different fashion.

Rescue is, however, at hand. Whilst this debate has been pursued, blow by blow, in the narrow world of European Community studies (which has always separated itself off rather too much from the intellectual worlds of both comparative politics/policy analysis *and* international relations/IPE), these other literatures have each moved on in a fashion which now offers up the prospect of forging a powerful blend of theories which, in harness, can at last provide a more or less satisfactory set of tools with which to analyse the behaviour of agents in and around state-led regionalist projects. I am thinking here, first, of the perceived convergence of contemporary theories of the state in the comparative politics literature and, second, of the revival of the old interest in transnational and transgovernmental relations in the international relations literature. Each has a lot of potential value to say about contemporary modes of governance and so let me now briefly explore the latest developments in these two fields.

The comparative politics strand draws attention to the extent to which there has lately developed a convergence between pluralist, elitist, and Marxist schools of thought in their thinking about the relationship between the state and civil society (Marsh, 1995). This is not to go so far as to suggest the emergence of a consensus. But, according to this argument, pluralists have increasingly come to accept that political competition does not take place on a level playing field and that there is such a thing as structured privilege which can be enjoyed by a particular individual or group on a number of bases. Equally, modern elite theorists do not see such clear and unchanging patterns in the circulation of elites as did their classical predecessors and modern Marxists have moved substantially away from the view that agents can only be understood as 'bearers' of structures to the point where they have largely embraced the notion that power relationships are contingent and thus require empirical explanation. In short, the effect has been to create a good deal of common theoretical ground whereby it is agreed that the state needs to be taken seriously, then located socially, disaggregated institutionally, and decomposed into its various component policy networks. All this, it hardly needs to be said, is a long way from Westphalia.

The international relations strand connects nicely with these conclusions because it resuscitates an interest in transnational relations without collapsing these into a society-centred view of the world which underplays the role of states. Keohane and Nye launched this line of enquiry in the 1970s, distinguishing between transnational relations, defined as transboundary relations involving a non-state actor, and transgovernmental relations, defined as transboundary relations involving sub-units of national governments (Keohane and Nye, 1971, 1974, and 1977). Yet the novelty of this approach was never fully exploited, even by its two instigators, both of whom were quickly drawn back into mainstream work. The subject has, however, recently been revived by Risse-Kappen in a way which focuses on the interaction between states and their internal institutional structures, on the one hand, and transnational relations, on the other (Risse-Kappen, 1995). This serves very effectively to 'transnationalize' many of the insights of contemporary state theory and renders them much more useable as research tools in international contexts.

To sum up, then, recent theorizing in these two separate parts of the terrain of political studies *together* provide a useful starting point for attempts to get to grips with the politics of regionalist governance. They take us beyond the tired exchanges of neo-functionalism versus intergovernmentalism and open up the possibility of discerning a number of different modes of regionalist governance. The next and last substantive section of the chapter constitutes an early effort in this direction. It draws on an emerging literature in respect of the EU and tries at least to ask the right questions in respect of NAFTA and APEC.

COMPARATIVE MODES OF REGIONALIST GOVERNANCE

'Multi-level Governance' in the EU

Over the last few years a number of scholars in different countries have started to conceptualise the EU as a multilevel structure of governance within which state and sub-state, public and private, transnational, and supra-national, actors all deal with each other in complex networks of varying horizontal and vertical density. This argument does not necessarily contest the claim that state executives and state arenas are still important or even that they remain the *most* important parts of the EU decision-making system. But it does firmly suggest that the state no longer monopolizes either in European-level policy-making or in domestic interest aggregation in member states. As a consequence, a new kind of polity is seen as being in process of formation, characterized according to Gary Marks and colleagues by the following key features:

First . . . decision making competencies are shared by actors at different levels rather than monopolized by state executives. That is to say, supranational institutions . . . have independent influence in policy making that cannot be derived from their role as agents of state executives. Second, collective decision making among states involves a significant loss of control for individual state executives [with] lowest common denominator outcomes . . . available only on a sub-set of EU decisions. Third, political arenas are interconnected rather than nested . . . Subnational actors . . . act directly both in national and supranational arenas, creating transnational associations in the process. States do not monopolize links between domestic and European actors, but are one among a variety of actors contesting decisions that are made at a variety of levels (Marks, Hooghe, and Blank, 1995: 4–5).

In this vision, the EU is thus presented as a dynamic, evolving arena of political interaction, not a stable order which can be reduced either to an intergovernmental or neo-functionalist logic.

Analytically, the implication of this approach is that reified state-centric accounts which set out out the preferences and bargaining strategies of whole countries have necessarily to be complicated by attention to the particular preferences of particular actors at a variety of points in the multi-level structure. As Marks, Hooghe, and Blank put it, 'there is no fixed recipe for disaggregating the state; it depends on the policy issue at hand' (Marks, Hooghe, and Blank, 1995: 8). Equally, there is no fixed recipe for assessing the role of the non-state actors who press themselves upon the various policy networks. However, what this also of course means is that there may still be policy areas where something closer to the old intergovernmentalist model remains appropriate. The baby does not have to be, and should not be, completely thrown out with the bath-water. Rather, the next step forward must be the elaboration and testing of hypotheses about the different conditions under which multilevel governance begins to take precedence over more traditional methods of government-to-government bargaining. A first stab at this has recently been essayed by Risse-Kappen (Risse-Kappen, 1996).

'Hub and Spoke' Governance in North America

As yet, no literature of any substance has emerged which seeks to analyse the institutional structure of NAFTA. This is partly just a matter of time (NAFTA was only inaugurated on 1 January 1994), but also reflects the very limited nature of the organizational apparatus which has been established to manage the treaty. Apart from regular meetings of trade ministers, environment ministers, and the like, this does not extend much beyond some rather frail dispute-mediation mechanisms and two commissions on different aspects of environmental co-operation, the significance or activism of which it is still somewhat early to judge.

However, if the focus of enquiry is widened somewhat, it is possible to argue that a nascent mode of governance is emerging in North America—and I deliberately say 'in North America' rather than in NAFTA. The key insight here is that the power of the US state is decisive in shaping the contours of governance in North America. Yet, as is well-known, the US state is composed of a myriad of different actors open to the influence of a complex range of social actors. One might even want to describe it as a multilevel structure of governance in its own right. In any deep analysis of US 'state strategy' it is thus clearly necessary to consider the relationship of US state policy-makers to the power of US national and transnational capital, to assess the role of various domestic and foreign pressure groups, to bear in mind all the time the balance of power between the legislative, the executive and the judiciary and between the different parts of the federal system, to weigh up the competing bureaucratic claims to represent the US of the White House, the State Department, the Pentagon, the CIA, the Treasury, the Federal Reserve, the Drugs Enforcement Agency and so on—in sum, to move on and away from the easy notion of there ever being a single US policy towards anywhere or anything and grapple instead with the many contradictions and variables—the many messy policies—that actually exist.

At the same time, as is equally well known, the US state structure is relatively easy to penetrate. US-based pressure groups have long understood this. But what has lately happened with increasing force and significance is that sub-state, state, and non-state actors outside the US but within North America (and thus deeply affected by all that the US state does or does not do) have caught on to the opportunity which this represents and have started to lobby their cases with the US *within* the US political system. Most particularly, other states in North America have realized that they have other options than to seek to relate to the US, foreign minister to foreign minister or diplomat to diplomat. Canadian state and other actors lobbied their positions extensively in Washington in the run-up to the negotiation of the US-Canada free trade agreement (as well as negotiating hard in the formal talks); the Mexican state did this brilliantly in the difficult months before the passage of NAFTA through the US Congress (Presland, 1997); and some of the small Caribbean states, which are much concerned about their trading position in the region after NAFTA, are slowly realizing that they may have a better chance of influencing US trade policy via a close collaboration with the two US senators from Florida than ritual twenty-minute meetings with President Clinton which is all that their size and relative importance to the White House can usually generate (Sutton and Payne, 1992).

I conceptualize this emerging process as a form of 'hub and spoke' governance to highlight the fact that ultimately the channels flow in and out of

Washington DC and the reality that it is the policy of the hub state that matters. But it is significant that a number of US states (of the union) are beginning to position themselves, as it were, as entry-points to the spokes, linking the US outwards, say, to Canada, Mexico, and the Caribbean Basin but also acting back upon the US policy process in good part on behalf of those other parts of North America with which, for geographical reasons, they have particular and often very sensitive social, economic and political connections (Munton and Kirton, 1996). From this point of view, an interesting comparative piece of research would be to examine, explicitly within the context of a notion of North American governance, the respective roles of political actors in Washington state vis-à-vis Canada, Texas vis-à-vis Mexico and Florida vis-à-vis the Caribbean Basin.

Pre-governance in Asia-Pacific

The academic literature on the political linkage between the domestic and international arenas within Asia–Pacific economic co-operation, whether defined broadly or by specific reference to APEC itself, is largely confined to the work of Richard Higgott (Higgott, 1993, 1994, and 1995). In a series of articles he has demonstrated that APEC is a form of 'market-led regionalism'; that, 'despite some institutional characteristics', it is as yet 'neither an institution nor a regime' (Higgott, 1995: 369); and that the act of conceding policy autonomy to a supra-national body is not even contemplated in the region. On a more positive note, what has driven the process forward has been the evolution of a region-wide dialogue about the merits of liberal economic co-operation dating back to the 1960s and encompassing in turn the Pacific Trade and Development Conferences (PAFTAD), the Pacific Basin Economic Committee (PBEC) and the Pacific Economic Co-operation Council (PECC). According to Higgott, this network of civil servants, university economists, and policy entrepreneurs has some of the characteristics of what Peter Haas has called an epistemic community. This was defined by Haas as 'a network of professionals with recognized expertise and competence in a particular domain and an authoritative claim to policy-relevant knowledge within that domain or issue-area' (Haas, 1992: 3). However, the problem with the literature on epistemic communities is that it lacks a theory of domestic politics and the state capable of indicating when and why such communities of professionals have an impact on policy formation. Higgott is thus surely right to assert that the 'network' which has emerged in Asia–Pacific around the concept of market-led regionalism is far from being a full-fledged regional policy network of the type recognized and analysed so extensively by pluralist writers on Europe and North America. Nor, it can be swiftly said, is there any prospect of the Japanese state playing the hub role in a regional governance system along the lines previously identified in respect of the US state within North America. In present and foreseeable circumstances, then, it seems appropriate to describe Asia–Pacific regionalism as being, at best, in 'pre-governance' mode.

CONCLUSIONS

The prime objective of the analysis offered in this chapter has been to lay the basis of a new research agenda. At this stage, therefore, conclusions can only be tentative and I will confine myself to making just three summary points.

The first is that globalization clearly does allow for new forms of governance. Indeed, it might even require such forms of governance. For whether the various new institutions of governance serve to facilitate the process of globalization, or to check and control it, or both, remains to be investigated in any depth. But even to pose the question is to strike a marked contrast to the picture of a world order that has slipped beyond the management of state actors favoured by proponents of the strongest version of the globalization thesis. I repeat, therefore, that it is an error to view globalization in too essentialistic or fatalistic a fashion. It should be viewed at root as a political process, as having an ideological character, and as giving rise to diverse, as yet largely uncharted, forms of governance. In short, research on globalization in the field of political studies must proceed in partnership with the notion of governance, using many of the conceptual tools set out in the earlier discussion.

The second point is that, manifestly, much of this governance now goes on at what I have called the regionalist level. Nobody can deny the political significance in the new global order of the EU, NAFTA, and even APEC. They collectively represent something new. However, as we have seen, no single mode of regionalist governance has emerged. Nor are any yet stable, with clear lines of political development laid down. Nor is there likely to be some linear process of development by which supposedly less advanced forms follow in the wake of the more advanced. It is a mistake, often implicitly made in the analysis of regionalism, to operate as if the EU was somehow showing the face of the future to other regionalist bodies. More comparative research unquestionably needs to be done, but it must be grounded in the realization that each of the three regionalist projects highlighted here (not to mention the many other existing *sub*-regionalist projects (Hook and Kearns, forthcoming)) has grown out of particular regional histories and cultures. In short, their differences (as between Europe, North America, and Asia-Pacific) are, and seem bound to remain, as striking as their similarities (deriving from the common regionalist thrust).

The third and final point relates to the overall picture, the overarching form of governance at the global level, likely to emerge from the globalization process. By virtue of its focus on the regionalist level, this chapter is limited in what it can hope to say in answer to this question. But what is apparent is that there will not be achieved any easy 'meshing' of the modes of governance in existence in the three major triadic regions of the world order, with the result that the option held out by some of building global governance in part via a 'minilateralization' of three structures of governsance (as opposed to a larger number of states in conventional 'multilateralism') will be very difficult to realize. As we have described them, the polities being brought into being via the various modes of governance of the EU, North America, and Asia–Pacific are not the 'like units' that states are deemed to be in conventional neo-realist international relations theory. As such, the vision of some kind of 'super G3' directorate being created out of the building blocks of the current three major regionalist projects is too simplistic and probably misconceived. Given the range of other players (state and non-state) and other levels of action (global, sub-regional, national, sub-national, local) that need to be encompassed in the analysis, a much more likely scenario is that the political economy of globalization will be accompanied by the emergence of a highly complex, 'plurilateral' system of governance (Cerny, 1993). What is certain is that, within such a system, regionalist governance is positioned to play a major role.

REFERENCES

Amoore, L., Dodgson, R., Gills, B. K., Langley, L., Marshall, D., and Watson, I. (1997), 'Overturning "Globalisation": Resisting the Teleological, Reclaiming the "Political" ', *New Political Economy* 2: 179–95.

BROMLEY, S. (1996), 'Feature Review of Paul Hirst and Grahame Thompson's Globalization in Question', *New Political Economy* 1: 129–33.

BULL, H. (1977), *The Anarchical Society: A Study of Order in World Politics* (New York: Columbia University Press).

CAPORASO, J. A., and KEELER, J. T. S. (1995), 'The European Union and Regional Integration Theory', in C. Rhodes and S. Mazey (eds.), *The State of the European Union*. Vol. 3: *Building a European Polity?* (Boulder, Colo.: Lynne Rennier).

CERNY, P. G. (1993), 'Plurilateralism: Structural Differentiation and Functional Conflict in the Post-Cold War World Order', *Millennium: Journal of International Studies* 22: 27–51.

COX, R. W. (1981), 'Social Forces, States and World Orders: Beyond International Relations Theory', *Millennium: Journal of International Studies* 10: 126–55.

—— (1996), 'Global Perestroika', in R. W. Cox, with T. J Sinclair, *Approaches to World Order* (Cambridge: Cambridge University Press).

GAMBLE, A. M. (1997), 'The New Medievalism' (paper delivered to an Anglo-Japanese seminar, the Kobe Institute, Kobe).

—— and PAYNE, A. J. (1996), 'Conclusion: The New Regionalism', in A. M. Gamble and A. J. Payne (eds.), *Regionalism and World Order* (London: Macmillan).

HAAS, P. (1992), 'Introduction: Epistemic Communities and International Policy Coordination', *International Organization* 46: 1–35.

HARVEY, D. (1989), *The Condition of Postmodernity* (Oxford: Blackwell).

HIGGOTT, R. (1993), 'Asia Pacific Economic Cooperation: Theoretical Opportunities and Practical Constraints', *The Pacific Review* 6: 103–17.

—— (1994), 'Ideas, Identity and Policy Coordination in the Asia Pacific', *The Pacific Review* 7: 367–80.

—— (1995), 'Economic Cooperation in the Asia Pacific: A Theoretical Comparison with the European Union', *Journal of European Public Policy* 2: 361–83.

HIRST, P., and THOMPSON, G. (1996), *Globalization in Question: The International Economy and the Possibilities of Governance* (Cambridge: Polity Press).

HOOK, G. D., and KEARNS, I. P. (eds.) (forthcoming), *Sub-regionalism and World Order* (London: Macmillan).

JAMESON, F. (1984), 'Postmodernism, or the Cultural Logic of Late Capitalism', *New Left Review* 146: 53–92.

KEOHANE, R. O., and NYE, J. S. (eds.) (1971), *Transnational Relations and World Politics* (Cambridge, Mass.: Harvard University Press).

—— —— (1974), 'Transgovernmental Relations and International Organizations', *World Politics* 27: 39–62.

—— —— (1977), *Power and Interdependence* (Boston: Little, Brown).

LEAVER, R. (1994), 'International Political Economy and the Changing World Order: Evolution or Involution', in R. Stubbs and G. R. D. Underhill (eds.), *Political Economy and the Changing Global Order* (London: Macmillan).

MANN, M. (1997), 'Has Globalization ended the Rise and Rise of the Nation-State?', *Review of International Political Economy* 4: 472–96.

MARKS, G., HOOGHE, L., and BLANK, K. (1995), 'European Integration since the 1980s: State-centric versus Multi-level Governance', (paper delivered to the American Political Science Association annual conference, Chicago).

MARSH, D. (1995), 'The Convergence between Theories of the State', in D. Marsh and G. Stoker (eds.), *Theory and Methods in Political Science* (London: Macmillan).

MUNTON, D., and KIRTON, J. (1996), 'Beyond and Beneath the Nation-state: Province-State Interactions and NAFTA', (paper delivered to the International Studies Association annual conference, San Diego, California).

MURPHY, C., and TOOZE, R. (eds.), *The New International Political Economy* (Boulder, Colo.: Lynne Rennier).

OHMAE, K. (1995), *The End of the Nation State* (New York: Free Press).

PAYNE, A. J., and GAMBLE, A. M. (1996), 'Introduction: The Political Economy of Regionalism and World Order', in A. M. Gamble and A. J. Payne (eds.), *Regionalism and World Order* (London: Macmillan).

PRESLAND, S. (1997), 'The Neoliberal Alliance in the Passage of NAFTA' (unpublished Ph.D. thesis, University of Sheffield, Sheffield).

RHODES, R. A. W. (1996), 'The New Governance: Governing without Government', *Political Studies* 44: 652–67.

RISSE-KAPPEN, T. (ed.) (1995), *Bringing Transnational Relations Back In: Non-State Actors, Domestic Structures and International Institutions* (Cambridge: Cambridge University Press).

—— (1996), 'Exploring the Nature of the Beast: International Relations Theory and Comparative Policy Analysis Meet the European Union', *Journal of Common Market Studies* 34: 53–80.

ROSENAU, J. (1997), *Along the Domestic-Foreign Frontier: Exploring Governance in a Turbulent World* (Cambridge: Cambridge University Press).

RUGGIE, J. G. (1993), 'Territoriality and Beyond: Problematizing Modernity in International Relations', *International Organization* 47: 139–74.

SUTTON, P. K., and PAYNE, A. J. (1992), 'Commonwealth Caribbean Diplomacy: A New Strategy for a New World Order', *Caribbean Affairs* 5: 47–63.

ZYSMAN, J. (1996), 'The Myth of a "Global" Economy: Enduring National Foundations and Emerging Regional Realities', *New Political Economy* 1: 157–84.

10

The European Union as Coxswain: Governance by Steering

ALBERTA SBRAGIA

Scholars of European integration have typically approached the study of the European Community and its successor the European Union from analytic assumptions rooted in either international relations or comparative politics (see e.g. Hix, 1994; Hurrell and Menon, 1996; Moravcsik, 1998; Sbragia, 1992*a*). Those working from an international relations perspective essentially view the Union as an international organization while those committed to a comparative politics approach view the Union as some type of polity.

Theoretical perspectives aside, many scholars argue that the Union is *sui generis* because it combines features of both an international organization and a polity with issues of sovereignty becoming very blurred. Sidney Tarrow points out that the contours of early modern Europe are a useful referent for understanding the European Union. In his words:

the European Union is best seen as a composite polity, which I define—following historian Wayne te Brake—as a system of shared sovereignty, partial and uncertain policy autonomy between levels of governance, and patterns of contention combining territorial with substantive issues (Tarrow, 1998: 1).

In te Brake's analysis, political spaces in Europe from 1500 to 1700 were not fixed—they were 'overlapping, intersecting, and . . . defined by the often competitive claimants to sovereignty' (te Brake, 1997: 13). That description is a rather accurate approximation of how many scholars of European integration view the political spaces of contemporary Europe.

That description of the political space also underpins much of the most recent work on the European Union. Simon Hix argues that scholars have moved on to what he terms 'the "new governance" agenda.' Hix's use of 'new governance' is roughly compatible with Guy Peters' discussion of that same concept in this volume. The emphasis, according to Hix, is on 'multi-level, non-hierarchical, deliberative and apolitical governance, via a complex web of public/private networks and quasi-autonomous executive agencies ...' (Hix, 1998: 54). If we accept Guy Peters' notion of 'old governance' as connoting steering and control, then certainly Hix's description of the EU would place it firmly in the 'new' category.

This chapter argues that the European Union exhibits a good deal of both 'old' and 'new' governance. What is striking about the 'old' governance is that the mechanisms used for steering and control differ from those of the traditional state, a feature which in turn shapes the way 'new' governance mechanisms actually work. In other words, neither the 'old' nor the 'new' in the European Union have counterparts in the member-states.

AMBIGUITY OF POLITICAL SPACE

The ambiguity of political space in Europe has to do with the unusual nature of the European Union. The European Community makes binding decisions but the symbol of its enforcement powers is the judge rather than the police officer or the soldier. It makes binding decisions in those policy areas in which the powers of the traditional state arrived rather late and is much weaker in those areas in which the traditional state first demonstrated its ability to use coercive power (Rose, 1976; Sbragia, 1997). Its system of decision-making incorporates the role of territorial units—the member-state governments—to an extent unknown in traditional federations (Sbragia, 1992*b*, 1992*c*). For those reasons, scholars of European integration argue that the Community/Union is neither an international organization nor a federation. Nonetheless, the key point for this chapter is that binding decisions are made, decisions which often will result in wrenching changes (especially) in the member-states' political economy.

The fact that political space is in fact contested, that hierarchical relationships are not the norm, and that a wide variety of networks have emerged in that relatively fluid space has underpinned the literature on 'new governance'. The European Union is viewed as a 'network organization', rather than one in which the 'state' is the key authoritative figure. It is perhaps not surprising that the German literature finds the existence of networks to be redefining governance, whereas the more Anglo-Saxon literature finds the existence of networks interesting but not as significant as German scholars.[1] The German literature begins with a different baseline of the powers and role of the 'state' than does the Anglo-Saxon. Both sets of literature however reject the old notions of governance in that 'unilateral steering' is viewed as highly unlikely or often actually impossible.

This chapter, however, argues that the European Union exhibits a good deal of 'old governance'. The activities and objectives of policy networks, however defined, are circumscribed by the 'old governance' features of the system. Thus, the Union does engage in steering—even without a proper government. But without a government, how does steering take place? This chapter argues that it takes place through the institutionalized exercise of judicial authority which operationalizes and enforces a policy norm, the operation of an institution designed to make strategic use of information unavailable to other actors, and the institutionalized lack of public money. These three mechanisms operate simultaneously, and it is their simultaneity which gives the Union the capacity to steer.

GOVERNANCE WITHOUT THE POLICE

Although the literature on comparative policy studies largely ignores it, the national state employs a coercive apparatus which underlies much of its other activities.[2] The state always enjoys the implicit threat of criminal and police sanctions; it is the ability to use those sanctions that differentiates it from other actors in any network. The events of the past few years in Italy have made that point very clearly as actors from all walks of life have been accused, arrested, and jailed. Only the state can dispatch the police.

The ability to use the police in a variety of areas has evolved over time in national states. Criminalizing behaviour has preceded such use of the police. In the case of environmental policy, we are now beginning to see such criminalization. In the Netherlands, for example, we find that although agreements between government and industry have been

---

[1] See Marsh, 1998. For an example of the German approach to the study of new governance in the European Union, see Kohler-Koch and R. Eising, 1999.

[2] I thank Albrecht Funck for bringing this entire field to my attention and for helping me understand how the coercive apparatus of the state works, how it is organized, and how it shapes the structures within much negotiation and bargaining between public and private action takes place.

concluded in innovative ways, the Dutch state has seen the need to create a
'green police' specifically designed to exercise police powers in the environmental field. The use of the police seems to be a function that states
eventually need to institutionalize.

In the European Union, the police power does not exist in the sense that
the EU itself controls no police. All enforcement of that type resides with
the member-states. The typical enforcement powers granted to even
decentralized federal states—a national customs service and a national
criminal code— are not part of the European Union. The Union can
neither arrest anyone nor criminalize behaviour (see Sbragia, 1997). (In
fact, the differences among the member-states in what is considered criminal behaviour leads to important implementation problems.)

The European Union therefore needs to govern without the ability to
threaten arrest. It lacks that basic attribute of state power. Yet, it is designed
to 'steer' national governments and private actors to act in ways in which
they usually would not if left to act unilaterally. How then does the Union
steer? To put it briefly, the Union does not have policemen, but it does have
judges. That dimension of coercion, in fact, is essential for the Union's
capacity to steer.

THE NORM OF ECONOMIC LIBERALIZATION AND
JUDICIAL POWER

The European Union has been designed to change the behaviour of both its
member-states and the firms which operate within those member-states.
The 'management of unequal state power' (Hurrell and Menon, 1996: 392)
was, and continues to be, addressed through a collective decision to promote a liberalizing economic order. The Treaty of Rome is noteworthy for
its commitment to an economic order very different from that which characterized Europe in the inter-war period. States with traditionally protected markets, France and Italy in particular, agreed to a set of rules and
institutions designed to open national markets more quickly than the
national political order would have done so if left to operate unilaterally.[3]
The fact that the 'constitutional order' of the Union incorporates a specific
policy choice and a policy direction provides the context within which a
discussion of governance must proceed.

[3] I thank Giandomenico Majone for this insight.

While national constitutions may protect the rights of private property holders, the Treaty of Rome is unlike national constitutions in that it deliberately sets out the road map for increased cross-border trade and the regulation of firms vis a vis their market share. The concern with eliminating barriers to trade—both formal and informal—is at the core of the European Union's policy apparatus. Its single market programme, with its aim of increasing European competitiveness, wanted to reshape what firms do. Mergers and acquisitions, inter-firm competition, increased cross-border trade, and price transparency across borders (to be achieved by the Euro) are all examples of what the norm of economic liberalization was designed to achieve in concrete, operational terms over the long term.[4]

Subsequent evolution of the Union has led to other policy goals such as environmental protection and consumer protection. None the less, all subsequent policy development has used the liberalization of economic activity as a cornerstone of the discussion. Any decision to limit that liberalization (such as in selected areas of environmental policy) is difficult and is always very carefully defined and bounded. The liberalization of the market, rather than its restriction, is the privileged position.

Thus, governance within the European Union—however defined—takes place within an institutionalized policy framework which structurally privileges certain policy content or at least policy norms. The fact that the Union is based on treaties—which are about policy choices—rather than a constitution is fundamental to understanding why the Union can steer in areas where national governments find it difficult. 'Treaties allow for much greater discontinuity in institutional development' than do constitutions (Sbragia, 1992c: 273), but they also privilege certain policy positions, or at least the principles which will undergird policy content, in a way that constitutions do not. While the unconventional way in which the Union is governed and the complexity of its decision rules is due to the power that the treaty-making process gives to national governments, that same process allows the norm of economic liberalization to be privileged in ways difficult to imitate in a constitution—writing process.

It also allows the executives of national governments to privilege economic liberalization in Brussels as opposed to their own national capitals

---

[4] During the negotiations over the Treaty of Amsterdam, for example, the German government wanted to protect its public sector banks against the competition rules which are basic to the norm of liberalization. Such protection was not agreed to by the other member states, so that only a legally non-binding declaration was accepted (Fisher and Tucker, 1997: 2).

(where networks of all types may view such norms as antithetical to their own interest.) It is not surprising that Lequesne, in his survey of top French civil servants, found that 'the internal market was clearly seen as a means of "cleaning up" and "rationalizing" outdated domestic public policies and of offering France "better conditions" in the context of the internationalization of economies' (Lequesne, 1996: 112). Nor is it surprising that the norm of economic liberalization, embedded in the Treaty of Rome, was reinforced and elaborated in the Single European Act and the Treaty of Maastricht.

Governance within the European Union, therefore, is not primarily concerned with the delivery of public services. Thus, at least one definition of governance provided by Rhodes, concerned as that definition is with service delivery, does not easily apply to the European Union.[5] In fact, much of the literature on governance understood as involving self-organizing networks is written by scholars of public management, service delivery, and the welfare state rather than by scholars of macro-economic management, government–industry relations, or regulation.[6] The first group are concerned with issues which are of only peripheral relevance to the EU. The Union is concerned above all with issues of what might be termed political economy, the functioning and regulation of legal, and increasingly of illegal, markets, exchange rate stability, the balance between public revenue and public expenditure, and external relations across a wide range of issues. It is about changing the behaviour of both governments and firms, of reshaping the relationships which have become entrenched among firms (typically bound by national boundaries) and between government and firms (as in areas such as public procurement).

The European Union channels market forces through regulation rather than by using, in T. H. Marshall's words, 'political power to supersede, supplement or modify operations of the economic system' expressed in the form of social policy (Marshall, 1975: 15). Social regulation rather than social policy typifies Union action. In Majone's (1993: 156) words:

---

[5] Rhodes writes that in his work on Britain, he 'sees governance as a broader term than government with services provided by any permutation of government and the private and voluntary sectors. Interorganizational linkages are a defining characteristic of service delivery and I use the term network to describe the several interdependent actors involved in delivering services' (Rhodes, 1996: 658).

[6] There are exceptions. In the field of government-industry relations, the policy network approach has been used. See e.g. Wilks and Wright, 1987; Grant *et al.*, 1989.

measures proposed by the Commission in the social field must be compatible with the 'economic constitution' of the Community, that is with the principles of a liberal economic order. This requirement creates an ideological climate quite unlike that which made possible the development of the welfare state in the Member States . . . The economic liberalism that pervades the Founding Treaty and its subsequent revisions gives priority to the allocation function of public policy over distributional objectives. Hence the best rationale for social initiatives at Community level is one which stresses the efficiency-improving aspects of the proposed measures.

While 70 per cent of all the business legislation in the UK is passed in Brussels, the same would not be true of British urban policy or of issues related to the British welfare state. As Cram (1997: 125) points out, 'there is no binding EU legislation in the areas of homelessness, poverty, family policy, old age or disability'. The welfare state remains largely in national hands[7] while the bulk of the EU's concern reflects the fact that 'markets are not natural phenomena but have to be politically constructed and politically maintained' (Gamble, 1995: 523).

The EU is in the business of constructing and maintaining new markets, while simultaneously developing a regulatory framework designed to channel those markets in fields such as health and safety, environmental protection, and consumer protection (Majone, 1996a, 1996b). Social regulation rather than traditional social policy is the instrument which the European Union uses to balance the power of the market. The principles underlying economic liberalization rather than the traditional welfare state, therefore, need to inform any discussion of European Union governance.

THE JUDICIARY[8]

Scholars interested in networks tend to argue that the state actors do not play a special role in the interactions among self-organized groups. As Rod

---

[7] For a discussion of how the EU is in fact beginning to affect national welfare states see Leibfried and Pierson, 1995.

[8] I am using the term 'the judiciary' loosely here. In continental Europe, constitutional courts exercise constitutional review while other courts do not exercise what is known as 'judicial review' in the US. Whereas any judge in the US can declare any law unconstitutional, continental judges cannot unless they sit on a constitutional court. In Stone's words, 'European judiciaries have never possessed jurisdiction over the constitution.' Constitutional courts (which are not formally part of the judiciary) were developed in order

Rhodes (1996: 660) points out, 'networks are not accountable to the state'. Beate Kohler-Koch argues that in 'network governance' 'the public administration is an actor which mainly organizes the arena for political exchange and agreement' (Kohler-Koch, forthcoming). The stress of authors writing in this vein is on the autonomy of private (societal) actors from public actors. Given that the Union does not have the traditional powers of the state, it would be expected that such autonomy would be even greater in the Union.

Yet if we define autonomy as the autonomy to exercise certain kinds of economic activity, we can argue that private actors have been fundamentally dependent on the institutionalized application of legal power. That power is grounded in the Treaty of Rome itself, the economic constitution of the Community, and the institutional apparatus established by the Treaty. Although the directives adopted by the Council of Ministers are the best known examples of the power of law, the judicial apparatus has typically provided the necessary (although not sufficient) condition for decisions by the Council as well as for decisions by the Commission to use its powers in competition policy. In sector after sector in which liberalization has occurred, action by the Commission or Council has been shaped by the European Court of Justice (ECJ). The Court has essentially defined the boundaries of autonomy within which firms can act (see e.g. Alter and Meunier-Aitsahalia, 1994; Egan, 1995; O'Reilly and Stone Sweet, 1998; Sandholtz, 1998).

The role of courts in structuring and facilitating the role of self-organizing groups is important and needs to be carefully delineated. Elinor Ostrom, for one, points out 'the importance of a court system that can be used by self-organizing groups to monitor and enforce contracts' (Ostrom, 1990: 25). Yet the role of the European Court of Justice goes far beyond that suggested by Ostrom. The Court has done more than monitor and enforce contracts. It has in fact 'constitutionalized' the Treaty of Rome so that its provisions are supreme in those areas covered by both the European Union and national government; national law must conform to Union law. In so doing, it has given the Union a privileged position in shaping the future contours of Europe's political economy—and institutionally has given itself an absolutely pivotal role. Over time, its decisions can cumulatively shape the contours of markets, hierarchies, and networks.

to exercise constitutional review while leaving the judiciary 'bound by the supremacy of statute' rather than the constitution. For a comparison of the American and European model of constitutional/judicial review, see Stone, 1995 (quotes from pp. 288–9).

Furthermore, the Court has provided access to claimants who feel they have been injured by the non-application of Community law. An economic constitution calling for liberalization would have lain dormant without the enforcement mechanism of a court which allowed individuals to bring complaints when that constitution was being violated.

Interestingly, most of the Court's landmark decisions have been made in the context of a case sent to it by a court (often a lower court) in a member-state. Courts in the member-states have aided and abetted the ECJ in its agenda of economic liberalization.

If one accepts that the judiciary exercises public power, its role in structuring relationships between private and public actors needs to be explored. In the field of environmental policy, for example, it is clear that environmental networks enjoy more power in the United States than in Germany because of differences in their legal standing. Environmental public interest groups can gain access to the courts in situations where their German counterparts cannot (Rose-Ackerman, 1995). The actual laws passed by legislatures, then, can be used as levers to force compliance in the United States more easily than in Germany. Non-state actors in the United States can use the courts to force public—and other private—actors to act in ways in which they would otherwise not act.

The role of the judiciary complicates the implicit dichotomy of autonomy/non-autonomy in much of the governance literature. Social actors may well be dependent on the judiciary to force action. Although they act autonomously in deciding to use the judicial system, their very dependence on its legally binding decisions in fact gives selected courts a 'privileged, sovereign position' (Rhodes, 1996: 660). Judges are important actors in steering non-state actors as well as public actors. Their decisions are often viewed as 'strategic' decisions in the sense that they eliminate certain options from the policy agenda while privileging others.

State theorists have not paid much attention to the role of the judiciary, partially because they have ignored the increasing role of constitutional courts in post-war continental Europe. As Alec Stone (1995: 287) has written, 'the consolidation of [constitutional] review in Europe after 1945 has definitively repudiated certain dogmas of continental state theory, the most important of which subjugated constitutional to legislative authority'.[9] As constitutional review has become more widespread in Europe, and as courts in member-states have sent cases to the European Court of Justice,

[9] For literature on the new role played by courts, see Jacob *et al.*, 1996; Shapiro and Stone, 1994; Volcansek, 1992.

the contours of the 'state' have changed in ways which are not yet well reflected in the literature.

In the European Union, the ECJ has been a major promoter of integration through its decisions which have privileged EU law over national law and through its decisions favoring liberalization of economies. The privileging of EU law has strengthened its own steering role as it is the ultimate arbiter of EU law. Furthermore, its decisions in the area of liberalizing national economies—the Dassonville and Cassis di Dijon cases being the best-known landmark decisions promoting economic liberalization—have empowered firms so that they now can sell where they could not before. The Court has also set the boundaries of the market through decisions such as that addressing the Danish Bottle Case.[10]

The activism of the Court has certainly eroded the capacity of national government actors to steer their own economy. The loss of steering capacity in national capitals has been replaced by steering in Brussels/ Luxembourg. The policy direction of that steering differs in the two capitals, so that liberalization is associated with Brussels/Luxembourg because of the Court and protection of markets is associated with national capitals. Ironically perhaps, the Court has been allowed to intervene because of the activism of courts within the member-states which have asked the Court in Luxembourg to intervene. That in turn has not only changed national 'politico-administrative cultures', but 'the expansion of the role of the judge over that of the technocrat' has provided a lever for rather profound change in the way 'government' operates at the national level (Meny *et al.*, 1996: 5).

THE ROLE OF INFORMATION

Numerous theoretical frameworks stress the importance of information, the difficulty and cost of obtaining information, and the strategic use that can be made of information. The network literature itself stresses the importance of the exchange of information. In the Union, information is brought from all

[10] The literature on the European Court of Justice written by legal scholars is rather large while that written by political scientists has only recently begun to develop. For the former, see Stein, 1981; Weiler, 1991. For literature written by political scientists, see Alter, 1996, 1998; Alter and Meunier-Aitsahalia, 1994; Garrett, *et al.*, 1998; Golub, 1996; Mattli and Slaughter, 1998; Shapiro, 1992; Stone Sweet and Brunell, 1998; Wincott, 1996.

sources to the Commission. Information flows toward the Commission which re-directs it in a variety of ways, uses it in the drafting of legislation, and considers it in shaping its discourse. While the Commission's formal power undoubtedly rests in its ability to monopolize the initiation of legislation, the effectiveness with which it does that and the reach of its influence would be far less if it were not at the cross roads of information flows in Europe. A Commission isolated from information would be significantly less powerful even if its formal powers were maintained.

The Commission obtains information from the numerous policy networks with which it interacts, from a variety of actors in the member-states, from critical international institutions such as the OECD and the various United Nations specialized bodies to which the Commission sends representatives (see e.g. Patterson, 1997; Zito, 1997), from research commissioned by the Commission, from the Council of Ministers meetings in which the Commission always participates, from public interest groups, from national political parties with which the Commissioners and their *cabinets* have contacts, from the European Parliament and the Court of Auditors, from sub-national governments, from its delegations abroad, and from the ever increasing number of letters of complaint written to it by citizens concerned about the non-application of Community law.

It is difficult to think of any institution in any traditional state which has access to the diversity of information gathered by the Commission. Flows of information almost invariably flow through the Commission. The Commission as an institution is at the very heart of a vast web of information sources: information from member-states flows to Brussels rather than to other member-states. All cross-border roads do lead to Brussels when it comes to information.

Thus the Union is, organizationally speaking, beautifully designed to absorb information from a huge variety of sources. Furthermore, information from within the member-states is transmitted in many ways, whether through 'national experts' seconded to the Commission, the innumerable committees drawing on a wide variety of experts from all the member-states which are involved with the Commission's and Council's activities, the work of COREPER (Committee of Permanent Representatives), the national experiences reported by the committees of the European Parliament, the informal visits which Commissioners and the Commission's civil servants make to national administrations, and the reports from national governments which are sent to the Commission on a wide variety of topics. Given the information which also flows in from outside the

Union, the Union, and most particularly the Commission, is in an extra-ordinarily favourable position for steering based on 'soft law' rather than control. The permeability of the Union, its comparative lack of insulation vis-à-vis the external environment, and its technocratic nature all give it a privileged position within the information flows of Europe.

The privileged position of the Union in the flow of information allows the Commission especially, but the Council of Ministers as well, to set the agenda in ways which disadvantage many of the member-states' current ways of operating. The phenomenon of externalizing domestic policy is well known, especially when it is done by the 'first mover' (Heritier, 1996; Wilks, 1996). Further, the process of compromise which is invariably involved in obtaining a legislative outcome often allows several member-states to contribute parts of their policy-making traditions to the final outcome. None the less, the final legislative product will not be what any of the member states would have approved if their national parliaments had been able to legislate unilaterally.

Information about different approaches, different assumptions, different national experiences is crucial to the Commission's policy formulation process and is subsequently important to the Council of Ministers' ability to fashion an acceptable compromise. The array of information sources allows the Commission to draft legislation in such a way that it pre-empts a good deal of potential opposition.[11]

The Union is therefore the repository of information available internationally, information collected and transmitted by governmental and Union actors , and information transmitted by societal actors. Moreover, that information is largely centralized in the Commission. The Commission has a privileged position vis-à-vis all actors in the sense that it holds more comparative information than any single other actor on any specific issue. It holds information about all the member-states whereas the member-states typically only have information about their own practices and experiences.

---

[11] Important information is also provided by private actors in their role as litigants vis-à-vis their own national courts and subsequently the European Court of Justice. Businesspeople are very knowledgeable 'policemen' when it comes to identifying non-tariff trade barriers for example. And briefs to the Court provide transparent information to an extensive network of lawyers who provide advice and counsel to business clients. Cases brought to the Court by businessmen claiming to have been injured by the inadequate functioning of the single market represent information which, as mentioned above, the Court can use to issue rulings which over time create real dynamics of change.

Although the Commission's own segmentation means that information is not used as effectively as it might, it is useful to remember how segmented most national governments are. As Rhodes points out, 'most ministers spare little thought for policy issues controlled by their colleagues unless their own department has a stake in them' (Rhodes, 1995: 21; see also Blondel and Muller-Rommel, 1993). Furthermore, bureaucracies do not typically view their role within a political system as one of using information to steer. As Olsen and Peters (1996: 3) have pointed out in relation to policy-makers:

Their ability or willingness to learn from experience is often limited. Students of public policy making, political institutions, and formal organizations report that causal and normative beliefs, behavioral patterns, and institutional designs do not easily change in the light of experience.

Steering requires information. It is not enough, but it is a necessary asset for any would-be governor. The privileged position held by the Commission in the area of information has often allowed it to set the agenda in spite of the fact that a politically driven Cabinet does not exist and neither do transnational parties. The agenda-setting powers of the Commission are directly related to its position in the flow of information, for it identifies problems before they come onto the political agenda and then mobilizes resources. If one compares the Commission to a secretariat, one realizes how important its role in receiving information is.

The information available to the Commission, the networks available to it for dissemination, and its powers to draft legislation combined with the explicit norm of economic liberalization which guides the Commission's thinking and the judicial enforcement of that norm, provides a powerful dynamic for change.

Information, however, is important beyond the agenda-setting stage. It is crucial for the successful crafting of compromises with the other institutions of the Union. It is crucial in helping to organize the national policy networks needed to implement Union policies. And it is crucial in changing the Commission's own practices, as illustrated by the use made by the Commission of the Court of Auditors' report criticizing the lack of an environmental dimension in regional policy (Mazey and Richardson, 1994). The Commission's formidable information resources provide an institutionalized forum to which all turn—networks, Council of Ministers secretariat, the Presidency, national administrations, parliamentary committee staffs, and so forth for all types of information and contacts.

BUDGETARY POVERTY

The Union is distinctive in the way it treats money. It eschews it. The budgetary limitations under which the Union operates are extraordinary given its ambitions. Its budget is by any measure tiny, and the range of activities for which it spends significant funds are also very limited.[12] Furthermore, the acceptance of the Maastricht convergence criteria by the member-states are also constraining the member-states, thereby cutting their own range of discretion.

The lack of money means that the Community can only provide a very limited set of side-payments compared to the side-payments which many national governments have routinely paid either labour or capital (or both), for instance. The member-states commit themselves to be steered without the prospect of financial incentives typical of those found in national systems. The reason countries are so happy to receive the relatively small amounts they do receive is because the pool of money is so small. Fiscal poverty forces the member-states to make commitments which, paradoxically, may be more credible than they would be if accompanied with Union funds. Other than the structural and cohesion funds, there are have been precious few other side-payments to member states which have taken the form of cash. If the member-states want to stay in the game, therefore, they have to stay in without the prospect of receiving the kind of funds sub-national units in federal systems feel entitled to.

As Majone has argued, the lack of funds privileges regulation over other forms of intervention which require funds. The costs of regulation are paid by those whom regulation affects rather than by public authorities. However, the lack of funds affects the Union in other ways as well.

Perhaps most importantly, the lack of money simply keeps many potential demands off the agenda. The Union's relative poverty in some sense serves the functional equivalent of the gold standard in the international system or the balanced budget requirements in American state constitutions (Sbragia, 1996). It forces a zero-sum calculation which, until very recently, had been foreign to national debates and conflicts about public monies. The intensity of the political conflicts over the structural and cohesion funds, the main examples of redistributive policies in the Union, ironically illustrates how much energy and political capital does not have to be

---

[12] For an excellent analysis of the finances which do belong to the EU, see Laffan, 1997.

spent simply because the regional funds are unique (Allen, 1996; Hooghe, 1996; Laffan, 1997: 106–21). If a plethora of policy proposals involving the redistribution of cash—or even the distribution of cash—were to be allowed onto the Union's agenda, it is likely that its 'steering' function as conceptualized thus far would be seriously undermined. The Union's relative single-mindedness would be diluted.

The same logic is at work in the way that Economic and Monetary Union (EMU) has been conceptualized. The concern with budget discipline in the post-Euro phase will act as a constraint on national governments akin to that of a constitutional semi-prohibition on borrowing. Whereas the Keynesian state was premised on the notion that public expenditure was relatively elastic, the Euro-political economy will be based on the opposite notion. At the national level, constraint is replacing elasticity, the discretion to accommodate interest groups demands is being replaced with a more zero-sum game, and the nature of public finance, deficits, and public sector borrowing is being redefined.

The frugality of the European Union is being projected onto the member-states. The latter cannot hope that Brussels will make up their shortfalls—for Brussels simply does not have the money. It is therefore impossible for social actors at the national level to 'socialize' the conflict over national public expenditure by going to Brussels, for expanding the arena of conflict over finance to Brussels will serve no purpose in the sense that Brussels cannot give them money.[13] Whereas social actors in the American states who felt left out of state spending programmes could bring pressure on Washington for funds, that option is largely closed to social actors in the member-states.

The budgetary poverty of the Union coupled with the constraints embedded in the Maastricht convergence criteria and the protocol for budgetary stability after the introduction of the Euro is leading to a transformation of how public finance has been linked to the satisfaction of demands by societal actors. To use Zukin and DiMaggio's (1990: 17) words, 'the role of shared collective understandings in shaping economic strategies and goals' is being addressed. Those 'shared collective understandings' are in the process of being re-defined because of decisions taken by the European Union.

---

[13] For a discussion of how conflict can be 'socialized' in traditional states, see Schattschneider, 1975.

POLICY NETWORKS

We have just argued that the Union is able to steer, that is to govern in a 'traditional' sense, because it has a court which implements the norm of economic liberalization, has access to a wide range of information, and has
taken a vow of fiscal (but not regulatory) poverty. Its ability to steer, however, does not preclude the existence of those networks which are central to
the discussion of 'new' governance. The literature on the European Union
is replete with studies of various networks of public and private actors. As
John Peterson (1997: 17) points out, 'a considerable amount of EU decision-making now occurs within policy networks'. In fact, Peterson finds
policy networks to be so important at the meso-level of decision-making
that he argues policy networks should be conceptualized 'as a tool for
analysing EU governance' (Peterson, 1995*a*: 71). Furthermore, some of
those networks may be composed of actors marginalized within their
national political systems but finding a voice by participating in a transnational group (Peterson, 1997: 6). Although scholars differ as to whether the
use of network analysis helps explain the dynamics of the policy process
within the Union (see e.g. Kassim, 1994; Peterson, 1995*b*; Rhodes *et al.*,
1996), it is clear that networks of public and private actors—whether
defined as policy communities or issue networks— exist in a wide range of
policy arenas. In fact, one could argue that their widespread existence renders the policy-making process of the Union more inclusive than many of
its member-states. How can such inclusiveness be reconciled with 'old
governance'? That is, how can so many interests, so many public-private
relationships, so many networks allow the Union to steer in the traditional
sense?

The answer to that question lies in the role networks play in the Union.
As Guy Peters points out in this volume, the role of societal actors in the
'new governance' paradigm can either be viewed as impediments to change
or as assets. In the Union, networks are typically viewed as assets, so much
so that the Commission actively encourages the formation of many networks. Essentially, they accept the European project, focus on decision-
making bounded by the norm of liberalization, transmit very useful
information to the Commission, and accept the vow of fiscal poverty.

Some networks are deliberately created by the Commission in order to
formulate and implement policy more effectively, to increase awareness of
certain problems at the national level, or give a 'European' dimension to a

problem which is still in the policy competence of national governments. Laura Cram, for example, argues that in the area of social policy the Commission has encouraged the development of transnational networks (Cram, 1997).

Interestingly, from her point of view, these networks do not seem to challenge the lack of fiscal resources available to Brussels. In a similar vein, the creation of networks has been a deliberate strategy on the part of the Commission in the area of gender equality (Bretherton and Sperling, 1996). Although networks are often thought of in terms of policy formulation, the Commission has deliberately created networks in the field of environmental protection so as to improve the implementation of legislation adopted in Brussels. In fact, networks are the Commission's primary response to the 'implementation deficit' which characterizes many EU policy arenas.[14] Finally, the Union's new regulatory agencies are also creating networks, acting as 'network coordinators', in order to ensure uniform implementation (Dehousse, 1997; Majone, 1997). The Union can better achieve its objectives with networks than without them and therefore the Commission deliberately and strategically creates them.

Of course, other networks are formed because the affected groups want to influence policy formulation and/or implementation. They bring with them information which the Commission can use to its own advantage. These networks may seek to cushion the impact of the Union's 'economic constitution' or to modify its impact. They typically support transition periods, for example, so that target groups are not asked to change quickly. Nonetheless, such networks accept the boundaries of that economic constitution. However, the overall *direction of change* in the Union is clear. And it is the clarity of that direction that speaks most eloquently to the capacity of the Union to govern in an 'old' sense—especially when contrasted with the inability of many of its member-states to set and sustain any such clear direction.

Policy networks, on balance, help the Union to steer more effectively by legitimating working together at the European level, gaining compliance from affected groups, and accessing a wide range of information not otherwise available to actors in Brussels. Policy networks, in effect, help the Union 'steer'.

---

[14] For a discussion of implementation and the 'implementation deficit' in the field of environmental protection, see Sbragia with Hildebrand, forthcoming.

CONCLUSION

The European Union governs in the sense of 'steering' because it is structurally designed keeps certain substantive questions off the table while insisting that others be kept on the table. The use of treaties rather than a constitution, the institutionalization of the norm of economic liberalization in those treaties, the creation of a powerful court, its unusual access to information, and the lack of public funds all help the Union steer.

To students of traditional states, the most striking feature of the Union is its vow of poverty. For analysts influenced by Schumpeter, for whom taxes were 'the heart of the state' the lack of public finance at the level of the Union requires analysis. In a democratic age, the implications of poverty for an entity with the power to make laws and enforce them through judges are profound.

Essentially, issues of redistribution are off the table while those having to do with economic liberalization are on the table. Fiscal federalism is not on the agenda while the single currency is. Regulatory policy is privileged while fiscal policy is subordinated. The ability of the Union to steer, therefore, seems tied to the absence of those features of statehood which have shaped the political conflicts of the nineteenth- and twentieth-century state. The Union's ability to govern in an old-fashioned sense, therefore, may be tied to the subordination of those issues which have defined such old-fashioned governance in the member-states.

REFERENCES

ALLEN, D. (1996), 'Cohesion and Structural Adjustment', in H. Wallace and W. Wallace (eds.), *Policy-Making in the European Union* (Oxford: Oxford University Press), 209–34.

ALTER, K. (1996), 'The European Court's Political Power', *West European Politics*, 19: 458–87.

—— (1998), 'Who Are the Masters of the Treaty? European Governments and the European Court of Justice', *International Organization* 52: 121–48.

—— and MEUNIER-AITSAHALIA, S. (1994), 'Judicial Politics in the European Union: European Integration and the Pathbreaking Cassis de Dijon Decision', *Comparative Political Studies* 26: 536–61.

BLONDEL, J., and MULLER-ROMMEL, F. (eds.) (1993), *Governing Together: The Extent and Limits of Joint Decision-Making in Western European Cabinets* (New York: St Martin's Press).

BRAKE, W. TE (1997), *Making History: Ordinary People in European Politics, 1500–1700* (Berkeley: University of California Press).

BRETHERTON, C., and SPERLING, L. (1996), 'Women's Networks and the European Union: Towards and Inclusive Approach', *Journal of Common Market Studies* 34: 488–507.

CRAM, L. (1997), *Policy-Making in the EU: Conceptual Lenses and the Integration Process* (London: Routledge).

DEHOUSSE, R. (1997), 'Regulation by Networks in the European Community: The Role of European Agencies', *Journal of European Public Policy* 4: 426–61.

EGAN, M. (1995), *Regulating European Markets: Mismatch, Reform, and Agency* (Ph.D. Dissertation) (Pittsburgh: University of Pittsburgh).

FISHER, A., and TUCKER, E. (1997), 'EU Treaty Joy for German Private Banks', *Financial Times*, 20 June, 2.

GAMBLE, A. (1995), 'The New Political Economy', *Political Studies* 43: 516–30.

GARRETT, G., KELEMEN, R. D. and SCHULZ, H. (1998), 'The European Court of Justice, National Governments, and Legal Integration in the European Union', *International Organization* 52: 149–76.

GOLUB, J. (1996), 'Rethinking the Interaction between National Courts and the European Court of Justice', *West European Politics* 19: 360–85.

GRANT, W., PATERSON, W. E. and WHITSON, C. (1989), *Government and the Chemical Industry* (Oxford: Clarendon).

HERITIER, A. (1996), 'The Accommodation of Diversity in European Policy-Making and its Outcomes: Regulatory Policy as a Patchwork', *Journal of European Public Policy* 3: 149–67.

HIX, S. (1994), 'The Study of the European Community: The Challenge to Comparative Politics', *West European Politics* 17: 1–30.

—— (1998), 'The Study of the European Union II: The 'New Governance' Agenda and Its Rival', *Journal of European Public Policy* 5: 38–65.

HOOGHE, L. (1996), 'Building a Europe with the Regions: The Changing Role of the European Commission', in L. Hooghe (ed.), *Cohesion Policy and European Integration: Building Multi-Level Governance* (Oxford: Oxford University Press), 89–126.

HURRELL, A., and MENON, A. (1996), 'Politics Like No Other?: Comparative Politics, International Relations and the Study of the EU', *West European Politics* 19: 386–402.

JACOB, H., *et al.* (1996), *Courts, Law, and Politics in Comparative Perspective* (New Haven: Yale University Press).

KASSIM, H. (1994), 'Policy Networks, Networks and European Policy-Making: A Skeptical View', *West European Politics* 17: 15–27.

KOHLER-KOCH, B. (forthcoming), 'The Evolution and Transformation of European Governance', *Analise Social.*

—— and EISING, R. (1999), *The Transformation of Governance in the European Union* (London: Routledge).

LAFFAN, B. (1997), *The Finances of the European Union* (New York: St Martin's Press).

LEIBFRIED, S., and PIERSON, P. (eds.) (1995), *European Social Policy: Between Fragmentation and Integration* (Washington, DC: Brookings).

LEQUESNE, C. (1996) 'French Central Government and the European Political System: Change and Adaptation since the Single Act', in Y. Meny, Pierre Muller and Jean-Louis Quermonne (eds.), *Adjusting to Europe: The Impact of the European Union on National Institutions and Policies* (London: Routledge), 110–20.

MAJONE, G. (1993), 'The European Community Between Social Policy and Social Regulation', *Journal of Common Market Studies* 31: 153–70.

—— (1996a), *Regulating Europe* (London: Routledge).

—— (1996b), 'Which Social Policy for Europe?', in Y. Meny, P. Muller, and J.-L. Quermonne (eds.), *Adjusting to Europe: The Impact of the European Union on National Institutions and Policies* (London: Routledge), 123–36.

—— (1997), 'The New European Agencies: Regulation by Information', *Journal of European Public Policy* 2: 262–75.

MARSH, D. (1998), 'The Development of the Policy Network Approach', in D. Marsh (ed.), *Comparing Policy Networks* (Buckingham: Open University Press), 3–17.

MARSHALL, T. H. (1975), *Social Policy* (London: Hutchinson).

MATTLI, W., and SLAUGHTER, A-M. (1998), 'Revisiting the European Court of Justice', *International Organization* 52: 177–210.

MAZEY, S., and RICHARDSON, J. (1994), 'Policy Co-Ordination in Brussels: Environmental and Regional Policy', in S. Baker, K. Milton, and S. Yearly (eds.), *Protecting the Periphery: Environmental Policy in Peripheral Regions of the European Union* (Essex: Frank Cass), 22–44.

MENY, Y., MULLER, P., and QUERMONNE, J.-L. (1996), 'Introduction', in Y. Meny, Pierre Muller and Jean-Louis Quermonne (eds.), *Adjusting to Europe: The Impact of the European Union on National Institutions and Policies* (London: Routledge), 1–22.

MORAVSCIK, A. (1998), *The Choice for Europe: Social Purpose and State Power from Messina to Maastricht* (Ithaca, NY: Cornell University Press).

OLSEN, J. P., and PETERS, B. G. (1996), 'Learning From Experience?' in J. P. Olsen and B. G. Peters (eds.), *Lessons from Experience: Experiential Learning in Administrative Reforms in Eight Democracies* (Oslo: Scandinavian University Press), 1–35.

OSTROM, E. (1990), *Governing the Commons: The Evolution of Institutions for Collective Action* (Cambridge: Cambridge University Press).

PATTERSON, L. A. (1997), 'Where is the Top in Top Down Policy Making? The Influence of International Organizations on the EU Policy Process' (paper Presented at the 'Europeanization In International Perspective' Conference, University of Pittsburgh, 19–21 September).

PETERSON, J. (1995*a*), 'Decision-making in the European Union: Towards a Framework of Analysis', *Journal of European Public Policy* 2: 69–93.

—— (1995*b*), 'Policy Networks and European Policymaking: A Reply to Kassim', *West European Politics* 18: 389–402.

—— (1997), 'States, Societies and the European Union', *West European Politics* 20: 1–23.

O'REILLY, D., and STONE SWEET, A. (1998), 'The Liberalization and European Reregulation of Air Transport', in W. Sandholtz and A. Stone Sweet (eds.), *European Integration and Supranational Governance* (Oxford: Oxford University Press) 164–87.

RHODES, R. A. W. (1995), 'From Prime Ministerial Power to Core Executive', in R. A. W. Rhodes and P. Dunleavy (eds.), *Prime Minister, Cabinet and Core Executive* (New York: St Martin's Press), 11–37.

—— (1996), 'The New Governance: Governing Without Government', *Political Studies* 44: 652–67.

—— BACHE, I., and GEORGE, S. (1996), 'Policy Networks and Policy-making in the European Union: A Critical Appraisal', in L. Hooghe (ed.), *Cohesion Policy and European Integration: Building Multi-Level Governance* (Oxford: Oxford University Press), 367–87.

ROSE, R. (1976), 'On the Priorities of Government: A Developmental Analysis of Public Policies', *European Journal of Political Research* 4: 247–90.

ROSE-ACKERMAN, S. (1995), *Controlling Environmental Policy: The Limits of Public Law in Germany and the United States* (New Haven: Yale University Press).

SANDHOLTZ, W. (1998), 'The Emergence of a Supranational Telecommunications Regime', in W. Sandholtz and A. Stone Sweet (eds.), *European Integration and Supranational Governance* (Oxford: Oxford University Press), 134–63.

SBRAGIA, A. (ed.) (1992*a*), *Euro-Politics: Institutions and Policymaking in the 'New' European Community* (Washington, DC: Brookings Institution).

—— (1992*b*) 'Introduction', in A. Sbragia (ed.), *Euro-Politics: Institutions and Policymaking in the 'New' European Community* (Washington DC: Brookings Institution), 1–22.

—— (1992*c*), 'Thinking About the European Future: The Uses of Comparison', in A. Sbragia (ed.), *Euro-Politics: Institutions and Policymaking in the 'New' European Community* (Washington DC: Brookings Institution), 257–91.

—— (1996), *Debt Wish: Entrepreneurial Cities, U.S. Federalism, and Economic Development* (Pittsburgh: University of Pittsburgh Press).

—— (1997), 'Governance, Credibility, and Federalism: The European Union in Comparative Perspective', (paper Presented at ECPR-APSA Workshop on

Regional Integration and Multi-Level Governance, Bern, Switzerland, 27 February–4 March).

—— with HILDEBRAND, P. (forthcoming), 'The European Union: A Story in the Making', in E. B. Weiss and H. Jacobson (eds.), *Engaging Countries: Compliance with International Environmental Agreements* (Cambridge, MA: MIT Press).

SCHATTSCHNEIDER, E. E. (1975), *The Semi-Sovereign People: A Realist's View of Democracy in America* (Hinsdale, Ill: The Dryden Press).

SHAPIRO, M. (1992), 'The European Court of Justice', in A. M. Sbragia (ed.), *Euro-Politics: Institutions and Policymaking in the 'New' European Community* (Washington, DC: Brookings Institution), 123–51.

—— and STONE, A. (eds.) (1994), Special Issue on The New Constitutional Politics of Europe, *Comparative Political Studies*, vol. 26, no. 4.

STEIN, E. (1981), 'Lawyers, Judges and the Making of a Transnational Constitution', *American Journal of International Law* 75: 1–27.

STONE, A. (1995), 'Governing with Judges: the New Constitutionalism', in J. Hayward and E. C. Page (eds.), *Governing the New Europe* (Cambridge: Polity Press), 286–314.

STONE SWEET, A., and BRUNELL, T. L. (1998), 'Constructing a Supranational Constitution: Dispute Resolution and Governance in the EU', *American Political Science Review* 92: 63–81.

TARROW, S. (1998), 'Building a Composite Polity: Popular Contention in the European Union' (Institute for European Studies Working Paper 98.3. Ithaca, NY: Cornell University Press).

VOLCANSEK, M. L. (ed.) (1992), Special Issue on Judicial Politics and Policy-Making in Western Europe, *West European Politics*, vol. 15.

WEILER, J. (1991), 'The Transformation of Europe', *Yale Law Journal* 100: 2403–83.

WILKS, S. (1996) 'Regulatory Compliance and Capitalist Diversity in Europe', *Journal of European Public Policy* 3: 536–59.

—— and WRIGHT, M. (eds.) (1987), *Comparative Government-Industry Relations: Western Europe, the United States and Japan* (Oxford: Clarendon Press).

WINCOTT, D. (1996), 'The Court of Justice and the European Policy Process', in J. J. Richardson (ed.), *European Union: Power and Policy-Making* (London: Routledge), 170–86.

ZITO, A. R. (1997), 'Expanding the EU Agenda from the Outside: A Study of the Role of International Institutions and Actors on EU Environmental Policy' (paper presented at the 'Europeanization in International Perspective', University of Pittsburgh, 19–21 September).

ZUKIN, S., and DIMAGGIO, P. (1990), 'Introduction', in S. Zukin and P. DiMaggio (eds.), *Structures of Capital: The Social Organization of the Economy* (Cambridge: Cambridge University Press), 1–36.

11

Conclusions: Governance beyond State Strength

JON PIERRE

As the preceding chapters have shown, governance theory has tremendous potential in opening up alternative ways of looking at political institutions, domestic–global linkages, transnational co-operation, and different forms of public–private exchange. Also, governance can be approached from a wide range of vantage points even within the same subfield of political science. One of the key research questions in this research focuses on the new or emerging forms of 'steering' that seem to be replacing more coercive policy instruments and command and control systems of institutional co-ordination. Governance theorists see the role of government in governance as a contextual phenomenon; the pursuit of the collective interest takes different forms in different political and institutional contexts and governments can be either the key, co-ordinating actor or simply one of several powerful players in that process.

The cross-sectoral comparison also brings out an interesting picture of the degree to which governance arrangements are institutionalized in different empirical contexts and our analytical understanding of such arrangements. In all subfields, there is a wide spectrum of degrees of institutionalization, ranging from ad hoc coalitions among key actors to more continuous networks (see e.g. de Bruijn and ten Heuvelhof, 1996; Marsh and Rhodes, 1992). These governance arrangements are sustained by normative notions about what characterizes good and democratic governance (March and Olsen, 1995). Given the voluntary, non-complying nature of contemporary governance, the normative structures are integral to governance because they offer legitimacy and political support to the existing model of governance and the intrerests pursued there.

GOVERNANCE AND THE STATE

The role of the state in governance is perhaps the most important issue in governance research, given the historical predominance of the state as the undisputed carrier of the collective interest. While there is much to suggest that this role of the state has changed, and continues to change, democratic government remains centred around the legitimacy of political institutions and the channels of representation, accountability, and consent between these institutions and the polity at large. As long as this remains the case, the issue of how the state transforms to accommodate emerging forms of governance remains a key issue in governance research (Pierre and Peters, 2000).

Several important conclusions concerning our ways of thinking about the state emerge from the analyses presented in this volume. There are three aspects of the state in a governance perspective which several contributors observed and elaborated. First, several chapters point at what seems to be a causal linkage between the relaxation of regulatory steering within the state on the one hand and the emerging forms of public–private exchange which are at the heart of governance on the other. We can, with only slight exaggeration, describe this development as a shift from a centripetal to a centrifugal model of governing. In the centripetal model, the political centre was the undisputed source of political power and institutional capabilities. In the centrifugal model of governing, however, the state seeks to increase its points of contact with its external environment as a means of conveying its objectives to the surrounding society. Important elements of this pursuit have been deregulation, deconcentration, and decentralization, and giving local authorities, agencies, and quangos opportunities to operate more closely to actors outside the political sphere in society.

Second, and more importantly, we need to reconsider our understanding of the sources of state power and the institutional capabilities of the state. Such capabilities, it seems, are to a growing extent contingent on the state´s ability to muster public and private resources—widely defined— and to wield public and private organizational capabilities towards common objectives.

Furthermore, several chapters point out that governance—to a greater or smaller extent—has emerged as an alternative model of 'steering' as a result of what appears to be a decreasing 'fit' between institutional struc-

tures on the one hand and recurrent patterns of behavior in the environment of these structures on the other (cf. North, 1990). The globalization of capital, to take the most prominent example of this growing discrepancy, has undercut much of the traditional leverage of national institutions such as National Banks. As Gerry Stoker argues in his chapter, our thinking about governance has in part been driven by globalization which penetrates previously closed and stable exchanges within a system of institutions. A similar pattern is demonstrated by James Rosenau in his analysis of global governance. Almost all systems of governmental organizations are still geared to a rule of law and regulation which in many cases has proved less and less desirable to the political elite. These institutional systems are also reflections of a state-centric image of society which has been called into question by the growing powers of networks; by sub-national authorities defining themselves as international rather than national actors; by the emergence of transnational systems of institutions; and, not least, by an ideological shift from the state and collective action towards the market and free enterprise.

This way of thinking about governance is closely related to normative institutional theory and its focus on the relationship between state structures and systems of norms, values, beliefs, and traditions (March and Olsen, 1989). The notion that the institutional arrangements of the contemporary advanced western democracies no longer reflect structured behaviour in the state's environment should constitute a powerful impetus for institutional change. And such change is precisely what we have been witnessing across the western world over the past couple of decades in the form of agentification, a growing interest in public–private partnerships and networks, and the 'hiving off' of functions which are not critical to the state (Peters and Savoie, 1998; Pierre, 1998; Self, 1993). This observation, in turn, is proof of the state's capacity to contain or adapt to external changes rather than surrendering to them (Mann, 1997).

Finally, as Paul Hirst and others note, governance has a 'post-institutional' or even 'post-political' connotation. While governance is a critical and defining feature of any advanced democracy, the role of government in such governance is not self-evident. That role seems to a great extent to be derived from traditional and historical patterns of exchange between state and society. In some political cultures, the role of the state has for a long period of time been defined above and beyond partisan differences; the state has arbitrated between social constituencies and organized interests and provided regulatory frameworks for markets

(Rockman, 1989). In addition, in some national contexts—primarily the Scandinavian and Dutch welfare states—the state has taken a higher profile in society, pursuing agendas of provision and distribution. The role which the state plays in governance is derived from this trajectory of its role in society and the economy.

This discussion touches on what Evans (1997) calls 'stateness'. While this concept remains surrounded by some degree of elusiveness and ambiguity, it is clear that 'stateness' is to a much greater extent a quality of society than of the state itself. 'Stateness' is about the legitimacy of the state and our willingness to surrender individual rights and freedom to collective institutions. Put slightly differently, the strength of the state is contingent on the degree to which society is willing to give its consent to the capabilities of the state. This is not a very novel way of thinking about the state but it is an approach which speaks directly to the governance image of 'steering'; one of the key questions coming out of the analyses presented hinges on the emergence of governance as a consequence of a decreased degree of 'stateness' in western society, or, conversely, on whether governance is a means of maintaining a fairly high degree of 'stateness' as a counterweight to globalization and deregulated financial and capital markets. To what extent emerging forms of governance are a cause or an effect of a decreasing 'stateness' in western society is one of several items on the governance research agenda. Let us now look closer what other important tasks lie ahead of us.

GOVERNANCE RESEARCH: THE NEXT ISSUES[1]

Governance and governance theory are still emergent features of society as well as in the social sciences. Governance as an analytical framework is still contested in several subfields of political science. In international relations research, as James Rosenau shows, governance is still regarded with some scepticism. Similarly, in much of American urban politics research, governance as an analytical approach still has to win broad acceptance in the urbanist community. This makes the need to carefully consider next steps in governance research all the more important. We can see four overarching sets of questions emerging from the preceding analyses.

[1] This section is related to a similar discussion in the closing chapter of Pierre and Peters, 2000.

First, while there are many good reasons why scholars of governance should study effective and successful cases of governance, we alo need to look more closely at the causes and consequences of governance failure, as Gerry Stoker points out in his chapter. In a way not too different from North's observation that poor economic performance is often explained by a poorly developed institutional framework (North, 1990), so governance research from a political economy perspective can highlight causes of declining competitiveness and growth by pointing at poor governance in sectors of the economy. Research from that vantage-point helps bring out the significance in non-complying co-operative arrangements between political and market-based actors. It also helps us understand the different roles of the state in the economy in a larger perspective (see Gamble, this volume).

Second, we need to know more about conflict management and conflict resolution in governance. As is the case with governance failure, we tend to focus our attention on consensual governance and infer that all governance is consensual. However, successful governance is predicated on a significant degree of conflict management; there is no reason to believe that alternative ways of pursuing collective interests will be any less contested and conflictual than was the case in the conventional models of democratic government. One aspect of these issues which we know fairly little about is how conflict avoidance and resolution are created and sustained in a governance system comprising autonomous actors brought together to serve a common purpose. What makes these issues particularly intriguing is how the broader collective interest is represented and taken into account by such co-operative structures. For instance, networks could be assumed to cater almost exclusively to the interests of those actors that participate in the network, a scenario which raises question about the long-term legitimacy of such governance instruments.

Third, and derived from the previous discussion, we also need to think more about how a shift from 'government' to governance affects the articulation of the collective interest. Is there a risk that the greater reliance of the state on societal actors blurs the collective interest, or, indeed, that it decomposes or fragments the collective interest? What are the long-term consequences of governance on democracy in this perspective?

Finally, the emergence of governance prompts us to rethink notions about 'stateness'. There are elements of 'stateness' which suggest that it represents the institutional manifestation of the collective interest embedded in a societal context. To the extent that that is the case, looking at those issues in a governance perspective yields an interesting alternative conceptualization of

'stateness' in which it is the collective interest *strictu sensu*, and not the state as the institutionalization of those interest which becomes the centrepiece of the analysis. Thus, governance theory helps us analytically separate the normative and institutional dimensions of the collective interest, or, to put it slightly differently, to separate the objectives of the collective will from the institutional structures of the state. Such a separation, in turn, opens up possibilities for a number of analyses of alternative strategies to pursue the collective interest, something which is at the heart of governance.

There are certainly many other important aspects of governance which deserve scholarly attention and this brief inventory of unresolved issues in governance theory has only identified a couple of areas where governance theory should be able to take our understanding of contemporary politics and societies further. We are only in the first phase in the development of what is already an intriguing sector of the social sciences.

REFERENCES

DE BRUIJN, J. A., and TEN HEUVELHOF, E. F. (1996), 'Policy Networks and Governance', in R. E. Goodin (ed.), *The Theory of Institutional Design* (Cambridge and New York: Cambridge University Press), 161–79.

EVANS, P. (1997), 'The Eclipse of the State? Reflections on Stateness in an Era of Globalization', *World Politics* 50: 62–87.

MANN, M. (1997), 'Has Globalization Ended the Rise and Rise of the Nation-State?', *Review of International Political Economy* 4: 472–96.

MARCH, J. G., and OLSEN, J. P. (1995), *Democratic Governance* (New York: The Free Press)

—— (1989), *Rediscovering Institutions* (New York: The Free Press).

MARSH, D., and RHODES, R. A. W. (eds.) (1992), *Policy Networks in British Government* (Oxford: Clarendon Press).

NORTH, D. C. (1990), *Institutions, Institutional Change and Economic Performance* (Cambridge and New York: Cambridge University Press).

PETERS, B. G., and SAVOIE, D. J. (eds.) (1998), *Taking Stock: Assessing Public Sector Reform* (Montreal and Kingston: McGill/Queens University Press).

PIERRE, J. (ed.) (2000), *Partnerships in Urban Governance: European and American Experience* (London: Macmillan and New York: St Martin's Press).

—— and PETERS, B. G. (1999), *Governance, Politics and the State: Rethinking Old Models* (London: Macmillan).

ROCKMAN, B. A. (1989), 'Minding the State—or a State of Mind?', in J. A. Caporaso (ed.), *The Elusive State* (Beverly Hills and London: Sage), 173–203.

SELF, P. (1993), *Government by the Market?* (London: Macmillan).

INDEX

Note: Page numbers in *italic* refer to tables.